VILLAGES
OF
SOUTHERN ARGYLL

To my mother, Winnie Pallister,
who gifted me her love of Argyll

VILLAGES
OF
SOUTHERN
ARGYLL

MARIAN PALLISTER

JOHN DONALD PUBLISHERS
EDINBURGH

First published in 2004 by John Donald Publishers
An imprint of Birlinn Ltd
West Newington House
10 Newington Road
Edinburgh
EH9 1QS

www.birlinn.co.uk

ISBN 0 85976 583 0

British Library Cataloguing-in-Publication Data
A catalogue record for this book is available
from the British Library

Typesetting and origination by Brinnoven, Livingston
Printed and bound by Antony Rowe Ltd, Chippenham

CONTENTS

COLONSAY

Scalasaig

Crinan·
Bellanoc
Ardlussa
Tayvall
Keills

JURA
Lagg

Port Askaig
Feolin
Craighouse

Kilberry

Bowmore
ISLAY

Clachan

Portnahaven
GIGHA

Ardbeg
Port Ellen

Tayinloan
Killean

Glenbarr

Sadde

Campbelto
Macrihanish
Drumlemble

Southend

| 0 | 10 | 20 | 30 Kilometres |
| 0 | 10 | | 20 Miles |

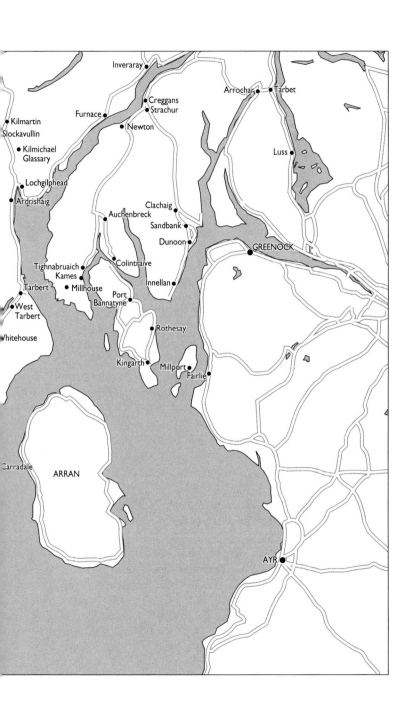

INTRODUCTION

The southern half of Argyll has been shaped as much by the religious and political leanings of its heritors (landlords) as it has by its geography and topography and I therefore make no apology for relating so much of its history in many of the chapters. Industries – whether those which relate directly to the land and the sea, those which respond to need or those which are developed with an eye on the main chance – are usually created by those with power and wealth. The poor man rarely stumbles on a money-making idea or if he does, it is only with the greatest of luck that he manages to develop it and make his fortune. The poor farmer ploughs a lonely furrow and manages to feed his family if the elements are kind to him. The rich landowner (or the landlord favoured by those even more powerful than himself) employs men to plough his fields, takes rent from them for living in his houses and demands a dozen chickens and a fine woven shawl into the bargain. And when he is sitting in his study in the evening, he might just design a new kind of plough which will improve production. Or if he is of a less technical bent, he will fire off a letter to the manufacturer of new ploughs to order one – and then write a note to one of his tenants saying he no longer requires two men to plough his fields so would the family kindly quit the premises by Whitsuntide.

Argyll, from Loch Awe to the tip of Kintyre and over into Cowal, has not been the site of great industries. Factory chimneys have been a rarity; cattle, timber and fishing the norm. Even in the centres of population, no buildings have been blackened by industrial pollution, no factory gates have opened to pour out thousands of men at knocking off time.

Campbeltown can claim to have met the criteria of 'industrial town' in its heyday of shipbuilding, herring fishing, whisky distilling, importing and exporting and all their ancillary trades. The villages of this part of Argyll, however, have thrown up much quirkier industries which seldom improved the lot of the working man and woman on a long-term basis. The mining at Drumlemble was discovered when a king wanted warm castles when he came to Argyll and was eventually developed by a prospecting landowner. Well into the twentieth century, the houses in which the miners lived remained as hovels without running water. Gunpowder manufacture was sited at Kames and Millhouse because English contractors saw this as a suitably remote area. The local death-toll at the works was devastating to such a small rural population. These industries came and went, sometimes leaving only a subsidence-induced crack in the cement of a modern farmyard as evidence that they ever existed. Only the village of Tarbert with its fishing fleet chasing the silver darlings has experienced consistency – although even there, politicians down the centuries have sought to control when and how men have fished and go on doing so to this day.

Landlords have sold feus and firs. They have exploited the natural resources and the people. Their politics have wreaked devastation on the land and their personal peccadilloes have shaped the destinies of generations. They have planted men as well as crops and they have dug up the roots of families so that farmlands could be enclosed or sheep grazed.

Of course, Argyll's heritors have not had an entirely negative effect on the county. Their estates and big houses *were* the industry of some villages and everyone from the parlour-maid to the blacksmith owed their livelihood to the laird. And when their own livelihoods were at stake, these lairds had the wherewithal to play interventionist games to keep an industry alive – as demonstrated when the Commissioners of Supply kept the black cattle market functioning at Kilmichael Glassary after Dumbarton traders tried to circumvent this ancient tryst.

Just as King James IV wanted warm castles and sent a collier to survey for coal, so the nineteenth-century lairds wanted modern lighting in their mansions and installed gas plants on their estates. They may not have offered as many jobs as Lochgilphead gasworks did, but in village terms one or two jobs is the equivalent of hundreds in an urban population – and the loss of that employment equally as ruinous to the rural community.

Some villages in Kintyre, Cowal and Knapdale were created; some grew organically; some have had short-lived fame and sunk back into obscurity; some took pounding after pounding for centuries and still came bouncing back. Now, tourism, trees and local government are the biggest sources of employment.

Today, the villages of southern Argyll are seen as idyllic backwaters – but the cottage industries of weaving and illicit distilling of bygone generations have been replaced by industries of a modern technological sort while craftsmen, artisans, farmers and fishermen fight to keep alive what Argyll author and historian Marion Campbell once termed 'the enduring heartland'.

1
SOUTHEND

The first footstep into Cantyre

Legend has it that Columba, the man credited with introducing Christianity to the west of Scotland, swore he would not settle until he could no longer see his native Ireland from the top of the nearest hill. His quest took him through Argyll to the island of Iona, where his homeland was no longer visible. Certainly, the hillside he is said to have climbed at the very tip of the Kintyre peninsula was far too close to Antrim for his spiritual and emotional comfort. The outline of the Irish coast, just a dozen or so miles away, can be traced even on less than clear days. His brief stay there gave a name to the scattered community which is now more plainly known as Southend, but then was Kilcolmkill – the first step on Columba's Argyll odyssey.

We are told that the shape of a shod right foot gouged in the rock at Keil Point marked his presence there. If the footstep really was made

The sight which met Columba when he landed at the tip of 'Cantyre' – Sanda and Sheep islands off Southend (*Maureen Bell Collection*)

by the missionary, his was not the first step taken on this peninsula by a long chalk. When Columba made his way north through the 42-mile-long finger of land then called Cantyre (in Gaelic, *ceann* means 'head' and *tir* is 'land'), he followed a well-trodden path. Then as now, there was much evidence of the mystical Celtic race which for three millennia before the birth of Christ had adorned its queens with jet beads of great beauty, buried its dead in chambered cairns, and erected strange stones which aligned with the sun at the summer and winter solstices. The footprint at Keil Point attributed by legend to St Columba could well have been a symbol of fealty hewn in the rock around 1,500 years before his arrival. In caves around Southend and a few miles north-east on the shores of a loch where Campbeltown would stand a millennium or so after Columba's landing, Neolithic tribes had worked extensively with flint. Traders and soldiers from the Roman empire had come this way, although they were never to subjugate Kintyre as they had England and the Lowlands of Scotland.

One man's landing place, however, is another man's point of vulnerability. Strategic importance created and developed this community. When the Roman general Agricola paid an unfruitful visit to the west coast in the summer of AD 82, he was neither the first nor the last to sail the coast of Kintyre with acquisition in mind. Irish invaders, who first colonised the area in the third century AD, saw the need to protect this somewhat too inviting landing place and Erc, the powerful Antrim prince, put his sons in charge of the three corners of Argyll: Lorn, Cowal and Kintyre. Their descendants quarrelled and heavily fortified their kingdoms. Dunaverty Castle, louring over Kilcolmkill, was already a crucial defence point for Gabhran when his Kintyre kingdom was attacked in 712 by Selbhach, leader of the tribe of Lorn.

The Romans knew the Mull of Kintyre as Promontorium Caledoniae. The Egyptian astronomer and geographer Ptolemy, who died in AD 168, called it Epidion Akron (promontory of the horse people), but the Antrim invaders brought their Gaelic language with them. 'Southend' may describe this village's situation well, but in a county named *Erc-gathel* (Argyll) in honour of the Antrim-born Erc, son of Gathel, where every hilltop and burn has a Gaelic name and most settlements, large or small, can be traced to Gaelic or Norse origins, the name is puzzlingly incongruous. In fact, this very English sobriquet was not in common use until the religious Reformation which swept Scotland in the 1500s. Chapels dedicated to St Columba and St Blaan gave the parish around Dunaverty Castle its early name of Kilcolmkill (*cille* meaning a chapel in Gaelic) and Kilblaan. In 1617 a Commission of Parliament united the parishes of Kilcolmkill, Kilchiaran and Kilblaan. The village today known as Southend was Monirua (later Moneroy) and in 1671 the parish of Kilcolmkill and Kilblaan became officially known as Southend.

Church and state have ruled ordinary lives throughout the very long history of Argyll, and Southend parish did not escape. This 10-mile wide strip of land across the tip of Kintyre was an attractive proposition for any would-be power. The east and west of the parish are hilly but as the Rev. Angus J. MacVicar writes in the *Third Statistical Account of Scotland* (1961), the glens, straths and seashore are 'good and fertile' land where dairy farms flourish. There were no dairy herds as we know them in the first Christian millennium, but that fertile land was precious. The seas around the Mull of Kintyre were treacherous for more reasons than weather. Successful defences must be sustainable and the land and sea here had the potential to feed the inhabitants of Dunaverty Castle.

In addition to fishers and farmers, a castle needs masons, carpenters, tailors and shoemakers. A mill was established at Machrimore to grind flour. To the list of occupations which grew around Dunaverty

Fishing was one of the earliest industries around the coast of Kintyre (*Maureen Bell Collection*)

Dunaverty Castle, fortress scene of massacre (*Maureen Bell Collection*)

smuggler can also be added. Down the centuries, long after Dunaverty was reduced to rubble, the smuggling of spirits, linen and other desirable commodities eked out meagre livings.

Dunaverty was important for local rulers, and so was Ceann Loch Cille Chiaran on the east coast of Kintyre. This settlement had, like the settlement around Dunaverty, been in existence since Mesolithic peoples fashioned their flint tools there. It took its name from St Ciaran and in time became Kilkerran, important as a headquarters of the Dalriadic kingdom. Then, like Kilcolmkill and Kilblaan, it came under the rule of the Norsemen.

Columba had consecrated Aidan, son of Gabhran, as the first Christian king of Scotland at Dunadd in what today is mid-Argyll. Aidan secured the independence of the Dalriadic kingdom in Scotland in 575, but after his death thirty years later, that independence was no longer guaranteed. Pictish wars were followed by Norsemen colonising Kintyre in the ninth century, and in 1098 Magnus Barefoot claimed the peninsula under a treaty with Scotland. Somerled, Lord of the Isles, eventually drove the Norsemen from Kintyre and other parts of Argyll before they finally left the whole of Scotland when Hakon IV was defeated at Largs in 1263 by Alexander III of Scotland.

Throughout these turbulent times, Dunaverty Castle was a pivotal defence.

While leaders of the various factions plotted their campaigns, the ordinary people of Kilcolmkill and Kilblaan were required to produce provisions and man the barricades. The Lords of the Isles, from their lair on the island of Islay, were to play games with the kings of Scotland for several centuries – land and property were the stakes played for, the population of Argyll dispensable pawns. No doubt the Scottish rulers saw the sense in indulging these games. Kintyre was the front line of mainland Scotland's defence and as such, its landowners had to be flattered or subjugated.

In 1249, Angus Mor was the first descendant of Somerled to acknowledge the superiority of the king of Scotland over Kintyre. He gifted Kilkerran Church to the Abbey of Paisley, which was then powerfully connected to the royal house.

The gift, he said, was 'for the weal of the soul of my Lord Alexander, the illustrious King of the Scots, and of his son Alexander'. These were kings Alexander II and III, and with an appropriately sycophantic touch, Angus Mor named a son Alexander (in Gaelic, *Alaster)*, the first use of the name among Highlanders. In 1266, when Norse territory was surrendered to the king of Scotland, Angus was given a place in the Scottish Parliament and was first in line to be in charge of Alexander's island possessions. His son, Angus Og (in Gaelic *og* means 'young'), made some judicious moves, too. He gave Robert Bruce refuge in Dunaverty Castle in 1306 and supported him at Bannockburn in 1314. As a reward, Bruce gave him Lorn but Angus Og was not pleased when Bruce put Kintyre in the hands of his nephew because it was such a strategically important area.

But the Lords of the Isles were not to be outwitted. John, son of Angus Og, acquired the Northern Isles through marriage to the heiress Annie Macruarie, then divorced her to marry Margaret Stewart, daughter of Robert II. His new father-in-law gave Kintyre to the couple in 1377, making the Macdonalds of Islay and Kintyre all-powerful. Marriage also brought the Glens of Antrim into the Macdonald family and perhaps the royal house saw this was a step too far. Kintyre was put under the sheriffdom of Tarbert and although John Cathanach Macdonald of Dunnyveg in Islay was knighted in 1493, Kintyre did not come back into his hands. Instead, the king re-fortified Dunaverty Castle under his own man.

Peeved by this move, John Macdonald hung the new governor of Dunaverty over its walls in sight of the king. He fled to Antrim but was eventually executed. It was then that the Campbells, royal favourites of the day, moved into Kintyre. Archibald, 2nd Earl of Argyll, was made Crown Chamberlain of the lands forfeited by the Macdonalds, including Dunaverty Castle and the new castle at Kilkerran.

In 1505, the Earl and the Bishop went to Ceann Loch Kilkerran and drew a list of the rental of Crown lands in existence. Among the main families were the Omays of Kilcolmkill. Cornelius Omay became rector of Kilblaan Parish at the Reformation of the Church in 1560. Alexander Cunningham, Master of Glencairn, was appointed governor with power to exercise the offices of sheriff and justiciar. His headquarters were at Dunaverty Castle. Soon, new names were to be added to this list as the 7th Earl of Argyll began an interesting experiment in social manipulation.

Politics and religion were greatly exercising royalty and nobility at this time. Archibald, the 4th Earl of Argyll who died in 1558, had been the first of the Scottish nobility to embrace the Reformation. His successor was a follower of the Catholic Mary Queen of Scots and became James VI's Lord High Chancellor. King James managed to be in dispute with both Presbyterians and Roman Catholics and in 1600 he introduced episcopacy to Scotland which was the root of violent dissent that century and into the next.

This 'remote' peninsula suffered directly from the social, political and religious changes formented in Edinburgh, London and Europe. Religious and political unrest manifested itself in Argyll as elsewhere and James VI requested the 7th Earl to begin what were known as the 'plantations' – the settlement of people from the 'civilised' Lowlands to control unruly Kintyre in the aftermath of the 1603 Union of the Crowns. The Macdonald lands granted to the 7th Earl in 1607 were ethnically cleansed and repopulation was done on purely political grounds.

By the time the 8th Earl (and only Marquess) of Argyll carried out a similar plantation later in the century, it was to repopulate a peninsula devastated by wars and disease. It was he who led the Covenanters against Charles I. Now he moved in influntial friends from Ayrshire and Renfrewshire and brought Campbells from other parts of Argyll. They brought with them their servants, their farm labourers and new agricultural ideas.

One of the most notable families to arrive was the Laird of Ralston who at first was given land around Saddell, north of Kilkerran in 1650. He was then granted lands in the parishes of Kilkerran and Kilcolmkill and Kilblaan, now becoming known as Southend. He came to an area where the contemporary Synod of Argyll recorded famine: the weather was bad in 1650 but the situation had been made worse by a succession of armies which had eaten what food was available.

This politicking with land was made easier by the Scottish tacksman system. The tacksman, often a relative or supporter, was granted a tack or lease by landlord chiefs such as the Campbells. In Kintyre, the tacks were bigger than average, usually over 20 merklands (by a 1585 decree, three merklands were 104 acres). Some stayed in one family for generations – the Macnachtens were at Gartavay in Southend parish from the 1500s to the 1800s – but Crown leases were for only three years.

In 1650, the Marquess of Argyll made a tactical change by giving out nineteen-year leases, which eventually became the norm. Ralston's tacks in Kilkerran and Southend were among the biggest, amounting to 44 merklands, or well over 1,500 acres. He was probably one of the last big tacksmen in Kintyre and he served his purpose. Although by 1678 there were still only 139 out of 421 merklands in Kintyre held by former Ayrshiremen and 103 by incoming Campbells, the effect was to dilute what the authorities saw as a politically dangerous Highland culture.

This manipulation was never, after all, simply a question of repopulation. The plantations went on during upheavals not seen before or since in Scotland. The English Civil War, the Restoration and the bloodless revolution of 1688, all inextricably linked with the Covenanters' struggle to be rid of episcopacy in Scotland – not to mention the settling of clan scores – left Scotland as a whole and Kintyre in particular in a sorry state.

There was no money, no trade and taxes had been doubled. When the Marquess of Argyll was executed in 1661 for complying with the English occupation, it took two years for the family to regain confiscated lands and titles. The ruling aristocracy balanced perilously on the frail religious and political line drawn by successive rulers. They incurred debts to pay for campaigns (massive in the case of the Campbells) and heads rolled. But the battles were physically fought by the fishermen and farmers and it was they who were left without nets and cattle or roofs over the heads of their children in the wake of the depredations carried out on the Clan Campbell and its followers after the failed 1685 rebellion led by the 9th Earl against James VII & II.

Most tenant farmers whose homes were visited by marauding Macdonalds did not even own the goods which were so wilfully destroyed. Tacksmen traditionally sub-let their land to tenant farmers, who paid rent but owned nothing – not even the cattle, horses, machinery or seed grain with which they worked the farm.

This so-called steelbow system lasted until 1710 and records preserve what was a common type of contract signed by a tenant of Malcolm Macneil of Carskey in the parish of Southend who was required to return everything when he left the farm he rented. The tacksmen made the money and began to create a middle class in Kintyre by paying for a university education for their sons. The tenants tilled the land and their sons followed in the furrows created by their crude wooden ploughs. Subsistence farmers operated under the old runrig system which lasted in Kintyre until the mid-eighteenth century. Although the Ayrshire and Renfrewshire lairds rotated their crops and used more modern implements than their Highland predecessors, at first they simply perpetuated the role of the tacksman, making a profit from the difference between the rent they charged the working farmers and the rent they paid the laird.

It was not until the 1730s in the time of John, Duke of Argyll and Greenwich, that the system was abolished and leases were given to working farmers for the first time. At the beginning of the seventeenth century, however, much of the rent was paid in 'presents': meal, cheese, malt, lambs and even cows. By the end of the century, when the political and religious upheavals had left the whole countryside reeling, those 'presents' had been given a set monetary value of £7 10s Scots.

In a more secular age, we are inclined to focus more on the personalities of history than the issues: John Knox railing against the Catholic Mary Queen of Scots; James VI & I and his failing for favouritism; the social excesses of Charles I & Charles II. The political and religious policies of these leaders, however, meant life and death to the ordinary citizen of Kintyre. John Knox's espousal of Calvinism was not simply a matter of principle but an attempt to combat economically and socially crippling Church corruption. He saw folk such as the farmers of Southend suffering at the hands of greedy tacksmen and corrupt Catholic priests and he demanded reform of a system which did not only demand the tacksman's rent and 'presents'. If a tenant farmer died, for example, his family had to pay 'calp' (*calpach*, a young cow) to the landlord and, on top of that, a teind or tenth of all crops and animals were due to the Church. The satirical reforming drama *The Thrie Estaites* showed this being paid in kind, but it was eventually converted into cash and written into the lease, the amount due being collected by the tacksman. These 'death duties' and tithes were devastating, especially if a tenant had more than one landlord. Although the 'calp' was abolished by an Act of Parliament in 1617, it was still being paid by charter in the 1670s in Kintyre.

Ecclesiastical reformers of the church may have been concerned with the intricacies of liturgy and hierarchy. For the Southend parishioner, the loss of a cow to the Church could make a widow homeless. And no matter what his own beliefs or allegiances may have been, a tenant was required to support his heritors (landowners) not just with his labour but with his life.

During the Civil War, so much associated with England's Roundheads and Cavaliers that Scotland's role is often forgotten, the religious and political vacillations of James Graham, Marquess of Montrose, and Archibald (known both as the Covenanting and the Cross-Eyed Marquess) the 8th Earl of Argyll, led in 1647 to the massacre of 300 civilians dragooned to defend Dunaverty Castle against Covenanter forces. The tacksman had to render service to his chief and the tenants had to render service to the tacksman. 'Service' included military duties, attending a landlord on hunts, cultivating his lands, carting his peats and his manure. It is not too difficult to guess which tasks were delegated to the tenants and sub-tenants.

Part of the 1643 rent at Machrimore Mill in Southend parish was geese and poultry. At Carskey farm, the account book refers to the 'Duke's straw'. Over 100 years later in his *General View of Agriculture in Argyll in 1798*, the Rev. Dr John Smith of Campbeltown condemned the social deprivation this still caused and spoke out against short leases and multiple farm tenancies, both of which he saw as a hardship to families and a hindrance to the advancement of agriculture. But it was the runrig system which left the fertile land around Southend underdeveloped for centuries. Today's deserted townships were once joint farms worked by sub-tenants. Each family drew lots for strips of good and bad arable land and pasture. The strips, called rigs, were worked by a plough and horses shared by all of the families. Poorer families might have had just one horse between them. The tacksman lived on the home farm, which was worked by hired servants and cottars. The other farms on an estate were sub-let to tenants who worked the land as a commune. These runrig farms began to disappear in Kintyre in the middle of the eighteenth century when land enclosure began. This was also a time of more 'plantations', when Lowlanders such as William Hunter and James Dunlop introduced dairy farming on the Southend parish farms of Machribeg and Ballyshear.

New farming methods, according to Dr Smith in the mid 1790s, meant that Southend parish had been able to reclaim 'more waste ground . . . than in any other in the county'. The local cattle were (despite being described as 'ugly' by Dr Smith) good milkers, but Lowland cows (like the Lowland human stock?) had, he said, an improving effect. The *Statistical Account* of Southend in 1790 records black cattle being brought over to Southend from Ireland and small black horses being traded in return. This trade in horses from Southend was evidently profitable. In 1809, 150 vessels sailed from Southend to Ireland carrying passengers, goods and 1,800 horses. Cattle drovers had passed through Kintyre from time immemorial. Marts (fattened cattle), which were part of the king's rents when he held lands in Kintyre as far south as Dunaverty in the sixteenth century, were driven overland to Stirling Castle under the supervision of the parish clerk at Kilkerran (Campbeltown), who had rent-free land as payment. It was not until the second half of the nineteenth century that the tradition of driving cattle overland to the great Falkirk tryst ended.

Southend parish was not able to develop its crops and its dairy herds, of course, until it was allowed breathing space to recover from the destructive political drama of the seventeenth century. Again, it was the fortunes of the major landlord which affected lives at grassroots level. The 2nd Duke of Argyll was one of the strongest supporters of the Act of Union of 1707 and he soon reaped the rewards. Campbell lands were restored, Lochhead on Loch Kilkerran became the burgh of Campbeltown and a degree of prosperity there spread around the peninsula. Under the now official Presbyterian Church of Scotland, no tithes were paid. The minister was paid according to the value of the lands owned by the heritors in the parish, so there was no dispute between the minister and his flock. 'Presents' were still expected, however, by lairds whose style of living was maintained by peats and hay, poultry, dairy produce, lint, wool, oats, meal, yarn, sheets and blankets – all produced by farm tenants who, according to Dr Smith, often had no leases and not enough to feed and clothe themselves.

The benefits of the agricultural revolution came first to the middle tier of farmers. In the mid-1700s, Southend parish tenants began to get leases and farms started to be worked as units rather than communes. Some of the poorest had already been forced out of farming, however. In 1714, a heavy tax was put on salt which badly affected the fishing

Southend, once known as Moneroy, the first link with the princes of Antrim (*Maureen Bell Collection*)

trade and, of course, those poor farmers who relied on fishing to augment their subsistence farming. If they paid the tax, it was not economically viable to catch and cure the fish – and if they failed to pay up, their cargoes were confiscated. Disastrous for Southend, it was more so for Campbeltown, whose growing prosperity was tied up in fishing. And if the burghers there were deprived of their living, who would buy the produce from the Southend parish farms?

Even so, the eighteenth century was undeniably a time of agricultural development. The 5th Duke of Argyll, who succeeded in 1770, was recorded by Dr Smith in the 1790s as having 'lately taken measures for erecting a village at Monirua in the parish of Southend'. His Grace, Smith said, was giving nineteen-year leases which went up in value when tenants signed for a second term. This was a period of planned villages – Bowmore and Port Ellen on Islay were contemporary examples – and part of the new ethos of developing estates on a sound economic basis. Elsewhere, this was the golden age of agriculture and the Duke brought Lowland ploughmen to his estate to improve ploughing skills.

But however much landlords might have sought to change subsistence into a land flowing with milk and honey, the weather would always be a defining factor. Just as the model village of Monirua or Moneroy (now Southend village) was exercising the Duke's imagination and new systems of farm enclosures, stone drainage and crop rotation began to improve the farmer's lot, bad weather knocked him for six.

In 1782, there was a disastrous harvest. The following year, the Duke of Argyll sent seed corn to tenants in Argyll to help them get back on their feet. And the cycle went on. No sooner had Dr Smith so admired the waving yellow of Southend corn than in 1820, fifty-two of the Duke's tenants in the parish petitioned for rent reductions after bad harvests and a drop in the grain prices. This must have come as a blow to Argyll Estates because the 6th Duke managed to spend the family fortunes during his tenure from 1806 to 1839 and appointed trustees had to pick up the pieces. Even in peacetime, the fortunes of the landlord affected the tenants. No wonder there were illicit stills hidden behind Southend kitchen dressers to make a little extra cash and keep up the tenant farmer's spirits.

Modern ploughs and fertilisers hardly impinged on the poorer Southend farmer's family, who in summer had to occupy himself and his family in digging peat for fuel, rent and for the children to take to heat the school in winter. In the parish, Macharioch farmers had to cut peats in Glenrea, six miles from home. Every farming task seemed to involve walking marathon distances. Sheep had to be walked miles to be sent to market. Produce had to be taken over the precipitous hill to Campbeltown.

By the days of the steamer in the nineteenth century, sheep were taken to Carradale to sail to markets in Lanark and Ayr. In the late 1700s, experiments with sheep had produced a successful cross-breed between the local flocks and black-faced tups. Leicester sheep were also being reared for domestic use on low-lying farms.

The 1840s saw potato crop failures in Kintyre, just as in Ireland, but because the political situation was marginally more sympathetic in some parts of the west of Scotland than in Ireland, the effects on the working man were not always so cruelly traumatic. Even so, there were mass emigrations and the population of Southend dropped between 1831 and 1881 from 2,120 to 955. People moved from the land into Campbeltown for work in the distilleries, the fishing, in trades and as labourers. They went overseas to Canada, America and Australia, joining the thousands more who left from all round Scotland. Southend could no longer sustain a growing population.

At the end of the eighteenth century, a man servant working in a laird's house earned £8 a year and a maid was paid £3. The ordinary farmer was paying £40 a year in rent. When things were going well, he could feed his family three meals a day of potatoes with herring or milk. If he felt he had done well that summer, he might salt a cow for the winter or kill a couple of sheep at the harvest. When the potatoes failed, he ate oat or barley (bere) bread. Dr Smith said in his report of farming in the county in the 1790s that in Kintyre it was 'customary to take some thin pottage or a little bread and milk before they began work in the morning and after dinner, should it even have been potatoes and herring, or flesh and broth, they have commonly a little bread and milk by way of dessert or supplement'. These customs, Dr Smith added, were known nowhere else in the county. Very unusually, the Duke of Argyll's tenants had permission to add venison to their diet – he told them in 1772 that he would rather have deer shot than that they 'wasted the bread of the poor' – in other words, ate subsistence farmers' crops.

But if farmers in Southend parish ate vension and pudding, a herdsman still earned just £1 a year. Implements were beginning to improve but many tenant farmers were still using the old clumsy ploughs they made themselves. Small's light plough was being introduced by 'gentlemen', according to Dr Smith, and driven by two horses instead of four, but the new machinery meant fewer men as well as fewer horses. And if up-to-date harrows and rollers were being used by the wealthier agriculturists, harrows with timber teeth tied to the tails of horses were more commonly used by their poorer colleagues. Thrashing machines were unknown and there were few brick kilns. The only draw kiln in Southend for producing lime as a fertiliser was built by an Englishman for his own use. Limestone was being imported to Southend from Ireland at that time to be processed into fertiliser because the journey was shorter than from many parts of Kintyre where it was quarried.

This is perhaps the most telling factor about transport in the late eighteenth century. Wheeled vehicles were a rarity. Peats, dung, corn and hay were carried on sledges or horseback, making the blacksmith at Machrimore (the MacCallum family worked the smiddy there for five generations until the 1960s) a vital member of the community. It was much cheaper and quicker to go by sea than to transport almost any commodity by road. The first wheeled farm cart in Southend was introduced by Christopher Thompson, one of the Duke of Argyll's English tenants who leased Dalabhraddean Farm in 1775.

Southend came into being to support Dunaverty Castle. The parish in later more peaceful centuries came to supply Campbeltown instead. A royal castle established Lochhead Kilkerran but the burgh's natural harbour gave it a life of its own. Fishing, shipbuilding, whisky distilling and their ancillary trades made Campbeltown a hub of activity long after fortifications disappeared; while the loss of Dunaverty Castle deprived Southend of its strategic importance.

Southend's milk and grain fed Campbeltown's creamery and distilleries. Whisky, herring and cheese become almost symbolic in the lives of local people. At funerals in Southend in the early nineteenth century, mourners, according to folk historian Angus Martin, were served with three rounds of drinks: whisky, rum and a whisky toddy. After the burial, mourners went back to the house for a feast of bread, cheese and more whisky. Martin records that widow Margaret MacMurchy, whose husband died at Achinsavill in Southend parish in November 1722, bought twelve boards for Donald's coffin from Malcolm MacNeill and four pounds of cheese and a pound of candles for the funeral.

The road to Campbeltown from Dunaverty was over Machrimore hill, a difficult route even today. A 1670 Act of Parliament required tenants and servants to repair the roads between 'bere seed time and hay time'. Even when Charles II commissioned the Duke of Argyll to enforce this law, little improved until after the Union of Parliaments in 1707. In theory, better roads meant fewer insurrections and after the second Jacobite Rising in 1745 there was a push for a better infrastructure in the Highlands. Thomas Telford created 1,000 miles of road and over 1,000 bridges and, at a local level, road improvements were required to be carried out by the heritors. Until then, Southend parish's industries took place at home. Milling, malt making, brewing ale and distilling aqua vitae (the precursor to whisky), weaving, cheese and butter making were all domestic operations until a better link was made to Campbeltown.

Life continured to be difficult, however, and the Rev. Angus J. MacVicar in his *Third Statistical Account* of Southend, published in 1961, records that the population of the parish fell from 2,120 in 1831 to 1,406 in 1851. During this time of emigration, crofts became vacant and instead of being re-let as they stood, they were joined to make larger farms. 'By about 1850', he wrote, 'most of the farms in Southend were practically of the same size as they are today.'

The emigrants were not only crofters. Some were ambitious

farmers who wanted to better themselves in the colonies. By the early 1850s, Southend families such as the MacKerseys, MacVicars and MacCowies had gone to Canada and settled around Chatham, Ontario. From 1850 to 1880, however, the Ayrshire cow was prospering in Southend parish and so were those farmers who remained. Butter and cheese making became the main industries and with plenty of cheap labour most farms were well managed. All the farm produce went to town on carts which then brought home domestic shopping, farm feed and artificial fertilisers. Nearly every farm now had its own limekiln and lime was being used in large quantities as fertiliser, along with imported Peruvian guano and seaweed carted from the shores. During this period of thirty years, the land lay in grass for three years then was ploughed and sown with oats the first year; potatoes, beans and turnips the next; and oats or barley undersown with grass and clover in the third year.

As always, there came the lean years resulting from forces which have parallels in today's developing countries. The so-called Great Depression which lasted from the mid 1870s to mid 1890s and beyond came in the wake of the repeal of the Corn Laws, which ended protectionism and allowed cheaply produced cereals from North America to swamp UK markets. The advent of cheap steam navigation brought prices down to levels with which landowners in Southend could not possibly compete. The poorer land in the parish went out of cultivation. Farm rents peaked in 1878 and by the following winter those landlords who had put people off their land to accommodate sheep were reckoning that the golden age of sheep farming was at an end. Because it was not worth producing grain, liming was stopped until 1906 when the market picked up again. There were advertisements in the *Campbeltown Courier* for 'Glasgow bread' and the distilleries were using barley not only from across the Altlantic but the Baltic and Normandy. The soil deteriorated so much that, according to MacVicar, some farms could not 'grow a crop of swedes'.

Yet this was a time when the working man for once benefited: cheap food increased the buying power of the poor. Landlord and tenant farmers suffered most , but they were forced to look to other sources of income. Milk, already part of the Southend parish production, became very profitable. Before the start of the First World War, Campbeltown again became the main source of income. Cash crops included potatoes, and barley was once again going to the twenty distilleries in the burgh.

Modern war and economic power games have wrought almost as much havoc as the conflicts of former times – although it is hard to imagine the terror of Southend farmers when the Earl of Sussex coolly wrote to Mary Tudor on 3 October 1588, from the ship *Mary Willoughby*: '19th September landed at Lowghe Gylkerran [Loch Kilkerran] . . . the next day, I crossed over the lande and burned twelve myles of lengthe on the other side of the Lowghe, wherein were burned a faire howse callit Mawher Imore [Machriemore] and a strong castle callit Dunalvere [Dunaverty].'

When most of the distilleries closed after the First World War, farmers again had to move with the times, while fishing, once a mainstay of Southend, dwindled by the 1950s to one man with a lobster boat who sold to London and Glasgow. Two fishermen operate lobster creels there today.

The tourism industry for well over a century has augmented Southend incomes. Towards the end of the nineteenth century, the steam boats which enabled the dumping of cheap grain and refrigerated beef on their doorsteps also brought tourists from Glasgow and enabled businessmen to set up second homes on Argyll's long coastline. In 1878, Eliza Hardie Brent, an American, stayed at the United Presbyterian Church manse in Southend with her sister Maggie Hardie, a convalescent former missionary. They took a boat from Greenock to Campbeltown and were picked up by a wagonette with one seat at the front and two behind. Their journey from Campbeltown to Southend took ninety minutes. During the visit, they made a trip to the Mull of Kintytre, where they saw 'thousands' of sheep grazing. Another day they went with their host, the Rev. Young, on a pastoral visit in a gig with two seats back to back and were given lunch at Drumavoulin. Mistress Brent recorded strawberries, cake and 'the most delicious milk.' The holiday was full of excitement. The wagon turned over and threw them out, they had to mix with the Glasgow Fair holidaymakers coming back from a trip to Edinburgh and Queen Victoria wrote to their neighbour, Major McNeal, related by marriage to the Marquess of Lorne, for the Bruce brooch, a famous piece of jewellery allegedly dating back to the time Bruce stayed in Dunaverty Castle. There was even a dip in the sea: the ladies of Keil asked the sisters to bathe with them on the Saturday, offering to bring bathing suits with them. There can be no doubt that Campbeltown artist William McTaggart (1835–1910), the grandfather of Sir William MacTaggart (1903–81), helped attract visitors to Southend with paintings such as his *Where Columba Landed.*

In the mid twentieth century, before package holidays proliferated, the Argyll Arms in Southend had grown from a modest coaching inn to a twenty-bedroomed hotel. Keil Hotel, built in 1939 and used as a naval hospital in the Second World War, flourished in the 1960s and 1970s. Today, the Argyll Arms has changed with the times, and is more pub than hotel. Keil Hotel closed in 1989 and is now a ruinous landmark for shipping – a far less dramatic beacon than the lighthouse built in 1788 on the Mull of Kintyre at the western extremity of the parish and repaired in 1820 by the Stevensons.

People come for the golf, the birdwatching, the loch and river fishing and to see seals basking on rocks where Columba may have clambered. Yet while a successful ferry was run by Edward Lloyd between Ballycastle and Southend in 1700, today it seems impossible to reinstate a ferry crossing between Campbeltown and Northern Ireland which would bring tourists to the area. Farmers say that without a ferry, diversifying into tourism is not viable.

The Rev. MacVicar predicted in his *Third Statistical Account of Southend* written in the 1950s: 'The decline in population is regrettable and can perhaps be checked only by a comprehensive scheme for small holdings or family farms.' Today, Robert Millar of High Catterdale Farm says the only way forward is to amalgamate family farms into bigger units. Tenants of the Duke of Argyll were able to buy their farms in 1955 when the Kintyre estates were sold off to pay death duties. Now farmers see the supermarkets as their exacting overlords and if it were not for Campbeltown Creamery taking Southend farmers' milk for niche market cheese production, few could remain in agriculture.

Southend landlords and landmarks have come and gone. Dunaverty Castle is a grim reminder of the effects of local, national and international politics. The ruins of Keil House recall a period stretching from the Reformation to the golden age of Scottish engineering. Owned from pre-Reformation times by the Omay family, which provided priests and ministers for Southend and Campbeltown, Keil was sold in 1819 to Dr Colin McLarty of Chesterfield, Jamaica, an island strongly linked with Argyll families, and the *New Statistical Account* of Southend reported in 1843: 'The farm of Keil has assumed a very improved appearance since it became the possession of the late Dr McLarty. When he entered into possession of this property

Keil School, where the engineers of Kintyre were trained (*Neil and Mary Kennedy Collection*)

about twenty-four years ago it was absolutely in a state of nature. He improved it in every way by draining and enclosures, planted trees about his farmhouse and gardens, and decorated the place with a variety of beautiful shrubs which has been an ornament to this part of the country.'

Keil estate then included Gartivaigh Farm. The next owner, James Nicol Fleming, a director of the City of Glasgow Bank, built a small Victorian mansion on the site of the laird's previous small house and in time added South Moil Farm. Mr Fleming was more interested in the house than the land, however, and in the late 1860s he turned it into what was considered one of the finest in the Western Highlands. But he overspent, borrowed from the bank (as apparently his fellow directors did) and was imprisoned after the bank inevitably collapsed, leaving shareholders responsible for £5 million worth of debt. Keil House passed to Ninian Bannatyne Stewart, another Glasgow businessman. On his death, the estate was broken up and in 1915 the house was bought by the trustees of the estate of Sir William Mackinnon, founder and chairman of the British India Steam Navigation Company.

Sir William had left money in his will to set up an engineering school for boys from Argyll and the Isles. Kintyre Technical School offered free education to less-well-off boys but the under-insured building was destroyed by fire in 1924 and the school was transferred to Dumbarton, leaving yet another ruin in Southend. Keil was sold at public auction in 1926 to James Barbour, a farmer from Gartfern in Stirlingshire.

Peter Armour, one of Keil's first students, recalled the breeze from the open dormitory windows lifting the bedclothes: 'No doubt we were healthy in the good Southend air.' That good Southend air, its wild coastal beauty and contrasting pastoral peace continue to attract visitors. Sometimes, however, its farmers – families who have sustained this 'peninsula on the end of a peninsula' for so many centuries through so much upheaval – must wonder if they can be sustained on good air alone.

2
DRUMLEMBLE

'. . . verify if colys may be wonnyn thare'

James Watt may have felt he had more to do with his time, in 1773, than sort out the problems of an unpromising coal mine in Kintyre. It was the year before his entry into a vital partnership with Matthew Boulton of Soho, near Birmingham, to produce a double-acting engine and he had a dozen other groundbreaking projects in preparation when he was invited by Charles MacDowall to carry out some surveys at Drumlemmen, known also as Drumlemon and today as Drumlemble. Mr MacDowall, called 'Crichen' after the name of his Kintyre property, had influence, however. He had been admitted as an advocate in 1734 and was later sheriff of Renfrewshire. The young James Watt was born in Greenock, Renfrewshire, in 1736, the son of a merchant and town councillor. He would have grown up knowing this pillar of the community. In the 1760s, Watt's best friend, John Robinson, tutored two of MacDowall's sons. Such early ties are hard to sever.

The engineer and inventor had already surveyed for the Forth & Clyde Canal and the Caledonian Canal and been involved in improving the harbours at Ayr, Port Glasgow and Greenock. Now, in the early 1770s, MacDowall tried to involve Watt in all sorts of Argyll projects, including the Crinan Canal. Eventually, he managed to get Watt over to Crichen to take a look at his mining and transport problems. On 8 June 1773, Watt sailed from Greenock on a vinegar boat. It was an inauspicious start to his Kintyre work – the boat was becalmed and did not reach Campbeltown until the 10th. He had a busy weekend, trying to cram in the work he would have done in those two wasted days. He spent the Friday and Saturday surveying, had the obligatory Sabbath off, took a look at some flooding problems around Campbeltown Mill on the Monday and Tuesday then concentrated on MacDowall's mining business: could he improve the pumps at the coal mine and work out a line for a canal to transport the coal to Campbeltown? By 21 June, Watt had started planning how to drain Loch Sanish on the low ground between Campbeltown and

Machrihanish. The next day he made a rough estimate of the canal and spent the rest of the week checking the best route for it. By the time he took a packet from Campbeltown back to Greenock, he had a notebook full of sketches and figures.

He set out on 1 July – and again was becalmed. He spent two days kicking his heels and watching whales between 'Cantyre' and Arran, not reaching Greenock until the 3rd. Even so, he sent plans and advice to MacDowall by August – but perhaps after experiencing such time-wasting travel it is not entirely surprising that Watt was only the nominal supervisor of MacDowall's mining and canal work.

This was the *belle époque* of development. Landowners and their wealthier tenants were pushing ahead with agricultural and industrial improvements and the Duke of Argyll was no exception. He was more than willing to lease land to MacDowall, who saw potential in reopening the Machrihanish salt-works which had closed in 1764. The process of salt production (a valuable commodity in a fish-curing area) involved evaporating sea water and MacDowall wanted coal to do it. To encourage the development of his estates, the Duke not only leased the local coal- and salt-works to MacDowall for twenty-seven years but agreed to take no rent until Whitsuntide 1773.

This had always been agricultural land but the Laggan Moss was also the largest area of extractable peat in Kintyre. Families from a wide area cut their peats here for winter fuel. Farms had developed at Drumlemmen and Ballycreggan, which may well have supplied produce for the royal castle at what was then Kilkerran, later to become Lochhead and then the modern Campbeltown.

Kintyre's castles were begun during the first Christian millennium, some replacing much older fortifications. They became the property of the kings of Scotland in due time, and those kings visited regularly. Today, road transport dominates and Kintyre is perceived as a remote destination. When water was the only way to travel, the peninsula was more readily accessible. Royal entourages frequently sailed up the Firth of Clyde to check on their vulnerable western outposts and independently minded clan chiefs. By the standards of the day, they were looking for comfort during these regal tours of duty and a few nights huddled over smouldering damp peat may have prompted James IV to send collier John Davidson to Kintyre in 1498 'to verify if colys may be wonnyn thare'. Davidson was given expenses to travel from Dumbarton and was paid to buy tools for his survey. Coals were indeed to be won there in the middle of Laggan Moss around

Drumlemmen and James ordered them to be mined for use in his Kintyre castles.

Three centuries later Davidson's discovery was to lead to Drumlemble being a vital linchpin in Campbeltown's prosperity. Village and burgh grew in tandem when men like MacDowall instigated the nearest thing to an industrial revolution Argyll ever experienced. The coal was the tail end of the carboniferous stratum which stretches from the east of Scotland to the Antrim coast. Never considered to be top quality, it fired Campbeltown's distilleries and eventually powered the peninsula's only railway.

This 'industrial belt' came within Campbeltown parish, which is bordered to the north by hills ranging to the height of Cnoc Moy's 1,462 feet. On the west coast, saltpans were worked at Machrihanish from the mid seventeenth century to the end of the 1800s, and Drumlemble's coal seams were just three miles from the burgh's boundaries. Coal miners appeared on the baptismal records in 1670 and in 1678 it was noted that Ballycreggan farm was 'parked [enclosed] for the colliers' horses' – long before any other land enclosure was undertaken. In the early days, the pits were known as the coal heughs and the salt pans were jointly tenanted by John Campbell, Chamberlain of the Earl of Argyll in Kintyre, and Alexander Forrester, proprietor of Knockrioch, who paid the Earl £1333 6s 8d for the tenancy.

Campbeltown itself had its roots in the mists of time. Ancient peoples working with flint tools and weapons around 6000 BC chose well to found their scattered community there. The sea loch, an inlet of Kilbrannan Sound, was a natural harbour. In time, it became an important centre of the Dalriadic kingdom and named for the Irish St Chiarran – *Ceann Loch Cille Chiarran* (Head of Loch Kilkerran). It was a sparse settlement for centuries but was strategic enough for Norse and then Scottish kings to encastellate themselves there.

For a time the lands were in the hands of the Macdonalds of Islay, but the support of Archibald Campbell, the 7th Earl of Argyll, for James VI & I meant he was granted rich Crown lands in Kintyre which the Macdonalds had forfeited. There had been an Act of Parliament in 1597 for the 'planting' of burghs in Kintyre, Lochaber and Lewis as a strategy of taming unruly Highland factions. In 1614 and 1615, Argyll suppressed the Macdonalds again and in 1618, newly designed 'Lochhead' became one of those 'civilising' burghs.

James Armour came from Ayrshire around 1665 and farmed Trodigal Farm near Drumlemble. One of his sons became a maltster in Campbeltown, another a still maker. As similar 'plantations' began to take effect towards the end of the century, King William approved the erection of the new town of Lochhead as a free burgh of barony. In 1700 it became the royal burgh of 'Campbeltoune' with a weekly market on Fridays and three eight-day fairs beginning on the first Tuesdays of August, October and November. Only the burgesses or those with freedom of the burgh could exercise trade or commerce in Kintyre and the adjacent islands. It was time to stop warring and start developing fishing, shipbuilding, distilling and coal mining.

The Rev. Dr John Smith wrote in his *Agricultural Survey of Argyllshire*, drawn up 'for the consideration of the Board of Agricultural and Internal Improvement' in 1795: 'Coals are found in the neighbourhood of Campbeltown but they have not yet been wrought to any great extent than what serves the town, which consumes about 4,500 tons a year.' He added: 'The coal is rather of an inferior quality. But it is said that better coal might be got by going deeper, and being at more expense.'

The coal was not sold throughout Kintyre. There were few wheeled vehicles in the peninsula and few roads other than bridle tracks or those used by drovers, so it was easier and cheaper to ship coal from Ayrshire. The small-scale mining at Ballycreggan Farm in 1670 was not developed until MacDowall started looking for a new and more accessible source near West Drumlemble Farm. The main market in the earliest days was Campbeltown's distilleries and MacDowall obviously saw there was enough potential to merit building a canal to transport the coal from Drumlemble to the east coast of the peninsula.

The development was not universally welcomed, of course. In 1788, Lachlan MacNeill, the tenant of Aros, was unhappy about paying a higher rent when his lease expired. He reminded the Duke of Argyll that when his rent had first been agreed, so many people were cutting peats on Aros ground that he was able to pay it easily. Since then, he wrote to the Duke, 'the Tacksman of the Coalworks of Drumlemon has erected a Fire Engine and Executed a Canal halfway to Campbeltown'. The presence of the canal, he claimed, meant that 'the inhabitants thereof are now so well supplied with coals that there is no demand for peats'. The canal was started in 1783 and was finished by 1791. It was able to take more coal at cheaper prices from Charles MacDowall's coal mine at Drumlemble into the burgeoning burgh – but it is doubtful if Lachlan MacNeill really was so much out of pocket as he claimed.

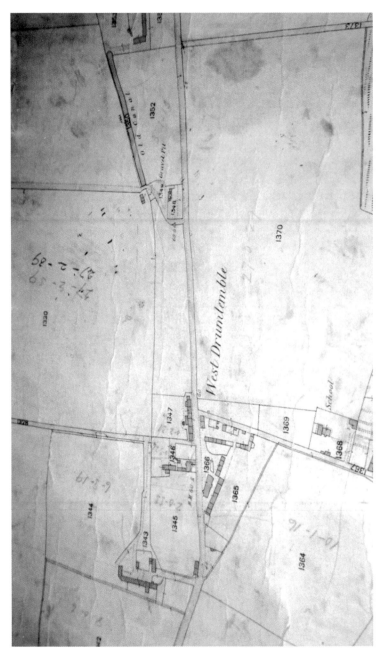

James and William Wallace's early nineteenth-century map of their farm at West Drumlemble showing the line of the canal

Poor people continued to cut their peats, spending, according to Dr Smith in his *Statistical Account* of the parish of Campbeltown, 'two or three months of the best season of the year . . . preparing a miserable and precarious fuel'. This in turn annoyed the Campbeltown Coal Company, which wanted a limit put on peat cutting to give local coal a chance on the market. A tax on coal transported by sea had done little to help promote the Drumlemble product, but after it was abolished in 1794, an export trade augmented the company's income from coal stocks sold to the distilleries and other local industries.

Change had come very quickly. There were only twenty-eight houses in Campbeltown in 1636. By 1692, a census of 'fencible' men (those fit for military service) showed seventy-six men aged between sixteen and sixty resident in the burgh. By 1791 there were 5,000 residents of Campbeltown and a hundred years later there were 8,235. The settlement of Lowlanders in Kintyre in the seventeenth century was one of the major factors which led to Campbeltown's growth, while the invention of the steam engine augmented its industrialisation. Without men of ambition and vision who, like MacDowall, could see the bigger picture, the town could have remained a backwater.

Whisky became synonymous with Campbeltown but the distilling of aqua vitae had been a home industry long before the existence of the burgh itself. In 1636, six quarts of aqua vitae (in Gaelic *uisge beatha*, the water of life) were part of the rent paid by Crosshill farm tenants to the town of Lochhead.

Brewing was also a cottage industry which gave poverty-stricken runrig farmers extra cash, but in 1770, Orr, Ballantine & Company built a brewery near the town mill and by 1772 there were twenty-two small licensed distillers producing 19,000 gallons of whisky a year. There was never enough barley for the whisky – and sometimes, as in 1683, there was not enough grain to feed the Kintyre population. 'Remote' is just a concept, and substantial armies marching the length of Kintyre right up until the time of the 1745 Jacobite Rising left famine in their wake.

The 1707 Union of the Parliaments led to a degree of peace and progress. Roads improved (if only to allow armies better access) but as early as 1702, the Rev. Lachlan Campbell, minister of the Highland Congregation of Campbeltown, had written to his friend, the historian Robert Woodrow, that there was at that time in Kintyre 'a certain Mathew [sic] Frew of Kilwinning, a noted engineer of coalworks, who had come as an undertaker in the building of some bridges'.

In its Kilkerran days, the town and surrounding area had prospered through cottage industries and fishing, although the tax imposed by the Scottish Parliament in the time of James IV on all herring catches had proved crippling. By 1663, however, one of the 9th Earl of Argyll's prizes for supporting the government was a tack or lease on the Assize of Herrings in all the western seas. He gave the job of collecting the Lochhead rent to John Yuill. Lochhead burgesses had been paying part of their rent in herring since at least 1636 when the 8th Earl's tenants also paid part of their rent with items like home woven horse rugs, poultry and eggs. A more industrialised herring fishing was now bringing the burgh prosperity and it has been said that, like Amsterdam, Campbeltown was 'built of herring bones'.

Warring factions would affect the peninsula until the 'Glorious Revolution' of 1688 as a result of which William and Mary took the British throne. In 1657, Sir William Mure of Drumlemble wrote that his son Alexander had been 'slaine in the warre against the rebels in Ireland'. But even so, the townsfolk were doing well enough in 1672 to shop with Donald Clark, one of Campbeltown's most important merchants.

Descended from the pre-Reformation parish clerks he not only was the proprietor of Drumlemble, which he held in feu from the Earl of Argyll, but also sold all kinds of agricultural implements, household goods and luxury items ranging from spices through French wines and tobacco to gloves, ribbons and silk. Mr Clark's customers earned their spending power in the ancillary industries which were beginning to grow alongside both the fishing and the distilling. There was a busy yard at Campbeltown from 1700, building and repairing ships. Barrels were made for fish and whisky. Nets were made and repaired. The Union of the Parliaments meant that Scotland's merchants benefited from changes in the English navigation laws which had previously reserved colonial trading rights for English merchants only. After 1707, Scottish merchants were also allowed to import coffee, tea, rum, tobacco and other goods from the colonies and sell them on to Irish and European markets.

This was when Glasgow's merchants made fortunes in tobacco and although Campbeltown merchants could never compete at that level, they did establish an exchange with the West Indies and North America. A 1745 Customs record shows William McKinley, a Campbeltown merchant who had been the burgh provost, exporting soap, candles, tallow and shoes for Hogson Legg & Company of

Belfast to Kingston, Jamaica, on the *Prince Charles*. Linen, tartans, copper stills, tallow and herring went out during the 1740s and 1750s to the West Indies, Pennsylvania and North Carolina, places which had been the destinations of Kintyre emigrants who now traded flax seed, oak and occasionally tobacco back to Kintyre.

There was a good trade in rum landing in Campbeltown for re-export to Ireland, from whence it was probably smuggled into England to flout high rates of excise duty. Charles McNeill made his money importing for Messrs Gallon & Thomson and Robert Orr traded for Thomas Gregg, another Belfast company. Orr and a merchant called William Finlay had become the main Campbeltown agents in this lucrative re-export trade by 1767. Campbeltown was now selling on everything from blubber to wooden staves and cotton wool but the burgh's key role in the rum re-exporting business was consolidated when the government bought the Isle of Man from the Duke of Atholl for £70,000 in 1765. The island had its own laws and duties and had been the centre of illicit trade, particularly with Ireland. Campbeltown filled this gap in Ireland's transatlantic trade links.

Of course, the loopholes were eventually plugged in 1772, making the illicit trade too risky. Then the American rebellion of 1776 made the Atlantic too dangerous and brought that era of trading to a close for Campbeltown. But its quay had seen great prosperity between 1765 and 1771, and that left a taste for enterprise which re-emerged through herring and whisky. Little wonder men like 'Crichen' MacDowall wanted a share of the action and were prepared to speculate to achieve that share.

MacDowall could not compete efficiently, however, if he had to transport his coal on the existing bad roads which became impassable in winter. The services of James Watt were needed to build a canal from Drumlemble to the heart of this prospering burgh. MacDowall's optimism was based on the discovery that one of the coal seams at Drumlemble was 6 ft thick. If the coal could be transported cheaply and efficiently to Campbeltown, there was surely more potential for exporting it from there, along with the linen and soap and copper stills, than there was from the harbours along the Ayrshire coast. Until 1774, some coal had been transported under sail from the open beach at Machrihanish, but then a zealous Customs surveyor seized an open boat carrying two tons of coal because it did not have a Customs docket. A canal was now a necessity.

MacDowall's major difficulties were Straw Water, which flooded, and the hills between the coal field and Campbeltown. Watt's expertise was to overcome both problems. The engineer took the most northerly pass through the hills into Campbeltown, and channelled Straw Water through a wooden aqueduct.

The canal rises to 37 feet above sea level. Too small for seagoing vessels, it started its journey of almost 4.5 miles beside a mine shaft which today lies under buildings at West Drumlemble farm. It was there that the barge horses circled at a terminus to make the return journey to Campbeltown. In 1797, a new pit was proposed nearer the village of Drumlemmen. The canal, which had no locks, was 9 ft wide at the bottom and 4 ft 6 in. deep. It could only take one boat, so passing places had to be built. By 1798 there were three flat-bottomed barges on the canal valued at £69. Watt made allowances for the difficult land the canal was to be cut through. If the Laggan Moss had been better drained as planned, the canal would have run dry. Three bridges over the canal were estimated at £30 each and two foot bridges cost £10. The estimate for the whole canal was £1562 16s, but prices were shown on the back of the estimate for variations for the Straw Water aqueduct (£104 13s and £159 5s 8d).

This 'back of the envelope' costing turned out to be for the most innovative part of the whole project. Straw Water was fed into what was thought to be the only wooden aqueduct built in the UK – an idea Watt may have recycled from an earlier design for an aqueduct over the River Avon on the line of the canal he surveyed between Bo'ness and the River Carron in 1771. The water level of the canal was so low that the river bed had to be dug out underneath the aqueduct to allow for flooding.

Watt had a disagreement with MacDowall over the materials to be used, wanting to floor the canal with old ships' planks or large stones. MacDowall would have none of it. He paid up for good mortar to support the aqueduct trough's support piers, but his lease was for just twenty-seven years and he said: 'All I want is to serve my time of it. I wish to be at no expense but what is absolutely necessary.'

And time was ticking away. After the coal-seizing incident at Machrihanish in 1774, the canal was the only way forward, but first Colonel Charles Campbell, a litigious neighbour, objected to it and then Campbeltown town council took out an interdict to stop MacDowall building the canal next to the town mill dam. If these were not obstacles enough, Drumlemble tenants sent MacDowall claims for damages to their land and property caused by the coal works. It was not until 1781 that the building was actually started with MacDowall's man following Watt's instructions and keeping within the bounds of the estimate. Meanwhile, in 1783, the Campbeltown boom years had a severe setback because of harvest failures and MacDowall did not even see his canal finished. He died on 11 September 1791. Records suggest the canal was not officially opened until 1794.

The coal, of course, despite the Drumlemble complaints, went on being mined. A cartload of coal weighed in at a third of a ton. In 1788, 31,418 cartloads were taken from Drumlemble. The next year it went up to 40,987 cartloads, but dropped back to 34,937 in 1791. By the end of the century, Campbeltown's upper crust was using the Drumlemble coal (much as the kings had used it in days gone by) while the poor stuck with their peat. Pack horses and ponies carried the peats to town (and there was a trade in them up to the twentieth century) while the barges toted forty cartloads of coal along the canal to town every day at a cost of seven shillings a ton.

There were, of course, plenty of poor around. In 1810, the Duke of Argyll asked a London land agent called James Malcolm to survey his estate. He found that even tenant farmers were living in houses with no floorboards and at east and west Drumlemble, the earth floors of farmhouses were below ground level, rather than packed in the traditional way above the level of the door. Even with a fire, the houses were always damp and Malcolm reported that people and cattle (sharing the same door) 'must wade through a sea of water' many months of the year.

While coal was being extracted from Drumlemble colliery, peat was being carried at the rate of 4,820 cartloads a year. This exploitation drained Laggan Moss and created improved farming land. The process was speeded up when some tenants in the area were offered a premium of £4 for every acre brought under cultivation.

In 1779, there were 162 farms listed on the Duke of Argyll's Kintyre estate, the biggest in the peninsula. Many were worked by several families and six on the estate had ten or more families attached to them. On Drumlemble Farm, for instance, there were fourteen families, two tenants, three tenants' sons, three servants, ten cottars, and eighteen others (women and children under twelve were not recorded). Were those who produced illicit whisky augmenting their meagre incomes, or simply blotting out harsh reality? Women had once spun flax and a village called Lintmill grew up to process it. But by 1772, they were distilling whisky while their husbands were in the fields. Folk historian Angus Martin records Nancy McArthur, Mary McKinven, John McMurphy and Bell McSporran running stills at Coalhill, while John McInnes had one at Drumlemble. Drumlemble women 'liberated' a still confiscated by an exciseman at Knockanty, throwing stones at him until he fled back to Campbeltown – while they returned the still to its 'rightful' owners.

It was not all subsistence farmers who ran illicit stills, however. The Armour family had a coppersmith business in Campbeltown and made stills, illicit and otherwise. The business records, *Still Books of 1811–17*, show that among those buying illicit stills were farmers, a miller, a shoemaker and an innkeeper. There were 800 separate transactions in the books, which would obviously have spelled disaster for these better-heeled folk had the books got into the hands of the authorities. After 1823, tougher legislation meant distillers were forced to take out licences and distilling became the new legal growth industry in Campbeltown. Coal had a major market again, but the collier's life never ran smoothly.

At the turn of the nineteenth century, 4,500 tons came into Campbeltown from Drumlemble daily. That figure rose to 10,950 tons in 1835. But by 1851, Drumlemble pit had been reduced to a care-and-maintenance situation and Watt's canal, now little used and overgrown, was abandoned in 1856. The pits themselves were closed between 1861 and 1863, but then a new pit was opened at Kilkivan by 1866. The colliery changed hands in 1875 and the new owners, in the spirit of MacDowall, built the Campbeltown & Machrihanish Railway, bringing with it a crazy period in the history of humble Drumlemble.

While the rest of Britain was beginning to bristle with branch lines, the age of steam had come to Kintyre by sea. This was to be the most isolated railway in Britain. The nearest rail line went via Dalmally to the railhead at Oban, 90 miles away. When a railway was mooted from Saltpans beyond Machrihanish through Argyll Colliery past Drumlemble, Lintmill, Stewarton and on to Campbeltown, it caused a sensation. This was a peninsula where wheeled vehicles had been almost unknown in the eighteenth century and where roads were narrow and often dangerous. The daily mail coach from Campbeltown to Tarbert battled against conditions which contemporary emigrants to America would have called primitive.

The new railway was the only narrow-gauge line in Scotland and the only Scottish light railway with its own rolling stock. It was built

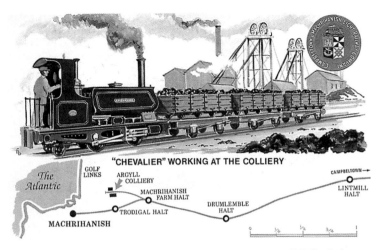

"CHEVALIER" WORKING AT THE COLLIERY

The route of the Drumlemble coal train (*Maureen Bell Collection*)

by the Argyll Coal & Canal Company, whose first action was to close the weed-choked canal and draw up another route for their tracks into town. The *Campbeltown Courier* reported on 29 July 1876: 'Operations were commenced this week for cutting out the new line of rails in connection with the Argyll Coal and Cannel (*sic*) company's works at Trodigal.' The aim was to provide a quicker service for Campbeltown distilleries, which in 1875 used 600 tons of coal a week. The whole district was using 1700 tons a week.

The railway was initially 4.5 miles long and was extended to 4.7 miles in 1881. The maximum gradient was 1 in 35 and the sharpest curve had a 150 ft radius, which somewhat limited the railway's capacity. In the early days there were level crossings, but cattle grids were eventually installed. The first locomotive was a 0-4-0 tank engine named *Pioneer* and built by Andrew Barclay of Kilmarnock. It arrived by steamer on 11 November 1876 and was taken to the coal works at Drumlemble. On 21 April 1877, a newspaper report announced: 'The new line of railway between Drumlemble and the town . . . is now completed'.

Wagons came on the steamer *Gael*, which docked at Campbeltown on Saturday, 19 May. The following Wednesday, coal was being delivered into Campbeltown by train. Household coal cost 8s a ton and dross was 2s 6d a ton.

When the pits at Kilkivan ran out in 1881, Messrs J. & T.L. Galloway opened new operations at Drumlemble, half a mile west, and the railway extended there. In thirty years, the coal business had gone from bust to boom and a new locomotive was brought in to cope with extra production in 1885 – another from the Barclay stable called *Chevalier*, which became the longest existing Kintyre engine. The railway had cost £900 a mile to build and £150 a year to run. In 1897 it was taken over by the Campbeltown Coal Company, running its eighteen wagons with a CCC logo on the side. The *Princess* was brought up from Stoke-on-Trent but after the company changed hands yet again in 1906, she was no longer in service and was stored away at Drumlemble.

The Kintyre spirit of enterprise saw that Drumlemble's coal was not the only attraction on this track. The sea breezes, the golf on offer at Machrihanish and the bird life on Laggan Moss could now be in easy reach for thousands of tourists and day-trippers from Glasgow, Greenock and far beyond – if only there was fast and comfortable transport once they disembarked from their steamers at Campbeltown. In 1901, a new turbine steamer called *King Edward* came into commission. The next year, the *Queen Alexandra* was plying the Firth of Clyde. With their high speeds they were revolutionising tourism, but once at Campbeltown, day-trippers had to go to Machrihanish by horse-drawn carriages. The first motor car had been seen in Campbeltown in 1898, but bad roads meant the combustion engine was not yet Kintyre's transport answer.

The railway, on the other hand, offered enormous potential and after talks with turbine builders in Dumbarton, the Argyll Railway Company was formed and the tracks which carried coal were now to be extended to the harbour in Campbeltown and the golf links at Machrihanish. In 1904, an application was made by the railway company to the Light Railway Commissioners and the green light was given for the Campbeltown & Machrihanish Light Railway Company. The board of directors included family members of the William Denny shipbuilding company in Dumbarton, a Glasgow coalmaster called James Wood, James J. Galloway, a Glasgow engineer, and James Ferguson, a Glasgow distiller. All possible interests seemed covered.

Four sections of railway were involved, creating a new passenger terminus at Hill Street in Campbeltown, a junction with the existing railway, and a new link to make coal shipment more convenient. There would be a 20 mph speed limit and passengers would pay 3d

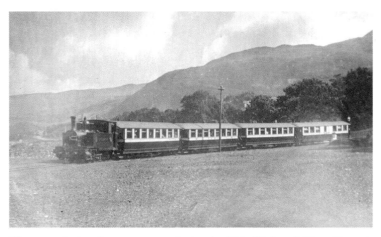

The most isolated passenger train in the UK (*Neil and Mary Kennedy Collection*)

a mile first class and a penny a mile third class. The scheme was passed by the Commissioners and Board of Trade approval was received on 8 May 1905. A prospectus was issued for 23,000 shares the next month.

The idea was to attract golfers and holidaymakers, but the 8,000 population of Campbeltown were also potentially passengers – and in 1905, 70,000 tons of coal were being carried by rail from Drumlemble to Campbeltown. It seemed like the start of a glittering new era combining the old and new industries of coal and tourism.

There were no conventional stations and the train refuelled at Limecraigs, where one local landlord assaulted an engineer to show his disapproval of this latest innovation during the building of the cutting there. The Limecraigs landlord was not the only objector, of course. A letter to the *Campbeltown Courier* in 1906 forecast that the railway would be cheap, nasty and dangerous. In the event, a 5 mph speed limit was fixed for the gradient between Limecraigs and the new Campbeltown passenger terminus. A 'special' was run for the miners' families as an opening gesture and although the tourist season was over, 10,000 locals took a trip during the first three weeks the passenger line was in operation.

It perhaps gives some idea of the status granted the line that the 'boat express' was advertised nationally (leave Glasgow Central at

8.25 a.m., arrive Campbeltown at 1.30 p.m. and take the train to the shores of the Atlantic), and that the world-famous *Bradshaw* ran the timetable. Three trains ran each way on weekdays with three more on Saturdays. Until 1930 there was no Sunday service. In the winter months, the Wednesday midday train was put back eighty minutes while the summer train connected with the steamer and did not stop at the halts on the express run to Machrihanish. On the regular run, the train stopped on request at Plantation, Moss Road, Lintmill, Drumlemble, Machrihanish Farm and Trodigal. Whenever a ticket for one of these stops was sold, the guard signalled to the driver. Did the day-trippers ever realise that their 'express' took exactly the same time as the regular journey? Presumably it added to their holiday excitement to think they were to reach Machrihanish by the fast train. Whether they were fooled or not, the 'express' ran most summers until the outbreak of the First World War and then intermittently until 1930. The economic situation which crippled the whole country after the First World War led to timetables which informed passengers there would be no trains if the colliery was idle. Even so, the tourist trade picked up after the war and eight trains a day ran in the summer months.

Sadly, the Royal Commission's estimate that the coal would last for generations was over optimistic. Then along came omnibuses and in the 1920s new bus services showed they could be more comfortable and more flexible than the train from Campbeltown to Machrihanish. There were bold ideas to extend the railway throughout Kintyre to make the single journey track more viable. As usual there was opposition from landowners, but there was never any real sense that this was a project with a future. The *Campbeltown Courier*, which had welcomed the railway in 1906, was now sagely declaring: 'The fact is that but for the presence of coal in the Laggan of Kintyre the present railway would probably never have been thought of.' Perhaps not, but it was a great idea while it lasted. It was all very sad when the railway company tried unsuccessfully to compete with the buses by buying its own second-hand vehicles. The railway finally closed for loss of revenue after the colliery shut down in 1929.

It had been an epoch of incredible enterprise. The era had starred characters such as Nan the conductor-cum-shunter-cum-porter and wee Ed McCable, the only person to wear a uniform, who rescued a train marooned in Chircan Burn. School trips and tourist bonanzas, church choirs and Sunday school picnics all went by the train. The

The miners' cottages at Drumlemble around 1890 – they stayed without running water and electricity until the 1950s (*James and William Wallace, West Drumlemble Farm*)

Hungry Hoose pub gave a free bannock with every dram en route – and all the while, Drumlemble coal fed Campbeltown's industries.

In 1923, 21,373 tons of coal were carried by train. After 1926, little coal was mined at all and miners drifted away to find work in a country on its knees. The financial loss to the railway when the pit closed in September 1929 was unsustainable. For the people of Drumlemble, it was devastating.

It was not only coal which had seemingly run out, however. The tourists were also in short supply. The *Campbeltown Courier* in June 1931 reported that two day-trippers had been spotted. Was there a need for the train anymore? The Labour politician Herbert Morrison, who had worked out a strategy for London transport, came to a meeting in the Territorial Hall in Drumlemble to hear the arguments which seemed to come down in favour of A. & P. Connachie, the local bus company.

In 1932, when the day-trippers began to drift back on the *Queen Alexandra*, no train was there to meet them. The land, wagons and plant had been sold to a scrapyard in June 1932. Three engines were broken up on the spot just fifty-four years after the first steam train had taken coal to Campbeltown. The *Pioneer*, said to have been stored

Train about to leave Campbeltown across Kintyre by train (*Maureen Bell Collection*)

at Drumlemble, apparently disappeared without trace. The men who had worked in the colliery could now only get seasonal work on the farms or odd jobs repairing the roads. Their houses in Drumlemble were little better than those surveyed by John Malcolm two centuries earlier. Miners' houses had huddled around Coalhill or were thrown up higgledy-piggledy around Drumlemble. In 1860 some primitive rows of dwellings had been built. They were overcrowded, had no electricity or gas, curtains instead of interior doors and water came from a pump in the street. In such desperate times, religion and music bring solace. Drumlemble had already seen a religious revival back in 1897 when Alexander Frazer, a student assistant at Lorne Street Church in Campbeltown set up a bible class at Drumlemble. Young farmers and farm servants and young miners made up the class, which soon turned into a series of evangelising meetings which attracted crowds from the town.

A report in *Revivals in the Highlands* says: 'With the exception of two or three, every miner in the village, which was formerly a Sabbath-breaking, godless place, was enlisted. The coal pit that used to ring with vile song and savage blasphemy resounded with songs, hymns and spiritual psalms. The day's work began with prayer and ended with song.' The 400-strong population ended up asking for a hall for 'religious purposes' and one was built by the five Presbyterian churches in Campbeltown for the village.

Did these tamed miners pass on their new way of life to their children? If they did, it would have been a happy day for the schoolmaster at Drumlemble General Assembly public primary school. The register for that establishment shows that throughout the second half of the nineteenth century, many of the children stayed away to help in the fields. On 12 July 1870, it records that children were needed to harvest potatoes for the Glasgow market, 'one woman receiving seven shillings last Saturday for her child's week's work'. A week later, the presence of Glasgow folk on their Fair holiday meant 'friends from a distance are visiting their relations here and this circumstance accounts for the absence of our scholars'. The schoolmaster had few teaching materials, had to contend with children spitting on the floor and bigger boys staying off to caddy for golfers at Machrihanish. In 1876, Her Majesty's Inpector's report stated: 'A good number of the Scholars belong to the migratory Collier class, and are difficult material to work upon.' Two years later with the role at 124 with one qualified and one pupil teacher, HMI recommended a female assistant. Outbreaks of diphtheria, miners' strikes and a disaster at the colliery in 1889 sadly served to keep a check on the ever-increasing number of pupils. No doubt the same situation was experienced at the church school up the hill. Yet at the close of the twentieth century, Drumlemble school came under threat of closure because of the low number of pupils in the district.

In the 1930s and 1940s, it was music which helped the folk of Drumlemble through difficult times. Willie Mitchell, son of a shipyard worker in Campbeltown, was a self-educated man who turned musician. He wrote the song 'Road to Drumleman' and performed it and many others at meetings of the Scottish Women's Rural Institute in Drumlemble's Mission Hall built for that religious revival at the end of the nineteenth century. Decades later, 'Road to Drumleman' was recorded by singer Anne Lorne Gillies, the Scottish band Ossian and the American folk group New Moon Ensemble.

Drumlemble was now struggling but just would not lie down. In 1945, at the end of the Second World War, the pit reopened and was developed by the National Coal Board, which promised 500 jobs and weekly outputs of 8,000 tons. In fact, it was worked until the 1960s, producing 3,000 tons of coal a week and employing 250 men. In 1954,

Famous throughout the UK as the Atlantic Express (*Maureen Bell Collection*)

130,000 tons came out of the pit, which met 80 per cent of the local market. It was closed as 'uneconomical'.

Campbeltown in the twenty-first century, having lost much of its industry, is now producing components for a new type of 'fuel' – propellers for wind farms at a factory within shouting distance of Drumlemble.

Many of Drumlemble's houses were removed after the Second World War, and not before time. When the council modernised the remaining houses in Long Row in the 1950s, they were in the same primitive state that they were built in the 1870s. Electricity and water went in for the first time and the village was included in council refuse collection rounds.

Today there is little evidence of Drumlemble's mining past. Willie and James Wallace live at West Drumlemble Farm, worked by their family since 1836. There is a crack in the cement outside their barns where a mine shaft has caused a little subsidence, and there is a ridge in the grass which shows the line of the old canal which terminated at the farm and had the turning point for the barge horses – not much to show for a whole industrial era. For many years the Wallaces were in dairying, until prices dropped so low that it was no longer a viable part of the farm. Instead, the twenty-first century sees them expanding the cattle finishing side of their business. They own three farms with a total of 550 acres in the area and grow some spring barley for animal feed. Bere, still grown for the Campbeltown distilleries when James was a youngster after the Second World War, is unknown in the area now and malting barleys are too expensive to grow because of transport costs.

Today, Laggan Moss is prime agricultural land and the season in Kintyre is longer than elsewhere. James says that before the mining began centuries ago, the Laggan was so boggy that most farms were up on the hills – and of course, they were very small because of the runrig system. Even in 1836 when his family first started farming at Drumlemble West, there were few animals and dairy cows, so much a part of Kintyre's more recent economic success, weren't kept there until around 1900. James misses the tight-knit community which still existed in Drumlemble village when he was young.

3
SADDELL

'To everything there is a season . . .'

About 1150, Cistercian monks founded St Mary's Abbey, close to the shore of the Kilbrannan Sound. The east coast of the Kintyre peninsula swoops and soars from Skipness to Dunaverty. The spine of Kintyre is a range of hills which peaks above Saddell in the 'hill of the boar' or Beinn-an-Tuirc. Today the 1,491 feet high hill boasts imposing electricity-generating wind turbines. Lower hills like Sgreaden and Bord Mor feed fertile valleys with tumbling burns that from the days of the monks turned mill wheels to grind grain. There were fish to be caught in Torrisdale and Glenlussa Waters as well as from the Sound.

Somerled, Lord of the Isles, is said to have been buried at the abbey after his death in 1207 (other legends claim his burial on Iona), but according to confirmations of the abbey's charters made by Pope Clement VII in 1393 and by James IV in 1498 and 1508, it was Somerled's second son Ragnal, or Reginald, who founded the abbey. This was the biggest ecclesiastical building in Kintyre prior to the Reformation in the sixteenth century – but then, most contemporary churches were tiny chapels. It was founded at a time when Europe was experiencing huge monastic growth and the Cistercians were an offshoot of the Benedictines. These monks were farmers and by 1200 Saddell was one of about 500 Cistercian houses in Europe. They employed lay brothers and became famous for breeding horses and cattle – and at Saddell agricultural activity seemingly outweighed the religious.

From Vatican archives it would appear that controversy surrounded the election of a new abbot at Saddell in 1393. It was a time of strife in the Church. In Rome, Boniface IX was recognised as Pope; in Avignon in France, Clement VII claimed the title. Saddell's mother house was Mellifont Abbey near Drogeda in Ireland and the abbot there was a Boniface supporter. When Saddell's Abbot Patrick died and one of their monks named Macratius was elected as his successor, Pope Clement sent word from Avignon on 12 July confirming the election. But when the Saddell monks told the Mellifont abbot who they had chosen – and who had confirmed his appointment – poor Macratius bore the brunt of the international politicking and was excommunicated. Although the abbey was large by Kintyre standards, this was a small community touched by big events.

It perhaps is not surprising that farming began to take up more time than religious matters. The abbey held lands from Davaar Island in what today is known as Campbeltown Loch, north to around Crinan in Knapdale, and on the island of Gigha off the peninsula's west coast. In an era when souls were believed to be saved through gifts to the Church, the abbey was over-endowed. Nigel, Earl of Carrick, and his wife Isabella gave the monks land in Ayrshire. Alexander, 3rd Lord of the Isles, gave them Gigha and Davaar, although Christina Caleni, great-granddaughter of Reginald, had already gifted Davaar previously. Duncan Campbell of Loch Awe gave them the lands around Crinan in the early part of the fifteenth century and similar gifts were still being given to the handful of monks who stayed on at the abbey even after it was closed in 1507. The abbey, by then little more than a commune of working farmers rather than a place of worship and meditation, had amassed strategic territory which could not be allowed to drift into the wrong hands. King James IV decided it should become part of the diocese of Argyll, not necessarily for religious reasons but because one of Scotland's most influential families was involved. The Bishop of Argyll was David Hamilton, an illegitimate son of James, Lord Hamilton, and the half brother of the 1st Earl of Arran. The bishop, a powerful and intellectual figure with national and international influence, had graduated from Glasgow University in 1492, studied in Paris, and by 1504 was witnessing royal charters and sitting on royal commissions. He travelled to Argyll on royal business in 1505 to 1507 and, in September 1507, the king confirmed his bishopric. His bonus was a charter giving him Saddell Abbey lands as a barony. Bishop Hamilton lost no time in building a castle on the shore half a mile from the abbey.

The Gaelic-speaking king was a frequent visitor to Kintyre and this corner of it could have been very different had his plans for Saddell gone ahead. James wanted Pope Julius to transfer the bishopric from the island of Lismore to Saddell. During his reign, the king had spent hugely on building, particularly at Stirling Castle. Now he proposed that a cathedral would be built at Saddell – and with a castle,

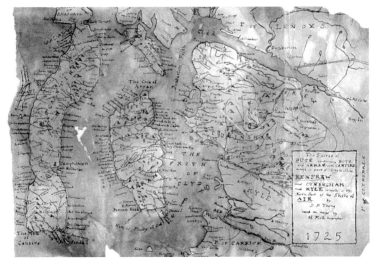

Saddell – the cathedral city that never was – was playing a secondary role to Campbeltown by the early eighteenth century (*Maureen Bell Collection*)

cathedral and Church power centred there, no doubt a splendid city would have grown in these green and pleasant valleys. The delivery of letters, however, was unreliable in the early years of the fifteenth century. Whether James's letter of request was intercepted on its way to Rome is difficult to prove, but it is now among the State Papers with Henry VIII's letters. With no response from the Pope and no follow-up because James met his end at the battle of Flodden in 1513, there was to be no religious seat of power at Saddell, no cathedral – but the castle had already been built by 1512 and became a valuable political pawn over the next century or so.

David Hamilton was still bishop in 1556 when his debts created a situation which would have farther-reaching effects on Saddell, Kintyre and, indeed, Scotland than the mere erection of a cathedral might ever have had. Back in 1475, King James III had stripped John of Islay, the last Lord of the Isles and head of the Clan Donald, of most of his possessions. Although the title of Lord of the Isles died with this John of Islay in 1503, the Clan Donald still had aspirations to power and James Macdonald of Dun Naomhaid (Dunniveg) in Islay still held lands in Arran.

When Bishop Hamilton found himself in debt to his half-brother, the Earl of Arran and Duke of Chatelherault, he gave him the whole Saddell estate in lieu of cash. In moved James Macdonald, suggesting a swap of his Arran lands for Saddell. The earl agreed, but there were strings: Macdonald was to pay the feudal dues on Saddell, collect rents and teinds in Kintyre, stay out of Arran affairs and play host to the Hamilton family at Saddell when necessary.

Two years after Macdonald took possession of the estate, Thomas Ratcliffe, Earl of Sussex and Mary Tudor's Lord Deputy of Ireland, came to teach him a lesson. Macdonald had been actively involved in Ireland's struggles against England, holding important Irish figures ransom in Scotland – perhaps even at Saddell Castle – and taking arms and men over from Kintyre to fight for his brothers: Alexander, Angus and Sorley Boy. Having fallen heir to the north-west corner of Country Antrim on the death of another brother, Colla, he gave this to Sorley Boy, who was a thorn in the flesh of the Earl of Sussex. Mary Queen of Scots obviously approved of Macdonald's activities against the English queen and gave ancient Macdonald lands in Islay and the barony of Bar in Kintyre back to James, adding to his domain of Saddell, Machrimore and Dunaverty. This jumped-up Scot interfering in the reconquest of Ireland was too much for Sussex. He sailed to Scotland in September 1558, and on 3 October reported by letter to Mary Tudor from his ship the *Mary Willoughby* that he had burned 'the hole countrye' of Cantyre. He had, he said, '. . . burned eight myles of leyngth, and therewith James McConnelles [an anglicisation of the Gaelic spelling of Macdonald] chief house called Saudell, a fayre pyle and strong'. He went on to burn Machrimore and Dunaverty castles at the tip of Kintyre.

When Elizabeth succeeded to the English throne in November 1558, Sorley Boy decided to offer his allegiance to her. James Macdonald was killed in 1565 and Sorley Boy took over his Irish estates. Saddell estate, however, stayed in the Macdonald family until 1607, when all the Macdonalds' Kintyre lands were given by James VI to the 7th Earl of Argyll in reward for services rendered. His successor, Archibald, the Covenanting Marquess of Argyll, gave the Saddell lands in tack to William Ralston of that Ilk in 1650 with the condition that he make habitable the castle burned by Suffolk. Ralston repaired the castle and put his Ayrshire relatives on the land to farm the tack.

The Marquess of Argyll was looking for political support when he included this member of the extreme Remonstrants sect of the Covenanters in his 'plantation' of Kintyre, but he also expected that

Saddell House and the castle where Lowlanders were planted after a violent
early history (*Neil and Marie Kennedy Collection*)

the agricultural expertise of the Ayrshire and Renfrewshire gentry
could improve the value of his lands.

Farming, fishing and, for a time, stone carving had gone on at
Saddell regardless of the political machinations of the landowners.
The Saddell Abbey school of carving began around 1425 and lasted
until the abbey closed, leaving a heritage of majestic and intricately
carved graveslabs which survives today. The stone probably came from
Kilmory Knap near Castle Sween. Never considered to be equal to
the Iona school, much of the carving may have been done by two lay
brothers who were itinerant stone masons. Some crosses commissioned
from Saddell survived only to be mutilated after an Act of the General
Assembly of the Reformed Church of Scotland, backed by an Act of
Parliament, laid down procedures to remove 'idolatrous' monuments
or deface them. Carved crucifixes were crudely chiselled off and the
basic crosses secularised, like the one used in 1700 as a market cross
for the new royal burgh of Campbeltown. Many more – like one
found in the sea at Southend – were simply smashed. The barbarity
of the Macdonald-led Dunaverty Castle massacre in 1647 may have
fuelled a backlash against Catholicism and inspired the iconoclasm
found in southern Kintyre at Southend, Saddell, Kilkivan, Kilkerran
and Kilchousland. Such iconoclasm may have been the only action of

rebellion open to subsistence farmers and poor fishermen who were constantly called upon to provide for the every need of their feudal landlords and to bow to their ever-changing political and religious allegiances, to the extent of laying down their lives.

Manipulation of populations affected every family in Saddell and the whole of Kintyre. When James VI & I inherited the problem of the Macdonalds of the Isles and their troublesome relatives the Macdonnells of Antrim, Kintyre was subjected to a 'plantation' of a different kind. James's intention was to divide and conquer by removing troublesome people and replacing them with loyal followers, as James IV had done before him. He had a degree of success when he confiscated lands in the north of Ireland and planted Lowland Scots and English there. He tried the same gambit in Kintyre but the ordinary people were either loyal to or fearful of their Macdonald overlords and the experiment did not work until the king put the job in the hands of his ally Archibald Campbell, 8th Earl and 1st Marquess of Argyll. Campbell was English-speaking and English in outlook. He was more than willing to oust his clan rival Macdonald but he was also sensitive to the fact that productivity could be improved on badly managed farmlands if Lowlanders moved in. He had an example to follow. In one of the first waves of 'transplantation', his predecessor had applied for a Decreet of Removal in 1609 to evict Kintyre tenants. But the Campbells were not the only 'transplanters'. On 26 February 1627, John Macdonald, a Knapdale landlord, issued a Precept of Warning to four tenants. Malcolm McIlgorme was one of those ordered by the sheriff in Kintyre to 'flit, remove with their spouses, bairns and stock', before Whitsunday. This warning was read out in church and the families scattered around the Kintyre peninsula. In 1685 they re-emerged in the record books when men had to take the oath of allegiance. Some were in Gigha, some in Glen Barr, while Angus and Dugald McIlguirme were on the farms of Ducheran and Barmollach in Saddell, then part of Killean parish. A century later, 'Blue' family (*gorm* is blue in Gaelic) members were emigrating because of high rents in Kintyre.

As if war and transplantation were not enough to deal with, what was called the 'plague' swept Scotland from 1644 to 1648. It was said to have arrived from Ayrshire at Dunaverty in a white cloud which spread over most of Kintyre – more realistically, it could have been spread by the civil war armies. It decimated Kintyre farms in

1647, leaving many without tenants. The 8th Earl found he had to repopulate as well as politicise his lands and Ralston got a tack of more than 23 merklands. The agreement was signed on 30 April 1650, 10 miles down the coast from Saddell in Lochhead, then still a fishing village but soon to become the burgh of Campbeltown.

The politically active Ralston went home to Ayrshire to campaign against Charles I, who was refusing to acknowledge the democratic form of government devised for the Church of Scotland by Protestants such as Ralston. Although he was against Charles's policies, Ralston was no republican and when Cromwell took power, he refused to follow him. The Earl of Argyll, however, decided to join the republicans and rather than lose Saddell over a disagreement about loyalties, eventually Ralston also joined Cromwell. He raised 220 horsemen for the Puritan cause in Kintyre in 1653. These men were ordinary tenants and farm workers required to answer their landlord's conscription call under the terms of their leases. What fear must have gripped the families of Saddell, as much at risk now as when Sussex torched the land they farmed. That summer, the Marquess of Lorne invaded Kintyre, marching down to Saddell and forcing Ralston to withdraw to Campbeltown, still known then as Lochhead. Lorne took a pragmatic view of the situation and decided not to hang his captives. As the son of the 8th Earl and Marquess of Argyll (who was executed in 1661 for anti-royal activities), he may have seen Ralston as the best man to caretake his Kintyre lands.

The seventeenth century continued to be a dark time for people of every class in Saddell. The monarchy was restored but Charles II still denied Scotland a democratically run church. The Covenanter Ralston was in the forefront of the resistance and with his Kintyre followers he was arrested on 12 October 1665 and imprisoned without charge or trial in Dumbarton Castle. Two years later they were all freed. Ralston had to pay a 10,000 merk bond ensuring good behaviour while his tenants and servants had to sign an agreement to keep the peace or pay a year's rent to the authorities.

By the time he retired to Saddell at the age of fifty-seven, Ralston's nineteen-year lease there was about to expire. The new earl decided to keep Saddell in Campbell hands and moved Ralston to a much bigger tack in the parishes of Campbeltown and Southend, where he died in 1691 at the age of eighty-one. As an old man in his seventies, he had seen the Macdonalds carry out their depredations against the Clan Campbell, sweeping through the whole of Argyll and leaving no house untouched. Farming and fishing implements, furniture, clothes and cattle were looted or destroyed along with the houses.

Politics, religion and clan rivalry conspired against the ordinary people of Saddell, and yet they continued to go to church and to educate children. The former must have proved spiritually painful and physically dangerous. At the beginning of the seventeenth century, Kintyre was still Roman Catholic Macdonald country and when the 7th Earl of Argyll was given charge of the peninsula, he did not enforce the Reformed religion because he had married a Catholic woman. There are no formal records of the Reformed Church before the Minutes of the Synod of Argyll, which start in 1639. There were Reformed churches in Kintyre from the middle of the previous century, of course, and when Franciscan missionaries came from Ireland in the 1620s they were given a hard enough time by Reformed ministers to have to hide out in the hills with their potential re-converts. When the Protestant bishop complained to James VI & I about these Irish fathers, the somewhat religiously ambivalent James said there was no need for anger with anyone converting the wild natives of Kintyre to Christianity, even if it came from Rome. The Kintyre Synod was held at Saddell in 1638 and the language spoken was probably Gaelic. But so great and so fast was the influence of the planted Ayrshire folk that in 1654 Saddell was the site of Kintyre's first English-speaking church. The Rev. James Garner, chaplain to the Marquess of Argyll, was inducted there on 17 June that year. Until then, the Lowlanders had gone back once a year to Renfrewshire and Ayrshire to take Communion and have their children baptised. The Gaelic congregation did continue, however, and was led by the Rev. Dugald Darroch with Lachlan McNeill Buidhe of Tirfergus the leading elder. William Ralston of that Ilk was the leading elder of the new congregation, which was represented at the first meeting of Kintyre presbytery in Lochhead on 15 August 1655. When Campbeltown became a royal burgh, it was not long before Ralston led the other Lowlanders in establishing a Lowland church there.

But the choice between an English or a Gaelic service was the least of the problems during the civil wars of the seventeenth century. The supporters of successive rulers lurched across the spectrum of Catholicism, Episcopacy and Presbyterianism, dragging their 'fencible men' and their families with them. It is not possible that the children of Kintyre could have been protected from the barbarity of the soldiers who marched up and down the peninsula during these bloody power struggles, yet this was a time when education was beginning to be offered to more than just the sons of the heritors. It was in the gift of the minister in Saddell parish to nominate the 'lesser gentry' and a few bright boys who would be educated at public expense at a school run by the General Assembly of the Church of Scotland. Ministers were not above nepotism and in 1640, the Rev. MacWharry nominated his own son, Donald. In 1649, it was James Campbell, son to the laird of Glencarradale who received the bursary. These boys grew up to experience a more peaceful era, although the Argyll dukes demanded still more 'fencible men' to support the 'bloodless' revolution which put William of Orange on the throne and were involved in the 1715 and 1745 Jacobite Risings. But from the Union of the Parliaments in 1707, Argyll began to be a county of progress rather than destruction. John Campbell of Saddell played his role in that progress as the first provost of Campbeltown after its erection as a Burgh Royal in 1700.

Although the 2nd Duke of Argyll, John Campbell, was a committed Unionist and away at war for much of the early years after he succeeded, the poorer and less influential proprietors of Kintyre stayed at home and cultivated their land. According to Dr John Smith's *Agricultural Survey of Argyllshire* published in 1798, in the first half of the eighteenth century 'luxury had not then reached us.' Hardly surprising, when most estate owners were still trying to salvage land decimated by the tramp of troops and properties which for almost the whole of the previous 100 years had been periodically burned and looted. According to Dr Smith, 'proprietors lived at home, and subsisted chiefly on the gross produce of their own lands.' By the time he was writing, however, things were different. 'An expensive mode of living is introduced,' Dr Smith said. 'Gentlemen resort frequently to the metropolis, and no reproach is attached to the loss of an estate, as the case is become so common.'

In 1751 there had been 200 proprietors in Argyllshire whose properties had a total rentable value of just over £9,924. The valuation determined the land tax, ministers' stipends, schoolmasters' salaries and other public calls on these heritors. There was some reorganisation of parishes in the middle of the century to take into account the changing status of villages and of Campbeltown itself. The parish of Saddell and Skipness was established in 1753, running the length of the east of the peninsula down to the Campbeltown parish border.

Heritors, or landlords, with very different agendas were moving into the parish, although the lands around Saddell itself were to remain in Campbell possession for another two centuries. John Smith felt the changes were a mixed blessing. 'Strangers with no attachment to the county' who could hand over £150,000 for a property but not 'reside there as did ancient owners' was the down side. It was a time when tenants could not afford repairs to what Smith called their 'mean and wretched hovels.' He forecast that if the needs of the 'hardy, virtuous and laborious set of people that is raised in the humble cottage' continued to be ignored, 'the nation will soon suffer'.

Those who could not get a living in Saddell or Carradale went to Campbeltown to seek a job. An Act of 1740 demanded that the heritors, ministers and elders of every parish make a list of all the poor in the parish and the heritors and householders had to provide a yearly sum for their maintenance. Ironically, the ministers themselves – and the parish schoolmasters – were so poorly paid that they had to do a bit of farming and grazing to support their families.

How much have things changed?

One present-day conservation-minded famer, Andrew Gemmill, is not breeding horses and black cattle as the brothers at the abbey did. He has not pursued a runrig system which condemned subsistence farmers to work communally on land of dubious quality. He describes Ifferdale as 'a run of the mill sheep farm' and expresses his interest in growing trees.

The Forestry Commission acquired this land in 1939, but today the mid-twentieth century plantings have just about been exhausted. However, through the enterprise of local farmers shelter breaks have been created with trees and hedgerows and the Rural Stewardship scheme is gaining adherents.

Today, Campbeltown has lost much of its modern industry and even the fishing, which also made Carradale a boom village, has virtually disappeared. In the 1700s, fishing was a real alternative to farming and offered men independence – a quarter share in a boat was more affordable than land. There were 600 fishing boats on Loch Fyne then and between £40,000 and £50,000 worth of fish was being landed in the county every year – an enormous sum by the standards of the day. During that era, Campbeltown was Argyll's success story. Just half a century old as a royal burgh, it was not only a major herring port but was importing and exporting commodities and luxury goods, building ships and distilling whisky. By 1792, twenty-

'Civilising' roadbuilding meant travel by boat from Saddell gave way, for some, to travel by charabanc. (*Neil and Marie Kennedy Collection*)

two small licensed distillers produced 19,800 gallons a year. But the poor always suffered and there were no social benefits then. Salt was too expensive for the poor to use to cure fish, so when George III offered a bounty of one shilling, later raised to two shillings, for every barrel of fish caught, the poor suffered.

By the early nineteenth century, potatoes were being grown around Saddell, particularly at Peninver on the Campbeltown side of Glenlussa Water from Saddell Abbey. But it was not until the steamers brought extra mouths to feed in the late 1800s that they would become a valuable cash crop. Then the new season's 'tatties' were lifted during the Glasgow Fair holiday in July when the population of Campbeltown was almost doubled by visitors coming on steamers from the city. One load of Peninver's finest was in the shops at 8 a.m., the next in the afternoon. The main crop was lifted in November.

But farming in this individual sense was never possible until the mid 1700s when steadings like those at Ifferdale were broken up and single tenancies were introduced. But the terms of those tenancies still included exacting terms. Tenants were all 'thirled' to a particular mill, for instance, which would have been built by the heritors. The millers had to pay their dues to the heritors and the tenants had to use the mill. Saddell mill, built in 1634, therefore became a focal point for the district.

Most Kintyre farms made malt for beer, which was drunk as we drink tea today, and of course, illicit stills produced whisky which no doubt rounded off a good day at the fair. In Saddell, the fairs were at Candlemas (2 February), Whitsun (15 May), Lammas (1 August) and Martinmas (11 November). The Whitsuntide and Martinmas fairs were when the rents were paid and farm servants were free to look for a new job. 'Feeing' fairs were when farmers hired servants for the next six months and people looking for a new job would walk to Campbeltown where in Main Street, Cross Street, Back Street (now Union Street) and the head of Longrow, labourers and farmers bargained their terms. If a farmer liked the look of a labourer, he would give him one shilling as 'earnest' money to seal the deal, but if the servant did not like the offer he gave the shilling back.

Dairy workers and cowherds were in much demand at Saddell – and were for another two centuries. At one time every farm had a dairy herd, a tradition introduced after the 'plantations' of Ayrshire farmers, although according to some of the early statistical accounts, Kintyre cheese was far from the excellent product which came to be associated with Campbeltown's creamery. Made with milk left for two days for the cream to separate, it often was sour. Cheese made with one-day-old milk could be tough and cracked.

Around Saddell, flax, potatoes and sheep seemed to do best for many years. Flax grown at Whitestone, just north of Saddell before Torrisdale, was processed at Lintmill near Drumlemble. The soil was well cared for at Whitestone, with seaweed ploughed in as a fertiliser. The MacKinleys were innovative custodians at Whitestone, building stone houses on the shore for their potatoes. That made it easy for Matthew MacDougall of Carradale, a potato merchant and relative of the MacKinleys, to ship their crop out. Another MacDougall relative was a fisherman and boatbuilder and one of his boats, *Mary and Agnes*, was used to carry Whitestone potatoes to Ireland in the late 1800s.

Today, sadly, no one in the district makes farmhouse cheese. Nor, although this land would have been worked for centuries by horses drawing simple wooden ploughs, are there any working horses in Saddell. In the old days, horse fairs were held at Campbeltown on the first Thursday in February, the second-last Wednesday of May, the second Thursday of August and the third Thursday in November –

Saddell Village in the late nineteenth century (*Maureen Bell Collection*)

perhaps more excuses to enjoy the whisky which Rev. Dr John Smith, author of the *First Statistical Account* of Argyll in 1794, deplored.

That is not to suggest that the people of Saddell were anything other than pillars of the community. A new parish church was built in Saddell around 1771 with 354 sittings. There was a Free Church at Carradale. There were four schools in the parish, although not all the children went all of the time – as elsewhere, they were needed to work at home on the land in the busy seasons and there was also the problem of weather. The lack of roads, the difficult terrain and a lack of shoes meant that sometimes fewer than half turned up. Today, all the younger children go to school in Carradale and secondary school children travel to Campbeltown.

Carradale today has become the focal point of the parish, with the village of Saddell shrinking to a few houses around the abbey ruins. With a tidal harbour where the River Carradale reaches Kilbrannan Sound, it was an ideal place for the herring industry to flourish in the days of smaller fishing boats. When James Watt came to Kintyre in 1773 to survey for the Drumlemble & Campbeltown canal, he also stayed at Colonel Donald Campbell's house at Saddell. Campbell wanted to know if improvements could be made to the river there and whether a jetty could be built at Carradale to make the harbour safer. Watt drew up plans for water supply improvements for Glen

The focus of population shifts from Saddell to Carradale (*Maureen Bell Collection*)

Saddell mill and for jetties to stop Carradale harbour silting, but the work was not carried out.

Saddell was a busy place in 1794, however, when the *First Statistical Account* recorded four millers, six tailors, eight shoemakers, nine weavers, three wrights, three coopers and a boat carpenter. Most of the young men were also employed in the fishing industry, but although Carradale and Saddell were prospering through fishing and farming, this was Campbeltown's day. The merchants there had holdings in as many as a dozen vessels as investments. Campbeltown-built ships traded around Britain, Ireland, Spain, Portugal and to America and in winter went to the herring fishing. One lawyer, Alexander McAlester, had an interest in four ships which on trips to America in 1770 and 1771 carried refined sugar, linen, shoes, stockings and barrels of Irish beef.

A century later, the centralising effect of Campbeltown meant the burgh was still flourishing but 'progress' had changed the profile of villages such as Saddell and Carradale. Sheep farming had peaked but the people had left the land. The population of Saddell and Skipness parish in 1801 was 1,767. By 1881 it was down to 1,163, of whom 789 were Gaelic speakers. Steamers revolutionised the herring industry which was focused on Campbeltown and sent fish directly to Glasgow, leaving Carradale to small boats and reduced trade.

The advent of the steamers led to tourists coming in growing numbers; indeed, it was possible to have a villa in a place like Carradale and work in the city. In the 1880s, when Campbeltown was busy importing barley, timber and general merchandise and exporting whisky, fish, livestock and potatoes, there were daily steamers in summer and one three times a week in winter. The boats called in at Carradale, making communication between Saddell parish and Campbeltown a much simpler and quicker matter than the tiring land journey. The easier journey also took more young people away from the parish, of course. Throughout Kintyre, those who were not bold enough, enterprising enough or desperate enough to emigrate left for jobs in Greenock and Glasgow – or for streets paved if not with gold then certainly herring bones just 10 miles from Saddell.

There were plenty of jobs in Campbeltown in the last decades of the nineteenth century. There were 1,607 fishermen and boys, as well as 45 curers, 10 coopers and 475 in allied trades. This was a time when the total value of boats, nets and lines in the burgh was £38,232. And there was work in shipbuilding; between 1878 and 1880, eight vessels were launched from the Campbeltown yard, six of them iron steamers. And although there were five fewer distilleries in 1880 than in 1850, there were still twenty offering limited employment and producing nearly 2 millon gallons of whisky a year for export around the world.

The work in Saddell parish, on the other hand, was limited. Carradale by this time had a post office, a telegraph office and a hotel and there was domestic work in the new villas where enterprising fishermen had invested money. You could get a job as a farm servant, go to the fishing, or work at one of the 'big houses'. At that time, John Neil Macleod of Kintarbert owned Glensaddell House opposite Saddell Castle. The estate extended to 12,805 acres and was valued at £2,935 per annum. It had been built in 1774 by Colonel Donald Campbell of Glensaddell for his retiral after a distinguished career in India and the castle, once a splendid edifice where kings and bishops took meat and board, was used to house the estate workers and servants.

The changing social scene, the cost of land, rising wages and increased taxes meant that most estates were now approaching the end of their glory days. No longer would kings – or even dukes – give grand estates to their supporters, as was the case with Ardcardle Castle at Carradale, which was built in 1498 and placed in the charge of the head of the Ayrshire Reids, Sir Adam Reid of Starquhyte and Barskimmine in Ayrshire. The Kintyre estates of the Duke of Argyll were sold off in the 1950s to meet death duties. Saddell was last owned as a private house by Dr Andrew Campbell of Johannesburg, who claimed connection with the original Colonel Campbell. In 1975, the estate was bought by Landmark Trust and the castle – windowless and with trees growing out of its crenellated walls – was carefully restored for holidaymakers. Tourism has grown in importance as an industry in the whole of Saddell parish, yet sadly, one of the most exciting parts of that industry – the daily steamer calling at Carradale pier and Saddell, where a ferry boat was in regular use – disappeared in 1939. After the war, the Gourock to Campbeltown service no longer called in at Carradale and the bus and car became the standard means of transport.

The old industries would go through change as well. The author Naomi Mitchison, a Carradale resident, wrote in the *Glasgow Herald* in a response to the publication of the 1961 *Statistical Account of Argyll* that the decline of the fishing industry was not, as was suggested in the Introduction, simply due to the disappearance of the herring from Loch Fyne but because 'the old fishing villages, where the sail boats were drawn up on the beach, have no facilities for the large modern boats. Nor has modern fishing any place for the old-fashioned crofter-fisherman'. She harshly criticised the Herring Industry Board for putting 'dozens of men out of work at the worst possible moment' in Campbeltown and Carradale. Today, the fishermen blame the Scottish Parliament for not fighting their corner fiercely enough in the European Parliament where the ruling half a century later is again to conserve stocks by restricting fishing. Have things always been thus? From salt tax to white fish quotas, the constraints on Argyll fishermen echo down the centuries.

The Forestry Commission bought up much of Saddell's hill land before the Second World War, employing around fifty workers and planting some 2,500 acres. In the 1950s, Saddell had fifteen farms and five crofts raising black-faced sheep, beef cattle and Ayrshire dairy cattle. Milk went to the Campbeltown creamery. The Forestry Commission severely reduced the number of sheep raised on the higher ground. Today that land is returning to farming and the sheep are being reintroduced as the season has come round for this harvest of conifers to be plucked.

An abstract of the Kintyre estates of the Duke of Argyll for 1790 shows that 150,000 quick thorns were imported from Ireland at a cost of £39 4s 10½d including packaging and postage. Most were planted on the estates – in 1774, Archibald Macdonald was paid £3 2s 7d for planting trees in Glenlussa, just south of Saddell abbey. Today Andrew Gemmill is again creating the hedgerows which the Duke of Argyll in the eighteenth century saw as one of the ways to improve his estates, as well as selling his own lamb, beef and pork at Campbeltown farmers' market. He can't imagine the 'enormous amount of effort' which was invested in getting sheep and cattle to distant markets in the past. This reduction in 'food miles' may sound like a modern concept to conserve the environment. In fact, Andrew Gemmill may well be farming more in the methods of the Saddell monks than any stewards of the land have done in the intervening centuries.

4
TARBERT

'*There is nothing which gives to one ashore such a profound impression of the riches of the sea as a herring-gutting scene.*' (*John MacDougall Hay*, Gillespie, *1914*)

The history of Tarbert, Loch Fyne, is one of boats, and perhaps the most famous boat of all is the one which King Magnus II – better known as Magnus Barefoot – dragged overland between West and East Loch Tarbert in 1098. He wanted to guarantee the inclusion of Kintyre amongst the lands acquired under a treaty with the Scottish King, Edgar, son of Malcolm Canmore, which ceded to Norway all the Scottish islands a ship could sail round. Magnus was shrewd enough to raise the sail on his lightest galley, stand at the helm and cross the isthmus. His underhand strategy meant that from 1098 until 1265, the frontier between Scotland and Norway lay along the line which is now the road from East to West Loch Tarbert. South of that line was a foreign country and Tarbert was a tough border post. Little wonder, then, that once the Vikings were defeated, the King of Scotland made the building of a castle at Tarbert a priority.

After the bloodshed and battles of the Vikings, the lands of Tarbert were in the hands of the MacGilchrists and the monks of Paisley Abbey held power over the ecclesiastical property. Like so many landowners of the day, in 1250, 'Donenald Makgilcriste, Lord of Tarbard' gave the monks the timber rights on his lands for his own salvation and that of his ancestors.

According to legend, when Robert Bruce fled west after his defeat by the English at Methven in 1306, he was saved from death on the bleak hills of Sliabhgaoil, a few miles from Tarbert, by the warmth of a goat which lay down at his side. He went south into Kintyre and sought refuge in the castles at Saddell and Dunaverty – but when he returned in triumph after Bannockburn in 1314 there was no hiding on hills in the darkness. This time he was said to have followed Magnus Barefoot's precedent and slid triumphantly across between the lochs at Tarbert on wooden rollers made from those MacGilchrist woodlands. A dozen years later, he would order the building of a

Tarbert harbour overshadowed by the ruins of Bruce's castle (*Neil and Marie Kennedy Collection*)

castle overlooking East Loch Tarbert, a fort at the head of the west loch and another at Cairnbaan in Knapdale. The castle replaced older fortifications and stood 100 feet above sea level. From its heights, Bruce could see the coasts of Bute, the Kilfinan peninsula from Ardlamont to Otter Ferry, and north to Ben Cruachan. It was lofty enough to give a lookout into West Loch Tarbert and any alien ships coming from the west. Friends and enemies were almost guaranteed to arrive by boat rather than over land.

The building work was not just a matter of centralised government passing orders to be carried out at local level. Bruce was a resolute monarch who came to Tarbert to supervise the castle, bringing with him friends in high places, including Bishop Lamberton of St Andrews, the Primate of Scotland. While he was there, Bruce received the annual dues of the sheriff, bailie and Customs officers and appointed John de Lany as Constable of Tarbert.

The local tradesmen had struck gold. Between the building work itself, furnishing the castle and creating roads for it – not to mention providing its residents with food and drink – there were jobs aplenty. Tradesmen were paid in cash and kind. William Scott received 20 merks for making a road between the east and west lochs, plus the price of a quantity of meal. Neil the smith received a year's salary of £12, Neil the plumber got 8d a day for thirteen and a half days, John the carpenter was paid 3d a day along with some meal and cheese and Hugh Dulp built the new mill for £3 and got cheese as a tip. Two roofers spent forty days roofing houses in the castle and were each paid 2d a day. This was at a time when the king's chaplain was paid £2 a year and de Lany himself was paid a shilling a day.

John de Lany's accounts are, according to *Origines Parochiales Scotiae*, the earliest account of domestic architecture and modes of rural life in Scotland – if the building of a castle can be called 'domestic'. In 1329, de Lany gave £2 to William Scott for making and maintaining a park at Tarbert, which may in the Scottish meaning of the word have been an enclosed paddock or perhaps an area for hunting. Whatever its purpose, Scott received a further £5 for finishing it.

On 20 July 1326, the completion of the building accounts showed a grand total of £518 13s 6d spent on Tarbert's new castle, which went up in just over a year. Included in the price were a chapel, a wine-house, a bakehouse, goldsmith's house, malt-house, brew-house, a mill with a pond and lade, and a moat. At the time, the Scots pound was about the same value as the English pound, although depreciation in later years meant that it dropped to a twelfth of the pound sterling.

Of course, Bruce did not fund the castle himself. Just as the monks of Paisley received lavish gifts of churches and woodlands, so kings received contributions from loyal followers who no doubt saw investment in the building of a castle as a career move. Dugald Campbell, Sheriff of Argyll and Bailie of Athole, was the main funder of the Tarbert project. Other contributors included Dofnald [*sic*], Neil and John McGilhorn of the Macleans of Duart family, Gilchrist of McAy [*sic*], who was an ancestor of the Mackays of Ugadale, the Bailie of Kintyre and the Abbot of Paisley.

It was perhaps wise for some of the locally based men to be seen as donors because Bruce came to the castle a number of times – in 1329 he ran up a bill for wine and salt while he was there and he paid out 18 shillings to a dozen men to bring one of his ships from Dumbarton to Tarbert. And although workmen, with their part payments of Islay cheeses and sacks of meal, were obviously valued, then as now it was the entertainers who were paid the big money. A court jester, Patrick the Fool, was summoned to Tarbert from England in 1329 and even the man who brought him was paid 18 shillings – the price of a dozen boatmen.

Tarbert was now a royal burgh, a trading centre for the Clyde ports and the islands, and a major tax-payer. With privilege comes responsibility, and Tarbert had to pay a war indemnity of £4 8s 10d.

Royal visitors and other men of importance called in at Tarbert Castle down the years, sometimes for pleasure, sometimes simply to exert authority in wild territory. Clan feuds made a mockery of Crown law and order and when James IV paid his three visits to the islands in 1493, he stayed twice at Tarbert. In April he ordered repairs to be done and put men and munitions into the castle. That July, he called Parliament to the castle for cabinet talks about the difficulties in Kintyre and the islands, making the highest in the land take the voyage up Loch Fyne.

Four years later, the king left Ayr in what must have been a chilly March to visit the new castle at Loch Kilkerran (later Campbeltown), and spend a week at Tarbert Castle. Later that year he sent a collier to Kintyre, again at a cost of 18 shillings, to look for a supply of coals to heat his properties. The king was back at Tarbert the following year to put his plans for law and order in Kintyre into action and this was when he gave Archibald, Earl of Argyll, powers over what he saw as the troublesome Macdonalds, styled Lords of the Isles. In 1505, Campbell was given more power still in the gift of the Barony of Tarbert, which was renewed several times throughout the first half of the sixteenth century. Tarbert Castle remained in the family of MacCailein Mor as feudal superiors.

Whoever was supposed to be in charge, however, one of its residents during the sixteenth century was Alan-nan-Sop (Alan of the Straw), a pirate and illegitimate son of Lachlan Catanach Maclean of Duart, clan chief of the Macleans. Whatever the legal rights of the matter, this residency at the castle was gifted to him by Macdonald of Islay, along with the island of Gigha and some villages around Loch Tarbert in exchange for the pirate's goodwill. This was a man who plundered as far distant as Loch Lomondside and Ireland and it is said that he held the Lord of Coll a prisoner at Tarbert Castle. This laird was famous as a poet and musician and the legend says he remained a prisoner until he answered the bold Alan's request for a song.

In 1503, an Act of Parliament appointed a sheriff to sit in Tarbert and Loch Kilkerran because 'the pepill ar almaist gane wild'.

Despite – or perhaps because of – this wildness and infighting, the shire of Tarbert was in existence from at least 1481. There had to be some rationalisation of local government, however, because north

Argyll came under the sheriffdom of Inverness, mid Argyll was in the sheriffdom of Lorn and Knapdale was part of Perthshire. After 26 February 1481, Tarbertshire took over Knapdale, Kintyre, Mull, Islay and Jura, Gigha, Scarba, Colonsay and the smaller islands off the west coast. It was run by a heritable lieutenant, a chamberlain, a sheriff and a coroner. Perhaps the latter had the most work to do on a day-to-day basis. An Act of Parliament in 1633 joined the 'shirefdom of Tarbett and shirefdom of Argyll . . . to be callit in all tyme coming the shirefdome of Argyll', which surprisingly has almost come to pass, give or take the temporary imposition of the region of Strathclyde and a few boundary changes down the centuries.

Even so, the wild men of Tarbert continued to refer to Tarbertshire for many years to come. In the late sixteenth century they would answer to James Campbell of Ardkinglas and Dugald Campbell of Auchinbreck when all able-bodied men of Tarbert (as throughout Scotland) were called to register at twice yearly 'wapinschaws' if they were capable of military service. Men who did not register were fined 100 merks on the premise that such penalties could kick the clan system. From 1579 to 1597, the fencible men of Tarbert were called out again and again to combat everything from Border reivers to 'enemies of the true religion'. They were provided with weapons and armour and the heritors (landowners) had to bear the burden of the cost. In 1582, Colin Campbell, Earl of Argyll, was sued because he failed to pay the tax levied for military provision on the shire of Tarbert. The privy council stipulated that if he did not pay up, the money would be taken from his estates.

The common man who did not meet the stipulations of the government often met a worse fate. When James VI planned an expedition to Kintyre and the Isles in July 1600 to subjugate the wild west, it was all hands on deck – or else. All those called up for military service were to wait for the king at Tarbert Castle, and all ferrymen and other able-bodied souls not already given a role in this expedition were to be at Port-a-Mhaidhe (Portavadie) on the Kerry peninsula to assist in ferrying the king and his army across to Tarbert. Those who did not attend were threatened with loss of lands, goods and life. At the end of the day, the expedition was cancelled. The excuse was that the king recognised the poverty and distress of his people in Scotland, but there were those who were inclined to think he was not prepared to risk it without the guarantee of sufficient troops. Instead, his answer to the clan problem was to strip the Macdonalds of their lands and replace them with Campbells in key local positions. It was a strategy which was to have repercussions throughout the rest of the seventeenth century as civil wars presented opportunities for inter-clan revenge. As always, the poor suffered most for the vacillations of the powerful.

In July 1615, with the Earl of Argyll away in England, battle lines were drawn 10 miles from Tarbert when Sir James Macdonald called his clan to arms. The government ordered a number of Campbell cadet families to raise troops to hold the situation in check until the Earl returned in September with 400 soldiers. Few Tarbert men joined the Earl's forces because they were Macdonalds or supporters of Sir James. The Earl planned to surprise the Macdonalds on the island of Cara and sent a fleet of galleys with 800 men to do the job. The same day, he reached Tarbert with the rest of his men and joined the other Campbell troops. Macdonald now moved some 400 men under his uncle Ranald to stop the Campbell forces on the east at Tarbert while the famous Coll Ciotach took three boats and sixty men to West Loch Tarbert. On both coasts, the Macdonalds were forced down into Kintyre and eventually Sir James had to retreat home to Islay.

The skirmish had its dreadful repercussions a generation later. In 1647, a dark year for Argyll, Alister Macdonald of Dunaverty, son of Coll Ciotach, was the only chief still fighting for the doomed King Charles I, the king who would be beheaded at Whitehall two years later. With more than 1,000 troops Macdonald wreaked such savage revenge on Kintyre – ostensibly because it was now fighting against the king – that General David Leslie, the Marquess of Argyll and their Covenanting forces were all despatched to stop him. They caught up with him at Runaherin on the west coast south of Tarbert and defeated him there. It was then that Macdonald retreated to Dunaverty, where the pursuing Campbell and Leslie forces massacred his 300 men as they sought refuge in the castle.

After Charles I was executed, Tarbert Castle found itself a Commonwealth stronghold. There is an intriguing story that when the castle was retaken by some of Argyll's supporters, the Roundhead garrison under a Lieutenant Gillot was out gathering nuts. The Earl's supporters took the opportunity to seize 10 barrels of gunpowder, 5,000 weight of cheese and 26 bags of biscuits, which sums up the priorities of both parties. After an apology had been accepted by the major-general in charge of the district, the earl had to pay hospitality to the troops and officers at the castle. Three years later, the 8th Earl paid a somewhat dearer price for his support of Covenanters and Commonwealth. The restoration of the monarchy saw the loss of Archibald Campbell's head on the gallows at Edinburgh. Charles II appointed six lieutenants in the shires of Argyll and Tarbert to keep the peace: at Tarbert, Cowal, Inveraray, Saddell, Craigness and Dunstaffnage.

The Argylls were not happy about the presence of this 'popish king' or his successor and the 9th Earl went off to Holland in 1685 to plot the take-over of William of Orange. Seeing Tarbert as 'a very centrical place' he planned to raise troops there against James VII & II at the signal of a burning cross from hills all over Argyll. The Duke of Atholl was tipped off by the Lord Lieutenant of Argyll and Tarbert to be prepared for the Earl's landing at Campbeltown via Kirkwall and Islay. The Earl marched from Campbeltown to Tarbert with 1,800 men on 27 May 1685.

Argyll had with him a portable press which he used to print propaganda against the King. His campaign was not, he said, to regain the lands of which he had been stripped, but 'to oppose and repress' the 'usurption and tyranny' of the King. The King's forces, however, were already strategically placed and there was no fight left in Campbell followers. Two days later the Earl fled Tarbert for 'the town of Rosa in the Isle of Boot' (Rothesay in Bute) before going on to fight at Greenock and then Kilpatrick . His army was broken up on 18 June and he was beheaded twelve days later. James had support from Irish troops who came over to Kintyre to suppress any remaining anti-royalist support, but William of Orange sent troops to Tarbert to send them packing back to Ireland.

William would not become King in Britain until 1688 and in the interim, his reciprocal support of the Argyll family was no safeguard against revenge by the Macdonalds. These 'depredations' were perpetrated against the Clan Campbell in 1685 and 1686 – and some of them were carried out by the men of Tarbert. Donald McIlvorie, a tenant of Archibald MacAlister of Tarbert, 'lifted' goods to the value of £773 6s 8d Scots (now just a fraction of the pound sterling but still a substantial plundering) from Neil Campbell of Ellengreig and his tenants at Colintraive and its neighbourhood. Horses, cows, sheep, geese, money, a ferry boat, a grey plaid, a dirk, plough irons, hides, an anchor rope, herring nets, meal, an axe, furniture and both full and empty barrels were among the plunder. Those who lost their boats that summer were subject to a double indemnity – there was a remarkable harvest of herring of which the looted Campbells could not take advantage.

But yet again, Campbell power returned to Argyll when William and Mary's 'Glorious Revolution' at last was effected in 1688 and as a reward for the family's support, Archibald Campbell was created the 1st Duke of Argyll in 1701.

This was to be – apart from brief interludes around the Jacobite Risings in 1715 and 1745 when Kintyre men were again called by their heritors to be on both sides of the political divide – the beginnings of peace and growth. It was a time when the 1705 Parliament of the new Queen Anne could pass an Act instituting fairs in the village of Tarbert as part of that process of 'civilising' which so many kings had tried before. There were to be four yearly fairs in May, July, August and October, each lasting two days, and a weekly market. Whether this pleased the inhabitants of Tarbert is another matter – despite the political violence of the previous century they had by tradition held three yearly markets on other dates.

There were other changes. The MacAlisters of Tarbert, the most substantial family in south Knapdale, had held feu charters from the Campbells, but now they were heavily in debt (a condition not unknown to the Campbells themselves) and the lands passed to several different families. MacArthur Stewart of Milton got Dael and Craiglas and Peter Dow Campbell of Kildusclan at Lochgilphead got lands north of Inverneil. Four farms went to Mr McFarlane of Muckroy and another three farms went to Campbell of Kintarbert. In 1746, the remainder of the estate, including the mansion house at Barmore, was bought by Archibald Campbell of Stonefield. By now, the once proud castle at Tarbert was dilapidated. It had been the MacAlisters' responsibility to maintain it under an old charter but there had been no spare cash to lavish on its upkeep.

It had, after all, lasted longer than many castles in Argyll, built as it was by Robert Bruce. Now his castle was crumbling – and a road was to be built along that difficult range where the goat gave her milk and her warmth and saved the man who would save Scotland. The 1794 *New Statistical Account* records that an English engineer was called in to survey for this road. And if Robert Bruce found the hill tricky, the Englishman was defeated by it. The *Account* says: 'The rocks were so precipitous, the ferns so gigantic, the Englishman so unwieldy, and so unaccustomed to travel such rough grounds, that, after much tumbling and scrambling, he was obliged to take himself to his boat and finish his survey by rowing along the shore.'

When he arrived at Barmore House, he told Sheriff Archibald Campbell that this was a road for Empress Catherine of Russia to build, not private individuals. Sheriff Campbell paid the man off and built the road himself. Although when we say 'himself', the reality was that heritors could still cause their tenants to buckle to and carry out the dirty work when needed, even if they could no longer demand clan fealty. This road, to which the Duke of Argyll also contributed in a fiscal sense, opened up Kintyre – a peninsula until then isolated to an extent from the rest of Argyll (although it could hardly have seemed so when the troops and raiders of the seventeenth century were trampling over the length and breadth of the county). The border drawn by Magnus Barefoot had long gone but the topography provided frontier enough.

But although Kintyre was seen to be cut off from Argyll it was far from cut off from the world. The Firth of Clyde was a gateway to the world rather than the barrier it is sometimes perceived to be in this road-dominated age. In 1809, Parliamentary Commissioners were told in no uncertain terms that the village of Tarbert was 'one of the most considerable places in the Highlands' because of its harbour and locality. It was then that the Commissioners agreed to enlarge

Weary fishermen made their way into the village along Pier Road (*Maureen Bell Collection*)

the quay, repair the land breast and remove rocks to improve the harbour entrance.

This is when Tarbert became a village of 'ordinary' people rather than a dependency of the great and the good (or the thoroughly dastardly, depending on villagers' politics and parentage). The old cottages had been scattered across the hillsides. Now they were built on the main street – although even after the Commissioners had done their best, they were still flooded by the winter tides. This was a village of fishers and farmers – perhaps not living quite such dramatic lives as described by John MacDougall Hay in his powerful novel *Gillespie*, but certainly against his backdrop of struggling agriculture and a booming, cut-throat herring industry.

Hay, writer and Church of Scotland minister, was born and raised in Tarbert at the end of the nineteenth century. The Tarbert at the beginning of that century was a village of paradox. Its houses were the thatched, earthen-floored, stone-walled hovels which had served the poor people of Argyll for centuries. Yet the old street was claimed to have been one of the first paved streets in Scotland – the perks of having a royal castle perched at the entrance to the harbour.

And of course, that harbour was Tarbert's *raison d'être*. Over a mile long, the East Loch has an island which makes a natural division between an outer and inner harbour. The narrow passage to the inner harbour proved difficult for the modern steamer, but provided security for fishing boats and kings' birlinns alike. An outer pier was built in 1866, bringing steamers to within less than a mile of the centre of the village – and opening up a third industry for Tarbert. To fishing and farming was added tourism. The front and back streets which went up in the middle of the nineteenth century provided housing not only for a population which had already grown to nearly 2000, but also for the influx of summer visitors who could walk or be driven by horse and trap into the village. Fine new villas were built along the waterside and in the 1870s over twenty new fishermen's cottages with gardens went up and shops were either built or improved, reflecting, as Dugald Mitchell says in *Tarbert Past and Present* (1886), 'an abundant faith in plenteous harvests being yet gathered from the sea'. The fishermen lived in these houses in winter and some rented them in summer to visitors.

A big attraction for visitors was the Tarbert Fair on the last Thursday in July. They came by steamer and road from as far as Campbeltown, Arran, Bute, Cowal and Kilmartin, and of course,

The intrepid took the mail bus (*Maureen Bell Collection*)

throughout Knapdale. Farmers sold their wool here, horses were traded and young people did their courting – the young men giving sweeties as 'fairings' to the young women of their fancy. There were sideshows and shooting stands and a circus – and when the visitors left on the steamers, the villagers carried on celebrating far into the night.

Henry Bell, the man who had the *Comet* built to bring tourists from Glasgow to his Helensburgh hotel, had proposed cutting a new canal at Tarbert in 1830, nearly thirty years after the opening of the Crinan Canal. It was not a new idea – James Watt had looked at the possibilities decades earlier. By 1845 a company had been set up with a capital of £150,000 and Parliament gave its approval. It would have been a great tourist attraction as well as making work easier for the fishing fleet, but the plan fell through when it was taken out of private hands and left for the government to complete it. The plan was revived again in 1892. Capital of £180,000 was called for and the profit was estimated at £12,000 – but the courage was not there to carry it through. East Loch Tarbert remained the terminus for tourists and cargo boats alike and the old pier saw shipments of wool, sheep, cattle and wood going out. The main prosperity of Tarbert, however, rested with the herring.

They say that Netherlanders came to Loch Fyne as early as 836 for salted herring, and they learned how to salt and cure here. In 1590, Professor Cosmo Innes wrote that Loch Fyne herring were highly appreciated in Scotland. By 1770, huge shoals of herring were being noted in the loch and 600 boats with four men to a boat were each making £40 for a season which stretched from July to January. The fish sold at £1 4s a barrel, although there was a salt tax on exports which penalised poorer fishermen. These were the days of drift-net fishing when the men had equal shares in their boats and nets. The boats went where nature signposted the fish – a basking whale, perhaps, a diving gannet or red plankton (*suil dhearg* in the Gaelic still spoken then by Tarbert folk). The nets themselves were hand made by the fishermen's wives and daughters and boiled to make them rot-proof in a concoction of leaves and resin.

Around 1830, ring-netting was found to be a quicker and more efficient way of catching the herring. They say it was Tarbert fishermen who hit on the ploy of using two boats to tow either end of a net into a ring as the boats moved together; perhaps too efficient – this trawling was seen as harmful to herring stocks and outlawed. For almost forty years from 1830, the Tarbert fishermen battled against the authorities who went on making tougher and tougher laws. Eventually this led to a Royal Commission in 1860 into fishing methods, several clashes in Parliament, a report in 1866 and compromises in 1867.

In a village like Tarbert, the wildness of the frontier bred into the very fibre of the place, the fishing families did not take kindly to this ban. Although the scientists were saying that too many fish were being trawled, the sight of immense shoals 'playing' in the waters so near to home was too tempting for men conditioned by a hand-to-mouth existence. Nets were hidden from the authorities but still men ended up in prison and it could have come as no surprise as the gunboats patrolled Loch Fyne to hear that a man had been shot dead.

The regulations prohibited herring fishing north of Ardnamurchan from 1 January to 20 May, and from 1 January to 31 May south of that remote west coast point. The Fishery Board could fine offenders between £5 and £20 and seize their nets. The Board also had the authority to extend the closed season at will. John Campbell of Kilberry took up the cause of the trawlermen, stressing to MPs that he did not think 'a trawler with his wife and children could live without food for the same period', and demanding if they had made provision to support the several hundred herring trawlers, their wives and children who had previously been encouraged to invest in nets and boats. Kilberry, along with William Campbell of Dunmore and Colin Campbell of Stonefield, were the only landowners in Argyll who supported the trawlers – for right or wrong. Dunmore added his voice by writing to parliament just a week after Campbell of Kilberry had made his impassioned plea. The curtailment of the fishing would, Dunmore said, 'occasion absolute ruin to the Tarbert men and their families.' Even so, boats were hauled up onto beaches, de-masted and the men left to fish from about thirty four-oared boats. This they did after dark and their illegal action led to the shooting of 22-year-old Colin McKeich of Tarbert, allegedly by Gunner Phillip Turner, a 34-year-old Cornishman, and Peter Rennie, 20, a marine from Hawick, who were patrolling Loch Fyne to ensure no herring were caught. McKeich had been at the tiller of the skiff *Annan*, pulling south of Skipness. They had no net but the crew had intended to help another boat if the weather was right. Turner and Rennie were tried for the shooting and in the wake of the trial, amendments to the fishing Bill were at last discussed in Parliament. Ring-nets were legalised in 1867.

The men of Tarbert were able to make £30 a night in the last third of the nineteenth century – an enormous sum for the times and not surprisingly it was not always spent wisely. Drinking, swearing and fighting were common on the streets of Tarbert when the boats came in – and it was not only the men who were capable of wild behaviour. Tarbert was a Klondyke – until 1884, all the herring went to Tarbert harbour and the buying, selling, gutting, curing, barrel packing, net making and mending, and the re-shipping of the fish made it a rough, tough, noisy place.

Then, suddenly, the harbour was silent.

By the middle of the 1880s, a fleet of fast screw steamers was picking up the fish caught by drift nets straight from the boats and delivering them to the city an hour before the city folk were ready for breakfast. This was good for Glaswegians and good for the steamer owners, who saw this as a lucrative enough business to send anywhere between half a dozen and sixteen boats to meet up with the Tarbert fishermen. But for the people of Tarbert – the women who had made the nets and stood ankle deep in fish-guts to keep their families together, and the men who had made the barrels or rolled them full along the quay to be shipped on to other destinations – it was the end of an era of financial security. Instead of the locally based fish curer (an entrepreneur who contracted everyone from the fishermen through the gutters to the coopers) calling the shots, now it was the Glasgow or Greenock steamer fleet owners who dictated the terms of the industry.

The drunks may have continued to spill out of the pubs onto the streets and the brass band may have promenaded with an air of bravado, but while some men still earned between £10 and £30 for a week's fishing, others, according to Dugald Mitchell in *Tarbert Past and Present*, 'may not have pocketed a pound for weeks together'. More and more, instead of fishing boats bringing in a pay packet the people of Tarbert relied on pleasure steamers such the *Columba* to bring visitors to the village.

Over the coming century, the fishing boats became bigger and the industry more sophisticated. In the post-First World War economic depression, faster boats meant poverty-stricken Glaswegians could eat cheap fresh herring from Tarbert and Campbeltown – but by the 1950s, only 3 per cent of men in Kintyre worked at the fishing. In his Introduction to the *Third Statistical Account of Scotland* (1961), Colin M. MacDonald said the departure of the Loch Fyne herring from their former haunts had left the various fishing communities on the

Tarbert – the kirk dominated the skyline but the public houses were the haunt of the fishermen (*Maureen Bell Collection*)

loch without 'any obvious means of livelihood'. Tarbert may have been one of the busiest villages to rely on fishing but others such as Lochgilphead, Minard, Newton and Ardrishaig also missed the rust-coloured sails of their fishing fleets. The peak of local prosperity was in 1948–9 when £200,000 worth of fish were landed in Tarbert. By 1950, the herring fleet mustered thirty boats, giving employment to about 200 fishermen, salesmen and road haulage workers. In 1957, there were just ten boats and sixty fishermen in the village. The post-war boom in house building, hydro schemes and road works provided employment which included the building of 100 new council houses after a 1940s survey showed that 40 per cent of Tarbert's houses were unfit for habitation.

This was an era of rural changes as well as change in the fishing industry. Tenants got the right to buy when the big estates were broken up and many were able to acquire their farms on favourable terms. Most of the new owners, who as tenants had lived by oil lamps, put in electricity. They raised a mix of blackface sheep and cattle and kept small herds of Ayrshire dairy cows.

Boatbuilding was still employing between forty and fifty men in Tarbert up to the end of the Second World War and a dozen men

Salting the silver darlings. But steamboats meant Glasgow could breakfast on fresh herring (*Neil and Marie Kennedy Collection*)

continued to repair and store vessels in the 1950s. In 1959, government grants allowed some investment. The fish quay was rebuilt by the harbour authority and the passenger pier was repaired. Although cargo vessels no longer called at Tarbert because road transport had taken over, a daily steamer still came from Glasgow via the Kyles of Bute. And if there was a drastically reduced fishing fleet there was a growing number of private yachts sheltering in the harbour.

Ronnie Johnson, a fisherman and author of a history of his Tarbert colleagues, has written that yacht owners find Tarbert an excellent stopping off place because of the 'beautiful natural harbour' – not to mention the hotels and shops along the the quay. From the 1860s to the 1960s, A.M. Dickie built yachts and small craft at Tarbert. William Burton Leitch founded a sail-making business in 1895, was succeeded in the middle of the twentieth century by Andrew Leitch, and now in the twenty-first century a third generation of the family is carrying on the business – another William Burton. With his wife, Willie makes sails, splicing and rigging for today's fishing boats and yachts. He says: 'Once the engines started going into the fishing boats, people began to see the leisure side of sailing. There are still twenty-four fishing boats that come in to Tarbert but the leisure boats dominate today. The villagers have to look to other means to support themselves than fishing.'

Willie does not want Tarbert to turn into a museum to the past, but he is keen that the old skills be retained. 'We are told to keep the old traditions but we have to modernise them or die,' he says. And so he uses computers in the design side of his work while the manufacturing is a reminder of days gone by. Old enough to remember milk being delivered by horse and trap round the village in his boyhood but young enough to have a son at college, Willie says the biggest change in the village has been the closing of the boatyard. He has seen the puffers disappear and welding and fish-processing factories start up. He believes that the modern Tarbert will survive through tourism and looks forward to the influx of visitors the West Coast Trail from Inveraray to Southend will bring. Hotels and self-catering properties have opened their arms to Tarbert's annual yachting event, the music festival and the seafood festival. Now Willie is hoping that a wooden boat rally during the seafood festival will add to Tarbert's attractions. He was instrumental in starting up the rally with the commodore of the yacht club and visitors to the seafood festival have been thrilled to see traditional boats from around Scotland and Europe.

Willie now has to travel with his skills to the Hebrides, Orkney and Glasgow because there is no shipyard or shipwright in the village to bring the boats to him. However, there is a positive side to this peripatetic way of living, because it revives traditions far older than those established by the first W. B. Leitch. In medieval times, the stone-carving schools of Argyll were linked with those of Govan – then a village in its own right rather than a district of Glasgow. The school was on the banks of the Clyde. Today, Willie is working with the GalGael Trust, which empowers Govan's marginalised young people to reclaim their culture and their traditional boatbuilding skills which were also practised on the Clyde for centuries. Willie makes the sails.

Back home in Tarbert, he sees young people with fishing still in their blood, desperate to leave school and go on the boats. 'They don't see the bad weeks,' he says. 'They don't see past the big earning weeks.' His son is studying marine engineering and Willie says the choice of a career will be his and his alone. 'I was given my choice,' he says. 'I told them at school I wanted to be a sailmaker. They said it was a dying trade and tried for three months to put me off. They even called my father to the school, but he simply asked me what I wanted to do and a sailmaker is what I became. I will carry it on, but I don't know if it will be carried on by the family. Prosperity for Tarbert comes in cycles. In the 1960s the family was exporting to East Berlin, Russia, Sweden and South America. Who knows what the future holds?'

5

TIGHNABRUAICH

Arthur's vision

There are some villages which have their roots in the mists of history. They have no real starting point but evolve according to the vagaries of time and circumstance. Tighnabruaich, by contrast, exists because Arthur Scoular had a vision.

It is easy to understand why he could see a future for this virgin territory, lapped by the Kyles of Bute and sheltered by wooded hills. Nowadays it would seem naked without its stately villas, manicured gardens and bobbing yachts – yet that is how Scoular must have seen this stretch of the Kerry peninsula when he arrived there in the first third of the nineteenth century. A man who could make connections and see potential, he saw it could be turned into a playground for Glasgow's burgeoning middle class.

The potential was there because of another entrepreneur. In 1812, Henry Bell had a hotel in Helensburgh on the Firth of Clyde. He wanted to transport his guests from Glasgow to Helensburgh as quickly and conveniently as possible and commissioned the *Comet* – a 39 ft boat with a high-pressure steam engine designed by John Robertson. This was the start of a new era of travel on the Clyde. It did not happen overnight, of course. 'Steamers' had to be developed to their full potential and the *Comet* played a role in that progress – she was given a bigger cylinder and lengthened so that she could travel from Glasgow to Fort William, but was not strong enough for sea journeys and foundered in 1820. As engineers refined the product, bright young men began to see the potential of this new fast form of travel. Today, Argyll is all too often approached by road, but monks, kings and merchants had always travelled there by water as the easy – indeed, the only – option. The steamer presented a liberating invitation to a much wider audience. After all, if visitors could travel quickly to Helensburgh hotels what, given a reliable boat, was to stop them speeding anywhere in the Firth of Clyde? What could now stand in the way of people setting up house in some of the most beautiful spots the country had to offer and travelling to work in the

The hillside behind Tighnabruaich as it must have looked before Arthur Scoular sold the feus (*Archie Smith Collection*)

city? These waters may have seen bloody battles in the past but now they could become the path to tranquillity.

The Kyles of Bute witnessed steam in its earliest years. The *Dumbarton Castle* had sailed through on a memorable journey from Glasgow to Inveraray in 1815, just three years after the *Comet*'s maiden voyage. But in those days, the quays on this side of the Kilfinan peninsula were too small for the new ships. Passengers and cargo for the handful of big houses and scattered farms had to be taken off the early wooden paddle steamers in rowing boats. Once the old wooden pier known as Tighnabruaich Wharf was built, however, ships began to land twice a day, but they mainly carried cargo and were in no hurry. During the 1820s and 1830s the first *Inverary* [*sic*] *Castle*, *Tarbert Castle* and *Dunoon Castle*, all owned by the Castle Steam Packet Company, plied these waters regularly and competed against other young companies. In 1839, that competition became fierce when Thomson and McConnell introduced a 'swift steamer' from Glasgow to Ardrishaig, the connection through the Crinan Canal to the Highlands and Islands.

The shipping companies now began to think in terms of passengers, excursions and tourism – an industry which blossomed in the wake of Queen Victoria and Prince Albert's sail through the Crinan Canal. Everyone wanted to sail the Firth of Clyde and swift steamers such as the *Dunrobin Castle*, *Rothsay* [*sic*] *Castle* and *Cardiff Castle* made it possible. In 1846, J. & G. Burns took over the Castle Steam Packet Company and Arthur Scoular stepped forward to shape the destiny of what was to become the village of Tighnabruaich.

Scoular had married into the area, and at this distance it is hard to know if his intentions were love or money. He came from Cambusnethan in Lanarkshire looking for a wife. He found Agnes Williamson, granddaughter of John Moody, a Writer to the Signet (solicitor) from Greenock who had come to Kilfinan Parish in the mid eighteenth century. In Moody's time, just as in 1506 when James IV signed a charter for Blair's Ferry, the only way to reach the place was by a boat with no form of mechanical propulsion. We know that Scoular came by 'modern' steamer when he wooed Agnes, an attractive lady as well as an heiress. John Moody, who had married Agnes Clark in 1742, bought Innens, or Tighnabruaich (Gaelic for 'house on the hill') Estate in 1773 from the Maclachlans, who had owned the land for 154 years. Mr Moody built Tighnabruaich House, a Georgian mansion and the ideal place to raise their three children. His granddaughter, Agnes, was to inherit the family fortune because her 'unreliable' brother Matthew had been cut off without a penny when he went off to Australia.

Alan Millar, a descendant of the family and resident of Tighnabruaich, says family wisdom labelled Scoular a 'rogue'. He was the second son of one Thomas Scoular and once established at the big house, he settled his relatives in too – Thomas at what was known as the Cottage, James at Rhubahn Lodge, and John at Inglewood. As the seminal figure in the development of the village of Tighnabruaich, the enterprising Arthur may perhaps be forgiven this 'planting' of Lanarkshire stock.

The Castle Steam Packet Company built Tighnabruaich pier in the 1830s then sold their fleet to the Burns Line and Arthur bought the pier from them with Agnes's money. Owning a pier meant being able to charge pier dues, but as more steamers were now calling here regularly, Arthur saw a far bigger picture. The Tighnabruaich Estate, now inherited by Agnes, owned the land along the shore. Arthur's vision was to sell individual plots to wealthy Glasgow and Greenock merchants who would take up at least part-time residence there and retain the feus for a quite respectable annual income. By the 1850s, enough property had been feued for the steamer companies to compete for runs which took in Tighnabruaich. Arthur stipulated in the feu charters that house owners could not operate a ferry in competition with their feu superior.

In 1851, David Hutcheson & Co. took over the Burns's West Highland fleet. One of the junior partners in the new company was David MacBrayne, a nephew of the Burns family and a name which was to become synonymous with travel in the Highlands and Islands. Under this management, the *Pioneer* called twice a day at Tighnabruaich wharf, followed in 1852 by a two-funnelled steamer called *Mountaineer*, said to be the fastest steamship in Europe. Older steamers were taken off the run and replaced by bigger boats such as the *Duke of Argyll*, and the red and black Hutcheson paintwork was applied to three Loch Fyne steamers taken over by the company. They had the contract for the mail run to Tighnabruaich (the first steam mail boat was the PS *Inveraray Castle*), but now that Arthur's feus were going like hot cakes, it was well worth Hutcheson's introducing the first packet service from the Kyles of Bute to Glasgow which returned to the Kerry peninsula in the evening. The steamer initially used for this run was called the *Sir Colin Campbell*. From 1852, a daily summer service was established to serve the new commuter class who were working in Glasgow and living in what was by now the village of Tighnabruaich.

Arthur's vision was coming to fruition.

Tighnabruaich certainly kept up with this rapidly growing steamboat industry. The pier built by the Castle Steam Packet Company in the 1830s was followed by one at Kames and another at Ormidale on Loch Riddon in 1856. Colintraive pier in the East Kyle was built around the same time. Later in the century, an iron pier was built at Auchenlochan which survived until 2001, when it was demolished by the Royal Engineers. It was a fast-growing community and many steamer companies were providing different services. The economy of the Kerry peninsula changed dramatically. This had been an area of agriculture and fishing operating under an almost feudal system of wealthy landlords and tenant farmers. Now there were new residents used to city standards who demanded servants to clean and cook and shops to provide everyday commodities. Steamships took fresh fish daily to Glasgow and new industry in Kerry Kyle was served by transatlantic steamers.

It was not only the economy which changed because of Arthur's vision. Young people saw city clothes and city manners for the first time and copied them. Much slower was the effect on language, but inexorably, Gaelic faded away until, in 1881, the census showed that a third of the population of this Highland village had no Gaelic and by 1911, there were only two people who spoke no English at all. When Arthur arrived at Tighnabruaich House, the domestic staff and local tenants would all have been Gaelic speakers who would have found his Cambusnethan English incomprehensible.

Kames became an overnight berth for the *Sir Colin Campbell*, which left at six o'clock in the morning for Auchenlochan, Tighnabruaich and Glasgow. Until September 1939, the Caledonian Steam Packet Company's *Juno* and *Jupiter* would take men to work in the city while their families lived their lives in Tighnabruaich – remembered by many children as the basis of an idyllic childhood. That summer 'commuter' run had begun in 1852. A decade later, Captain Alexander Williamson became involved in the steamer scene. The family is unsure if he was related to Agnes Scoular's father, John Williamson, but he was certainly a man with the same entrepreneurial skills as her husband Arthur. From 1853 to 1862, he owned a steamboat with Captain William Buchanan. Then he went solo and built up a fleet of steamers known as the 'Turkish' Fleet' because of their exotic names: *Sultan*, *Sultana* and *Viceroy*. These sailed to all the Clyde resorts and became known as the most reliable of the Clyde steamers, working in cautious opposition to the Loch Fyne cargo boats and the Hutcheson steamers. When the Glasgow & South-Western Railway started a service from Glasgow to Prince's pier in Greenock, links were made with Captain Williamson's Turkish fleet to provide connections to the Kyles of Bute. As many as nine steamers a day called in at the different piers and Tighnabruaich was no longer a sleepy backwater but a bustling resort.

Arthur and Agnes lived at Tighnabruaich House with her younger sister Ruth Isabella. When Agnes died in 1865, Arthur did not let the grass grow under his feet. He was the heir of both Agnes and her sister and within a year was married again, this time to Margaret Gilmour, another heiress who came from Lanarkshire. Arthur himself died on 12 June 1875, having contributed to the creation of one of the most attractive destinations on the Clyde.

In his lifetime, nineteen owner-occupier houses were built, including Craigengower, owned by Adam Black, MP, the publisher of the *Encyclopaedia Britannica* and the Waverley novels. Arthur saw the population of Tighnabruaich grow from a handful to 398 and he watched the steamers vie to serve them. Alongside Tighnabruaich was another new village – Auchenlochan, the result of a venture similar to Arthur's. In 1853, John Malcolm of Poltalloch, a mid Argyll estate on the parallel peninsula to the west of Kerry, decided to build a road on property he owned between the lands of the Lamonts in Kames and Auchenlochan Farm, which touched on Arthur's property. When the road was completed in 1859, Malcolm began selling feus on the roadside and some handsome villas were built on them, creating a village of around eighty people. Between the two communities, there grew the need for shops, a bank, and a post office. Clean water was installed and after Arthur Scoular's death, his widow and daughter carried on his work by introducing electricity to the village in 1896.

This was run by a petrol-driven generator and there were lights on poles. The newspapers had a field day. 'The English Torquay', one wrote, 'will have to look to its laurels or it will be left behind in the matter of attractive lighting by its Scottish prototype.' The Scoulars were not entirely altruistic in installing the lights and had hoped to recoup the £500 it cost to install and to encourage villagers to pay for running costs. Sadly, the people of Tighnabruaich felt they could live in the dark and after two years, the lights went out because there were no contributors.

In 1841, Archibald Lamont of Ardlamont Estate had employed fifteen servants and a gardener and it is hard to say whether the incomers initially provided as many jobs as traditional heritors like Lamont. But by 1864, the Royal Hotel had opened in Auchenlochan and there was a hotel in Tighnabruaich. Certainly, builders were needed for all those new houses, but new feus were limited because of the steepness of the hillside.

The progress of Tighnabruaich was not entirely smooth. In 1878, the collapse of the City of Glasgow Bank devastated the fortunes of some of the very people Arthur Scoular had seen as rock solid. The directors of the bank had played fast and loose with their investors' money. When it folded on 22 October, rumour had it that the postmistress of Tighnabruaich went to the bank to withdraw her savings before delivering the telegram which bore tidings of the crash and the order to close the branch. In later years, the Royal Bank of Scotland opened up and sold Anchor Line tickets on the premises – much in keeping with the Tighnabruaich spirit of enterprise.

The building boom did not necessarily provide jobs for local people. The masons came from as far as Roxburgh, the island of Uist and Anstruther. As the villas went up, the last of the traditional

Building and mending boats has run in the Smith family. Archie sports the moustache (*Archie Smith Collection*)

thatched cottages disappeared and the last sailing ships disappeared from the waters which Tighnabruaich fronted. But there were still the local fishermen's yellow boats with their red-brown sails which were moored over the weekend while their nets dried on poles stretching from Tighnabruaich to Kames. Arthur Scoular's era could be said to have ended when a new Tighnabruaich House (1895) and Kames Parish Church (1898–9) were built – the last major projects of the period.

Despite the bank crash, the new residents recovered and in the run up to the First World War they enjoyed stable prices and low taxation. They had money in their wallets and were happy to spend it on their Tighnabruaich houses and yachts. They had maids and part-time gardeners and they supported the church and local charities. In 'good works' they were led by the Scoular family, whose involvement with the Boys' Brigade, which camped every summer on the peninsula, ran to providing tea in the garden of the new Tighnabruaich House.

There were those who chose to let their properties rather than live in them, introducing a less wealthy layer of Edwardian society to the peace and tranquillity of Kerry Kyle. Locals used to move into sheds at the back of the houses and let their houses. In 1908, the rent of a furnished villa with eight rooms and the use of a rowing boat was £20 for the summer, while a season ticket on the steamers could be had for a few shillings. Holidaymakers could shop in Andrew Irvine's emporium, which had opened in 1885 and stayed in the family for five generations, and buy the produce grown in Irvine's market garden. They could watch the Tighnabruaich Regatta, which was established in 1900 and as the years went by there were dances, cinema showings and ceilidhs in the three village halls. Tighnabruaich Golf Club was established in 1894, followed by the Kyles of Bute Golf Club in 1907, and the Kyles of Bute Sailing Club became internationally renowned.

Within seventy years, new technology and one man's vision had transformed a rural backwater into a famous centre of recreation – but not for everyone.

For some, life went on as it had always done. In 1868, the teacher's log at the local primary school read: 'A number of new pupils who entered today were unable to answer the questions I put to them for want of English.' On 28 March, fourteen-year-old Robert Scott left school to attend to the sheep on his father's farm. This area may have been 'little Torquay' for some but for others it would remain a place of fishing and farming. Many residents would think nothing of taking the steamer every day to Glasgow, but the teacher would write in June 1868: 'The tinker's two boys leave the school today. They are emigrating to Glendaruel [a few miles distant within Cowal] for the winter.'

Some would be considering having a yacht built and would have a house in town as well as a grand villa in Tighnabruaich. The teacher would write in her log on 14 June: 'Effie the tinker comes to inform me she will not be able to pay me my fees just now as "times are hard" and "trade dull".' Some would have a clean water supply and a maid to fill the bath in the morning. In the Medical Officer's *Report of the Sanitary Condition of Tighnabruaich* in 1880, Dr John Mackenzie would write: 'Privies and ashpits need immediate attention. The present system of water closets without an ample supply of water is really defective and in my opinion highly detrimental to public health.'

But the incomers brought some benefits which affected the whole population rather than the privileged few. Their presence meant a new school had to be built in 1873 because Tighnabruaich had 156 children of school age – almost three times the number at most rural

The village grew as Arthur Scoular's masterplan took shape (*Archie Smith Collection*)

parishes in Kintyre and Knapdale at the time. And the steamers meant that those without a job could travel elsewhere to seek one. In 1891, Peter Crawford worked Otter Ferry, charging 1s 6d to reach the steamer. This ferry had originally been for cattle; now fifteen people could sail out in the big boat to the steamer waiting in Loch Fyne. But employment grew in Tighnabruaich with the establishment of two yards building yachts – later to be requisitioned, like the yachts themselves, during the Second World War.

The concentration of population in Tighnabruaich meant changes for the church, too. In ancient times, Kilfinan was the centre of the parish. In the thirteenth century, the local rulers, Lawman, son of Malcolm, and his uncle Duncan, son of Fercher, gifted the church and all its properties and rights to 'God and St James and St Mirrin of Paisley and the monks who serve God there'. The Paisley monks were powerfully involved with the Scottish royal family at the time and a number of landowners were currying favour with such gifts, specifying that such generosity was 'for divine charity and the salvation of my Lord Alexander, illustrious King of Scotland'. If the gift did not have its effect in this life, the hope was there for the next. But while Paisley Abbey became rich through such donations, local parishes such as Kilfinan were left so poor that they could not put a roof on the church. In 1351, the parish found a supporter in Martin, Bishop of Argyll, who stopped payments to Paisley because the Abbey had neither repaired the church nor sent suitable priests. The matter went to Rome but Kilfinan was never to get a good deal under the Paisley regime. In fact, the church was in such a remote area that the Rev. David Kellas, parish minister in Tighnabruaich until 2004, believes that communal worship did not exist because the church was too far away and too small for the medieval population.

The Reformation in 1560 brought huge change and the political and religious dramas of the seventeenth century touched Kerry as elsewhere in Argyll, but it took the developments of the nineteenth century to shift the focus of worship in Kilfinan parish. As Tighnabruaich grew, the population in the west of the peninsula declined. The Rev. Joseph Stark was minister of Kilfinan Parish Church from 1832 until he 'came out' at the Disruption which split the Church of Scotland in 1843. Mr Stark continued as minister of Kilfinan Free Church and his brother, the Rev. Alexander Stark, retired at the age of seventy from the Free Church Ministry in Closeburn, Dumfriesshire, and came to live with him in Tighnabruaich in 1856. By then, members of the Free Church who spent their holidays at Tighnabruaich were ministered to by Joseph, who had a degree in Greek, spoke fluent French and Gaelic but was not approved by the moderator of Dunoon Presbytery because he was not a Highland man by birth. He used to walk seven miles to Millhouse, preach there in Gaelic and English, walk back to Tighnabruaich to preach again to the growing number of visitors and permanent residents, and then tramp four miles across the moor to Achrossan. Alexander, who had been ordained in 1808 and was considered to be the father of the Free Church, took on the ministry of Tighnabruaich, sometimes preaching in a carpenter's shed, sometimes in the open air, most often on the lawn of Craigengower. A century later, Mr Black's house had been converted into a Church of Scotland rest home for 'tired mothers'.

Joseph appealed for funds to build a church and a manse. The cash came rolling in both from individuals and from wealthy city congregations and by 1863 the work was completed at a cost of £1,600. The small wooden building which had gone up as an interim church was moved to a place behind the church as a vestry and session house until 1877. Alexander continued as an unpaid minister until he retired at eighty-five in 1871. The first minister called to Tighnabruaich was the Rev. James Young, who was inducted in 1877.

When the Free Church of Scotland joined with the United Presbyterian Church in 1900, the Tighnabruaich congregation elected to join the new United Free Church of Scotland. In 1929 at the union of the Church of Scotland and the United Free Church, the congregation decided to join the reunited Church of Scotland. This was when the Tighnabruaich *quoad sacra* church was renamed the High Church and the parish church became the East Church. The congregations united in 1931 and used the High and East churches on alternate Sundays. Enviably for twenty-first century ministers, in summer so many people thronged Tighnabruaich that both buildings were used for services. All good things come to an end, however. During the Second World War, Kilfinan parish was full of servicemen. Ardlamont Estate (originally home of the Lamonts, the descendants of that 'Lawman' who gave Kilfinan Church to Paisley) was cleared of residents to house troops training for the Normandy landings and one of the other mansions, Caladh House, became home to Navy personnel on navigation training and renamed HMS *James Cook*. Tighnabruaich House became a military hospital. Italian prisoners of war and evacuated children were sent to Tighnabruaich from Glasgow, Greenock and Clydebank. Tragically, one parish priest felt the children were missing home too much and took them back just in time to face the Clydebank blitz.

The High Church was closed in 1942 'for the period of the war'. When Millhouse homes were evacuated to house soldiers, it was requisitioned as a furniture store. Like Caladh House, it was never the same again. Neither building was maintained properly and by 1948, the High Church had deteriorated so much it was sold to the council to be used as a gym and assembly hall for Tighnabruaich School. It had been built as a chapel for the Poltalloch District in 1862 and disjoined from the Parish of Kilfinan that year. It was served by young ministers of missionary status for twenty years before the parish got its own first minister, the Rev. Norman Macleod McFie. From 1957, Kilfinan and Tighnabruaich parishes have been linked and served by one minister just as in those far distant days when the church belonged to the monks of Paisley.

Wartime changed everything, although there were still eighteen steamers on the Clyde with a passenger load of 24,000 and one remaining MacBrayne mail steamship sailed under the British Railways flag. Pre-war, MacBrayne's had become the number one company, but other steamers belonging to competing railway companies had their own terminals and up until 1939 there were twelve steamers a day calling at Tighnabruaich in summer and even the winter service took people to Wemyss Bay and Gourock.

After the war, social and demographic change meant few either wanted or could afford to live the double life once enjoyed by Glasgow merchants. Death duties finished off even the Tighnabruaich Estate. Holiday patterns changed, too. Air travel meant package holidays to sunny climes. In 1969, the new road from Tighnabruaich to Ormidale offered a fast route for cars and timber and cattle trucks through Glendaruel to the Rest and Be Thankful – General Wade's military road which in the eighteenth century had linked Lowlands and Highlands. As a result, the mail steamer was no longer viable. Roll-on roll-off ferries between Dunoon and Gourock and East Kyle at Colintraive meant cars and freight could reach the Kilfinan peninsula quickly by a second route and suddenly the era of pleasure cruising was coming to a close and just as in the days of James IV, the short ferry crossing was the order of the day.

Pleasure cruising has not gone forever, of course. The *Waverley* paddle steamer still makes forays into the Kyles of Bute and is over booked every time, but even in 1946 a steamer company survey showed that it was no longer financially viable to operate pre-war services. In 1973 when the Caledonian Steam Packet Company took over David MacBrayne and became CalMac, there was an undertaking to provide lifeline services to the islands and peninsulas but cruising was an optional extra which fell off their agenda in later decades. Eventually, after much starting and stopping of services, Tighnabruaich as a 'lifeline' service was dropped in 2000.

Even private yachting is no longer quite the same, although yachting and the Kyles of Bute will always be synonymous. Throughout the Second World War, yachts were requisitioned by the Royal Navy. When war ended, they sat sadly in Rhubahn Bay waiting to be sold or scrapped. Chester Currie, who with his brother was a noted yachtsman in summer and a scallop fisher in winter, remembered that in 1929–30, 100 fishing smacks had called in at Tighnabruaich and herring were still caught in the Kyles in number up to the 1950s. 'It was a beautiful sight at night seeing the fleet all lit up in the Kyles,' Chester said – but perhaps once the electricity made a comeback, that sight would not have been so impressive.

After the war, electricity was no longer the prerogative of a paternalistic landlord but was installed by the Hydro-Electricity Board,

Looking across the Kyles from the Smith yacht slip (*Archie Smith Collection*)

with eighty-two street lamps between Tighnabruaich, Auchenlochan and Kames. Clean water was available to all, not just the rich, from reservoirs in the hills above the villages. There was a head post office in Tighnabruaich and a police constable in Auchenlochan.

Today, although many of the shops have disappeared, victims to the big supermarkets in Dunoon, and the steamers no longer turn a journey into an adventure, tourism is still an essential Tighnabruaich industry and many of the old villas are once more owned by those of means who want a bolt-hole from the city. This time around, they are more likely to be artists and actors than city merchants – but they are still looking for the peace and tranquillity offered by Kerry.

Most of the piers have completely disappeared, along with the the herring fishing, but in November 1999, Tighnabruaich Pier Association was formed and a partnership has been made with Argyll & Bute Council to conserve and develop that first plank in Arthur Scoular's vision. If Arthur Scoular was the name of the nineteenth century, Chester Currie and Archie and John Smith were synonymous with Tighnabruaich in the twentieth. Chester and his brother Duncan were the adventurers, captaining boats in the glamour days of sailing and racing 'J'-class boats. Chester, his wife Pat and Duncan brought back the *Endeavour* from the United States and were feared lost at sea when they lost ship-to-shore connection. The Smiths were immortalised by

The twentieth-century boatyard served racing professionals and boating amateurs (*Archie Smith Collection*)

Argyll author Neil Munro's famous Para Handy character, who after one of his exploits was in need of a new boat and said it had to be 'a genuine Archie Smith'.

Archie and John opened a yard at the turn of the twentieth century, repairing, cleaning and fitting out boats ready for the spring. As business flourished, Archie lived in the house Stroncarraig and opened another yard to build dinghies and small yachts. His grandson, another Archie, who was born in 1935, recalls the whole family working in the two yards and he served his apprenticeship as a boatbuilder there in an era when it took ten men to manipulate the old bogeys which pulled the boats out of the water. Clients came from far and wide for small cruising boats and 18-ft racers like the *Marula*. When today's Archie was just a tot, grandfather and Uncle John were commissioned by the laird of Caladh House to build a 35-ft motor launch with bunks as a wedding present for his son Bobby.

The original Smith Brothers' yard was knocked down in the 1980s to make way for the lifeboat station. Today, most boats are fibre glass and some of the old skills have been lost. But Tighnabruaich still repairs boats – and Archie says modern machinery means two men can do the job of ten and handle far more boats than Smiths ever could. As many as 100 boats are re-fitted in Tighnabruaich each season and there's a second yard at the old Kames gunpowder quay.

Local farming, forestry and fishing jobs have almost disappeared, but those who live in plots first sold from the Tighnabruaich Estate a century and a half ago are happy to share the Scoular vision of peace and tranquillity.

6

MILLHOUSE AND KAMES

For whom the Dolphin Bell tolls . . .

The *Glasgow Herald* of the day called it the biggest works of its kind in Scotland and it was built in the parish of Kilfinan because the area was so rural and remote. But the gunpowder production which began on their doorsteps in the early nineteenth century was not 'remote' from the communities of Millhouse and Kames – any more than the Trident nuclear installation is remote for the twenty-first century inhabitants of Argyll, however far it may seem from central government – and between 1846 and 1922, sixteen men died in explosions at the Millhouse Works of the Kames Gunpowder Company. Another four were drowned when the works' steamer *Guy Fawkes* was sunk in 1864. Today, their names are listed on a commemorative plaque under the Dolphin Bell – the timekeeping bell used at the gunpowder works from around 1839 until its closure in 1921.

The bell is now silent and rural peace has long since been restored to the Kerry peninsula. But for almost a century, this gentle backwater became a centre of industry, of changing lives and changing landscapes. Today there is little more than the Dolphin Bell and the remnants of quayside activity in Kames to remind us that men like William Pike, Alexander McGlashan and John McGilp lived and died against a backdrop of consignments of saltpetre landing from South America and thousands of tons of gunpowder being shipped out each year in glistening japanned canisters to all parts of the globe.

This invasion of the Kerry peninsula could not have taken place without the steamer, which was causing a revolution of a very different kind on what had been the Tighnabruaich estate just a brisk walk from Kames and Millhouse. But while the cargo delivered to the new Tighnabruaich pier was the very best of Glasgow's business world seeking a stress-free zone, the boats pulling into Kames, by contrast, were trading in commodities which would bring jobs to local men, cause the creation of a previously unimagined infrastructure, and stave off the kind of land clearance and emigration-induced

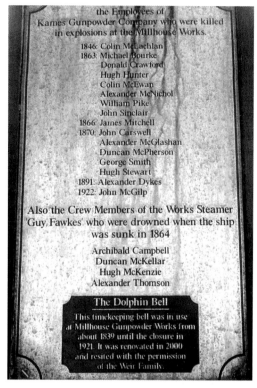

the Employees of
Kames Gunpowder Company who were killed
in explosions at the Millhouse Works.

1846: Colin McLachlan
1863: Michael Bourke
Donald Crawford
Hugh Hunter
Colin McEwan
Alexander McNichol
William Pike
John Sinclair
1866: James Mitchell
1870: John Carswell
Alexander McGlashan
Duncan McPherson
George Smith
Hugh Stewart
1891: Alexander Dykes
1922: John McGilp

Also the Crew Members of the Works Steamer
'Guy Fawkes' who were drowned when the ship
was sunk in 1864

Archibald Campbell
Duncan McKellar
Hugh McKenzie
Alexander Thomson

The Dolphin Bell

This timekeeping bell was in use
at Millhouse Gunpowder Works from
about 1839 until the closure in
1921. It was renovated in 2000
and resited with the permission
of the Weir Family.

For whom the Dolphin Bell tolls (*Author's Collection*)

population decrease which other parts of Argyll experienced during the same era.

This finger of land which from ancient times was the parish of Kilfinan had escaped some of the wildest excesses which history had visited on neighbouring peninsulas. Kilfinan stretched from Ardlamont Point to Otter Ferry on Loch Fyne on the west and Loch Riddon on the east. In the Gaelic, *ceithir* (pronounced keh-hir) means four. The English corruption of that word – Kerry – came to mean the Ardlamont peninsula, which was the fourth part of the region assigned to Comgal (Cowal), grandson of the Dalriadic leader Fergus Mor. There were early settlements on Fyneside (Cowal was accessible only by sea and few pushed on into the hills) where people left evidence of their lives in the shape of ruined forts, standing stones,

chambered burial cairns and ancient tools. These fingers of land
pierced by lochs had been left behind by two ice ages. Nomadic
hunters came here 7,000 years ago to take advantage of a climate
warmer than today's and of wooded hillsides wealthy in game. They
were followed by Neolithic farmers who not only worked the land
but created strange works of art in the shape of cup-and-ring carved
stones and had knowledge enough of astronomy to align great stones
with the all-powerful, life-giving sun.

Some 2,000 years before the Christian era, there were people
living in Kerry who had industries of their own, fashioning tools
in copper and then bronze. Cultivating the land, however, became
the main sustainer of life as a succession of invaders seized power
and left their mark. The Romans came to Cowal and so did the
Irish and the Vikings, who may not have been able to claim all of
Cowal as a province of Norway but nonetheless left their heritage in
names like Ormadale (dale of the snake) and Ascog (bay of the ash
tree). In medieval times, monks built tiny chapels named Kilfinan,
Kilmodan and St Marnock after the early Celtic saints. There were
clan chiefs who created their own little kingdoms here away from
the eyes of greater rulers, developing communal land use that would
become the runrig system which still marks the terrain – look for it
above Tighnabruaich on Duin and on the moors travelling east from
Portavadie ferry.

Black cattle and four-horned sheep were the wealth of this land and
their owners were as little given to subjugation as those of Kintyre.
The chiefs demanded loyalty from their extended families and used
the men to watch their cattle and fight their battles – staged mostly
at sea in oared boats called birlinns which developed speed and
agility during the 370 years of the Viking presence to outclass the big
Norwegian galleys. The main family by the thirteenth century was
the Lamonts, who stemmed from Laumon, a grandson of the local
Celtic ruler Fercher, but whose name had a Norse ring to it – Lauman
in Norse is lawman. By 1266 all the warring between Norway and
Scotland came to an end with the Treaty of Perth and the government
had to begin the difficult work of taming the western frontier so
long dominated by the Norsemen. A Charter of James III confirmed
the barony of Inveryne as being in the hands of the Lamonts. Their
seat at Ardlamont is first mentioned in 1432 and most of the farms
in existence today were named by 1472. *Camus na Miclach* (or in an
updated Gaelic *Camas na Muclach*, the bay of the swine or possibly

Ardlamont House, ancient seat of the Lamonts, main Kerry heritors, was commandeered for troops in the Second World War (*Alan Miller Collection*)

even the 'sea pig', or whale), however, was already mentioned in a charter in 1295 and would become the village of Kames.

This being Argyll, there can be no history without the name of Campbell making an appearance, and in the parish of Kilfinan they were at loggerheads with the Lamonts. Lauman supported the English King Edward I in the thirteenth century and most Lamonts and their followers (by choice or by reason of feudal dues) fought against the Scottish leaders during the wars of independence – picking the 'wrong' side at the battle of Bannockburn in 1314. With the grace of hindsight we can see that it was inevitable that the Campbells would be ordered in by Robert Bruce to sort out the Lamonts on their home territory. The Lamonts won the battle, but lost their lands around Dunoon. The subsequent gift of the church and lands of Kilfinan to the abbot of Paisley in 1331 could be viewed with some scepticism. There may have been pious words about saving souls to accompany this gift (which brought with it rent to be paid in corn, cattle and hides by those who farmed the church lands) but as there was a major link between Paisley and the Stuarts, who would become Scotland's kings just forty years hence, it may have been made cynically.

The Lamonts held their own in Kerry, fielding their own little navy of birlinns – that of the clan chief very evident with its targe and banner fluttering in the wind in the Kyles of Bute. Some of these boats, which could range in size from eight to as many as fifty oars, were made in Kerry and they were not only boats of battle but of trade, bringing cargoes into the peninsula and exporting local produce to the central belt – the only viable route being by sea. By the seventeenth century, however, the cooler climate meant the peninsula had less to offer the world and after the Union of the Crowns the economy declined and the building of boats for war came to an end.

Throughout the sixteenth and seventeenth centuries, the Lamonts and Campbells remained on opposing sides as the bigger political picture unfolded across the British Isles. The Lamonts were to gain from the Reformation, taking the kirklands of Kilfinan after Paisley Abbey was burned in 1559, but, as always, it was their tenants who would lose most devastatingly during the various skirmishes which were fought in the name of taming the west. In 1603 when Dougal Campbell of Auchinbreck raided Bute from Kames, the people of Kames did not escape. Marion Stuart's farm was burned, Wester Kames was besieged and crops were burned around Ardmaleish. A dozen years later, the Earl of Argyll took 1,000 men to subdue Sir James Macdonald and the Kerry men were obliged to fight for the Lamonts against them. By the middle of the century when the civil war was enveloping the country, Lamonts jumped from side to side. Because the Earl of Argyll was playing a similar game (and seemingly settling old scores as a sideline to the war by removing 3,000 of Lamont's black cattle) there was little cohesion in the county. After Campbell was defeated at Inverlochy, Lamont decided to support the doomed King Charles and fought against the Campbells on the Holy Loch and at Strachur before 2,000 Irishmen joined him at Kilfinan. He seemed to be on a winning streak until the king was defeated on both sides of the border and Lamont had to withdraw to Toward and Ascog. The Campbells of Ormsary invaded Kilfinan parish and again, the followers bore the brunt of the subsequent orgy of bloodletting. At Ascog Castle, a three-day battle resulted in an 'honourable' surrender but with 200 survivors taken to Dunoon and hanged. At Toward, the gates were opened to the Campbells and men, women and children were slaughtered. At least thirty-six Lamont supporters were hanged at Toward but Sir James Lamont himself was given a promise of safe conduct for the surrender of Ascog Castle. In the aftermath, the Lamonts were gradually replaced in the Kerry version of Campbell human plantations by Lowlanders .

Despite the bloodshed, this period in Kerry's past was also one of prosperity and progress. In 1550, Loch Fyne was jumping with herring. New corn mills were built in the area: one at Mecknock, which was to become Millhouse, and another at Meldalloch. These were to replace the old querns and strict rules of payment were imposed. There were now rules governing the strength of beer, too, and Johnne Lawmont was fined the hefty sum of £25 for making and selling malt above the price authorised by the Crown.

It was little short of miraculous that the Presbyterian church in Kerry became more solidly established under the governance of the Marquess of Argyll, the one known as the Covenanting Marquess or cross-eyed Archibald. It was his ambivalence which had gained this 8th Earl his title of Marquess from Charles I. He then joined the Parliamentary side, defeated the royalists in 1645 and was asked to form a government in Scotland by Cromwell. Then, having crowned Charles II King at Scone, the Marquess rejoined Cromwell when the Scottish army was defeated at Worcester and so was to lose his head when Charles II was restored to the throne.

In the middle of all this these troubles, the aspirationally egalitarian Presbyterianism brought the prospect of general education and Kilfinan got its first school. But, of course, boys were needed in the fields and men were needed in battle and there was rarely time to savour the fruits of education or labour. There may have been a brief respite from bloodshed after the restoration in 1660, but times were hard. The 14th Clan Chief of the Lamonts, Sir James, came back to Ardlamont after his incarceration in Inveraray and then Dunstaffnage for his own misjudgement of the political situation. He was by now so much in debt that rebuilding the Toward and Ascog properties was never an option, although Ascog remained in the family until Mrs Ann Lamont, the widow of a Glasgow University professor, bequeathed the whole estate to the Church of Scotland in 1996.

By 1685, more trouble was brewing for the innocent bystanders of Kerry. When the 9th Earl of Argyll plotted from Holland to overthrow King James VII & II, he arranged to meet 2,000 supporters on Bute. Defeated by the Earl of Atholl, he withdrew to Eilean Dearg (red island) at the entrance to Loch Riddon where 500 barrels of gunpowder exploded in the ensuing fracas. With another Campbell's head rolling from the block, his successor deeply involved in the plans to bring William and Mary from Holland for the 'glorious revolution' of 1688, and Kerry's feudal lord once more sitting on the 'wrong' side of the fence, deeply in debt, the parish of Kilfinan was going to rack and ruin.

It is almost certain than none of Kilfinan parish's tenant farmers, tied by short leases within the runrig system of communal production, would have had the means to invest in the disastrous 1695 Darien venture, but many were affected by it nonetheless. The Company of Scotland aimed to raise the enormous sum of £400,000 (about half the capital of Scotland) to establish a Scottish colony. In the first day, £50,000 was raised and the rest came in over the following five months. The company sent five ships and 1,200 men to Darien on the isthmus of Panama, which was to be called Caledonia. When the ships arrived, the men began to build New Edinburgh, but this secret destination, known only to the directors until the ships' captains opened their orders on sailing, turned out to be not the promised land but a graveyard for hundreds of Scots. When a second expedition arrived in 'Caledonia,' little was found but graves and deserted huts – and perhaps some of the useless cargo of wigs and woollen goods which was to have been the foundation of the colonists' fortunes. After some months, those who survived surrendered to a Spanish force and were allowed to leave – but those who had invested were left destitute and the general economic depression which followed speeded up the Union of Parliaments in 1707. From Kilfinan parish, the lairds of Evanachan and Auchagoyl had died in this disastrous ploy. Only after the Union was the economic situation to improve and Kilfinan began to see changes.

Perhaps the most notable would be the slow move from the runrig system to single-unit farms with tenants on longer leases. Stone walls were built to enclose properties and farming practices gradually improved. Men worked on land and at sea to achieve a decent living. Millhouse (then still Mecknock) got a school and another opened at Otter Ferry. A road was built from Ardlamont to Otter Ferry and from Otter Ferry over the Bealachandrain. There was to be no more obligation to serve in the militia but now tenants could be called out to build the new roads which were (like so many other schemes in previous centuries) intended to civilise the west. None of this happened with the speed intended by central government. By 1755, there had still been just 20 yards of the Lochfyneside road completed. On the other hand, it seemed to be a much quicker task to build inns for travellers' needs, and there were now eleven of somewhat questionable quality in the parish.

It was not all plain sailing. John Lamont of Kilfinan actually joined with Campbells – the heritors of Eilean Dearg and Glendaruel – to support the Jacobites in 1715, while Lamont of Inveryne was on King George's side with MacLachlan of Innens and Stewart of Ascog. In 1745, the Lamonts were on the Hanoverian side while the MacLachlans of Castle Lachlan north of Otter Ferry raised 150 men for the Stuart cause. It is said MacLachlan did not actually fight at Culloden because his wife poured boiling water over his legs just before he was due to leave.

Nothing moved fast in Kerry. In the *First Statistical Account* of 1794, the parish minster the Rev. Alexander McFarlane said that tenants were so much 'attracted to the ancient mode of cultivation that modern improvements can scarcely be said to have found their way into our latitude'. Although the English plough was to be seen in some Kerry fields, little manure was ever spread on them and the stones were left because they were believed to warm the soil. Lamont of Lamont grew wheat successfully in 1750 but oats, barley and potatoes remained the main crops. Where the runrig system still survived, Mr McFarlane reported that five or six families subsisted on each small property which was overstocked with ill-fed animals. The market for crops was Greenock, but Kerry imported more than it exported and although fishing brought in between £50 and £100 a season, it was seen to take the men from the land from July to Christmas.

In 1755, there were 1,793 people living in Kilfinan parish. Many were leaving because the land was being given over to grazing. The smuggling which had been rife in the area – trade in brandy with the Isle of Man had been profitable – was diminishing and if any real change was noted by the minister, it was that the end of the eighteenth century was more peaceable than the beginning. By 1815, General John Lamont tried to put a stop to emigration from the peninsula – a rare move favouring people over sheep. He believed that population growth was the only way to prosperity and so he created more crofts and allowed fewer farm amalgamations. Even so, farmers still had to supplement their incomes with fishing.

There was little else to provide a living. Coal mining had been tried at Kildavaig without success, and to date the new steamers had not brought sufficient newcomers to offer any significant number of domestic posts. Gradually, however, Loch Fyne fishing's link with the steamers as a means of getting catches to the major conurbations in record time did bring work to Kerry. Most fish were landed at

Inveraray or Tarbert, but by 1840 there were sixty-eight boats working with drift nets from the Kilfinan parish bays. That was work for over 200 men and half of them were from Kerry. The area had already got its own fish curer in 1838 – that all-powerful figure who made the contracts, employed the workers and processed the fish from loch to table. He was employing over ninety workers, including gutters, packers, cleaners, dryers and coopers. After 1867, when legislation allowed trawling, catches became even bigger and two years later there were eighty-one skiffs registered in Rothesay which had Kerry owners. The 1871 census reported 126 Kerry fishermen.

It was something of an irony that at a time when the population of Kerry was on the increase again that it should be decided that this was a location remote and isolated enough to be suitable for a gunpowder factory. The company was looking for cheap labour, a good water supply and access to the sea for transport. The idea of such a factory and the employment which it would bring was not universally welcomed. The Ardlamont laird initially took legal action to prevent industry on his land, although in 1839 when the gunpowder mill was given the go-ahead, Lamont completed the road from Kilfinan to Ardlamont, which finally linked Kames Farm with the shore. He also had conditions built into the building of the quay at Kames: it was to be for the use of his tenants as well as for the powder mill.

Between 1839 and 1921, 410 people were employed in the production of gunpowder. Not all were local – many who had worked in the industry elsewhere came for jobs. The 1861 census shows that many were from England and there were mechanics, engine smiths and coopers from the Glasgow area. There were jobs for women to pack the casks of powder.

The works were founded by Thomas Buchanan from Glasgow and John McCallum, who had been born locally in Acharossan. The land and premises were owned by the Lamonts initially, but Buchanan and McCallum bought them in 1850. The dispute between France and Russia over the Palestinian holy places which led to the outbreak of the Crimean War in 1853 meant more work for Millhouse and Kames. In 1854, Britain joined in the contentious conflict and peace was not concluded until 1856, by which time these little villages on the same latitude as Moscow were experiencing a boom. A second loading pier, the Black Quay, had been built and more workers had been taken on.

There is little to show of the intense nineteenth- and early twentieth-century industrial activity at the old gunpowder manufacture at Kames and Millhouse (*Author's Collection*)

But, of course, peace is no good thing for a gunpowder factory. By 1872, the company was in financial trouble and had to be transferred into the hands of a Glasgow trust. It was bought in 1876 by a firm called Curtis & Harvey from Faversham in Kent which paid £25,000 for the business. This was just a year after the Explosives Act had been passed laying down safety standards in gunpowder mills. Factory inspectors came and demanded alterations to the water supply from Loch Ascog and other safety measures – although, as can be seen from the toll recorded beneath the Dolphin Bell, these did not prevent deaths in this complex operation.

Gunpowder was needed not only for military conflicts, but also for a variety of tasks in an increasingly industrial world. In Argyll itself there was quarrying and the mining areas of Lanarkshire and Ayrshire used gunpowder in their blasting processes, but there were clients much further afield looking for the product made in Kerry and cargoes went as far as New Zealand. The latest technology was used to create the powder and there were several steam-powered engines on the different sites. The workers specialised in a number of complicated processes and then there were the ancillary jobs: the timekeepers, the magazine keeper, the carters who went between Millhouse and Kames

The saltpetre works which were an integral part of the gunpowder manufacture at Kames and Millhouse (*Alan Miller Collection*)

with the raw material and the finished product, the laboratory team and even the boot-makers and laundry workers who were at times an integral part of the safety operations.

From quiet backwater to industrial powerhouse, Kerry's gunpowder production stretched over five sites. The potassium nitrate (saltpetre) used in gunpowder production usually came from Bengal in India. The saltpetre for this mill came from South America, with deep-sea steamships soon taking over from sailing vessels. Most of the charcoal used in the process had to be imported but some was produced from local alder woods: Millhouse was an ancient centre of charcoal burning.

The first production process took place at Kames where the saltpetre works was built beside the pier. The rest of the processing and the warehouses and dwelling houses for the workers and managers were spread over around Low and High Mills, South Auchagoyle and part of Millhouse, including Barnafaud croft, and north of the Kames–Millhouse road. The buildings had flat corrugated roofs and packed earth or yellow pine plank floors. Because this was a round-the-clock operation, a wall was glazed and oil lamps hung outside it for safety. The production site itself was inside a seven-foot high wall. Craignafioch Burn was damned into two reservoirs to provide water for the High Mill via lades and an aqueduct. In earlier years there had been a woollen mill at Mecknock which had closed before the advent of the gunpowder mill and it had been powered by water from Loch Ascog.

The saltpetre and charcoal were mixed and blended at Millhouse and the powder was then pressed, re-granulated, glazed, dried and dusted. It was packed into canvas bags or japanned canisters and stored in the main magazine for shipping. Millhouse had a narrow-gauge railway with horse-drawn trucks but at Kames one-horse carts were used to transport nine-barrel loads between the mills and magazine. Carts returned to the works with coal, charcoal, sulphur and saltpetre. The men worked twelve-hour shifts six days a week and 60–70 full cartloads went up and down from Kames to Millhouse every day.

The mills got through twelve loads of coal a day and there was a contract with a company called Ross & Marshall to deliver 150 ton loads each week on puffers – the little Clyde cargo steamers made famous by Inveraray-born author Neil Munro in his *Tales of Para Handy*. These particular puffers had names such as *Skylight* and *Twilight* and they also took some of the finished gunpowder away. To meet regulations governing the loading of explosives near the mainland, however, the packed barrels were usually taken out from Kames's Black Quay to vessels moored off the Bute coast.

One of the tragedies recorded on the Dolphin Bell memorial plaque happened in 1864 when the *Guy Fawkes*, which was owned by the Kames Gunpowder Company, sank. Archibald Campbell, Duncan McKellar, Hugh McKenzie and Alexander Thomson drowned. The 120-ton vessel had been used to take gunpowder to Liverpool and pick up raw materials there.

From this 'remote' corner of Argyll, between 3,000 and 4,000 tons of gunpowder were shipped each year and by the 1870s the government had accepted Curtis & Harvey's T.S. No. 6 powder specification as the standard for the Martini-Henry rifle and the company was a main supplier. Little wonder that Kerry was now the most populated area of the parish and had a healthy economy.

Of course, the presence of such industry did not work to best advantage for everyone. Lamont must certainly have felt there was a gunpowder plot working against him. He had serious financial difficulties and in 1862 he mortgaged the Ardlamont estate for £10,900. He also tried to sell 'very beautiful feus' in the manner of Arthur Scoular round in Tighnabruaich, but few of Glasgow's industrial barons wanted to spend money building a rural haven next to a

Kames village store served the gunpowder factory workers (*Alan Miller Collection*)

gunpowder factory. However, for the grocers, the tailors, the cobblers, the spirit merchant and innkeeper who were now able to sustain their businesses in Kames, life was more rosy. In 1871, the census recorded that 190 males and ten females were working at the Kames and Millhouse plant. But although there was prosperity for these workers, fear must always have been present. It was not only that the materials they were working with were so volatile that an explosion such as the the one which killed seven men in August 1846 could happen so very easily. There was the weather to contend with too; the disaster in December 1863 happened after lightning struck one building and gales swept the flames on to others, killing yet another seven men. That night the local GP, Dr Fletcher, looked after the injured but the company also sent the *Guy Fawkes* to Rothesay to seek Dr McLachlan to asssist. In 1870, yet another four men and a boy were killed in the works. In 1883, there was news from Furnace on the other shore of Loch Fyne that there had been a serious explosion at the gunpowder factory there, closing it permanently, and back in Millhouse, neighbour and workmate Alexander Dykes would die in 1891.

Little wonder that no one wanted to tempt fate, and when garden plots were allocated to workers in 1894, they made No. 13 the washing green. Among those who cultivated the other twelve plots were Donald Weir the engine keeper, Walter Brown, one of the millkeepers, and engineer Charles Millar. There was still a Donald Weir with the company when it finally closed in 1921, but this one was a glazer. He had been with Millhouse Gunpowder Company for between forty and fifty years – was it the same Donald, who had stepped down from the more strenuous engine-keeping job to keep the works glazed instead? All the employees were made redundant and received severance deals according to the job they had done and the length of their service.

Sadly, there was a final death when the mill was being dismantled. John McGilp's name appears on the Dolphin Bell memorial for the year 1922. He died in hospital from powder burns.

With the closure of the works came the end of an era of industrialisation in this 'remote' rural corner of Argyll. Within two decades, its isolation would once more be its selling point. During the Second World War, Millhouse's cottages were evacuated along with all the inhabitants of Ardlamont peninsula to make way for the 25,000 British and American troops who came to Kerry to train for the 1944 Normandy landings. The Millhouse folks' furniture went into store in Tighnabruiach and the mansion house of Caladh was also requisitioned by the Royal Navy as being distant enough to carry out secret training.

The *New Statistical Account* of 1843 had recorded that Kilfinan parish had no market town, and 'strictly speaking, no village in the parish', no turnpike roads, no quays or harbours except the pier at Otter Ferry. Instead there were clachans of a dozen to fifteen families served by half a dozen schools and a post office in Kilfinan. Arthur Scoular changed all that by selling the Tighnabruaich estate feus and the gunpowder factory turned Kames and Millhouse into villages, too. But while Tighnabruaich continued to prosper, Kames and Millhouse lost ground when the factory closed. Many families had transferred to other works in Ayrshire and by the time the *Third Statistical Account* was written by the Rev. George Cairns in 1955, many of the homes in Millhouse were occupied only in the summer. Schools at Millhouse, Ardlamont and Kilfinan closed because there were no pupils (or teachers) and the children went instead to Tighnabruaich. One thing had not changed – the coal was still being discharged at the powder works quay at Kames.

That quay came into its own in the 1920s and 1930s when there was an upsurge in the herring industry. The late Chester Currie, fisherman and yachtsman, recalled the fish being gutted and salted by up to a hundred 'fisher lassies' on the powder works quay at Kames and on the Auchenlochan pier in 1929-30. They worked in the old Powder Mill buildings on the old quay. Many came from Fraserburgh and a lot of the herring went to Germany.

Apart from the growing industry of tourism, the area continued to return to these labours of a previous era – to farming and fishing. Some of the larger farms were now over 1,000 acres and in the 1950s there were thirty-two full-time and ten part-time farms operating. Forestry plantings swathed the Ardlamont peninsula in the 1950s but even then the Forestry Commission knew it would not yield a fortune. The population of Kilfinan parish, which had peaked at 2,709 in 1911, had dropped to 1,253 in 1951.

Augusta Lamont of Knockdow estate, who died at the age of eight-five in 1958, said: 'Rural depopulation seems to be correlated with the introduction of motor transport, which facilitates ever-increasing centralisation, and this in turn affects almost every phase of life.' Employment went outside the parish, coal came by lorries instead of ferries and even shopping habits changed – buses took people to Dunoon, and the Rothesay shops suffered.

Today, Catriona Maxwell says it is as if the gunpowder works never existed. Apart from a testing cannon in the middle of a field, there is scant evidence of the old industry. Catriona, born in the early years of the Second World War and brought up in Millhouse, remembers being evacuated to Kilfinan because of the troop activity in the area. She remembers seven living in a room and kitchen in the village and recalls them as happy days. 'When we were little, unknown to our parents, we went to the old works. You could see all the ruins of the buildings then and I suppose they were quite dangerous. Now it feels odd that this was once an industrial area. It's hard to believe we had a school here, a church up the road, a post office, a shop and the joiner's shop. Quite a lot of people would like to see some new industry to give the place more of a buzz.'

Secondary school students go to school in Dunoon and few come back because there is precious little employment in the area. Catriona Maxwell lists tourism and the fish farm at Portavadie as the main sources of income. Timber is now being taken out from the area by water from Portavadie but the work is done by contractors rather than local labour. Local roads are being upgraded to allow coaches into the area and this could mean more trade for local shops and eating places but this type of tourism can never offer the number of jobs which once were available in the bigger houses of Tighnabruaich, the mansions and of course, the gunpowder works.

7

COLINTRAIVE

A crossing for kings and cattle

Colintraive is tucked away in the maze of waterways which ooze out from the Firth of Clyde. It sits halfway down the middle finger of the Cowal peninsula – not the eastern finger with its potentially important seaboard facing the industrial central belt of Scotland; not the western fringe with Kilfinan church and the Lamont stronghold; but the one defined by Loch Striven and Loch Riddon, a small deep sea loch which flows into the east of the Kyle of Bute. If the ice ages had dealt a fractionally different hand, Colintraive may have been on the island of Bute: its position on the mainland just 200 metres from that royal island is what created its status as a vital ferry port. They say that few ferry journeys are shorter than the one from Colintraive to Rhubodach and this convenient stepping stone made it a gateway to Cowal and the mainland in the long centuries before the A886 swooped and soared its way down through Glendaruel Forest. The strait may be a daunting 61 metres deep, but it is so narrow that in the days when black cattle constituted the wealth of this corner of Argyll, the beast were swum across from Rhubodach to Colintraive at the start of their journey to the great markets of Crieff and Falkirk. Colintraive is an anglicisation of the Gaelic *caol an t'snaimh*, the strait of the swimming.

Patricia Watt, who took over the Colintraive Hotel at the beginning of 2004, says Bute has a stronger influence on the village than Cowal and that is not only because every time she enters the hotel's front door she is reminded by the imposing armorial achievement above the door that this was once a hunting lodge on the estate of the Marquess of Bute. Rothesay is clearly visible from the single-track road around Strone Point. Bute islanders pop over on the ferry to dine in style at the hotel. As was ever the case before motorised travel, this is yet another Argyll village where the instinct is to travel by sea, not through difficult hinterland.

It is also another Argyll village where tourism has become the main industry. There may be a builder, a fencing supplier and families

Colintraive village (*Argyll and Bute Library Services*)

making their living from the fertile soil that narrowly fringes the peninsula, but around 30 per cent of the property in the area is let as holiday homes. The ferry, the church and the hotel are the modern focal points of the village. Young people travel out of the area to work and about a third of the residents are retired. The houses are strung out along the shoreline of the Kyle, their stately appearance and manicured gardens a reminder that the hidden nature of Colintraive was its attraction to the industrial barons of Glasgow and Greenock who built them as holiday homes from the first third of the nineteenth century. Tourism has been the key to prosperity for almost two centuries – but it got off to a bad start.

In 1827, one of the first tourists to come to Colintraive was the 1st Lord Teignmouth, who recorded after his visit, 'The Kyle of Bute offers no scenery worthy of notice.' Perhaps the hospitality at the inn was so good (or so bad) that Lord Teignmouth was rendered incapable of seeing the Kyle at all, let alone in a good light. Perhaps the 200-metre crossing was too stormy for him. It is hard to imagine what he was searching for, but in the years since then visitors have developed an appreciation of the dramatic views, the stillness and freshness of the air, and the peace and tranquillity punctuated only by the quiet throb of a CalMac ferry engine. In the 1850s, Victorian steamers came to Colintraive pier and disgorged the families of the wealthy for their summer stay. Papa spent the week in the city consolidating the family fortunes while Mama, the children and a retinue of maids enjoyed a month or two away from the industrial smog of Glasgow or Greenock. Later, day-trippers noisily trooped their way around the village, but for them the preferred destinations were the growing resorts of Rothesay or Dunoon and its neighbours. The start of the Second World War saw the end of the steamer era in Colintraive – the small piers on the Clyde were closed and never reopened. Yet although the road may have created links through the hinterland of Argyll and beyond to the rest of Scotland, Colintraive is still best reached via Bute from Wemyss Bay and then that 200-metre stretch of water from Rhubodach.

It is probable that the very earliest settlers reached this part of Cowal by similar routes as they split into their various factions. Bute lays claim to being the first island of the Scottish Highlands because geologically, the Highland Boundary Fault lies between Rothesay in the east and Scalpsie Bay on the west of the island. Historically, it was the front line of a troublesome western seaboard. For 7,000 years before Christ there had been nomads and settlers inhabiting Bute and Cowal. They left behind their artefacts and their monuments – there is a large Bronze Age cairn in a field east of the ferry terminal in front of the hotel at Colintraive – but major trouble did not begin until the Irish princes decided to colonise the land so near to their own territory across the narrow strip of water which led to Argyll. It was Comhghall, grandson of the powerful Antrim Prince Fergus Mor and son of Erc, after whom Argyll was named, who was given this quarter (*ceithir,* which became Kerry) and whose name was anglicised into Cowal. Then castles were built to replace the forts of the earlier settlers. There was one at Dunoon (*dun*, fort; *amhuin*, stream – the fort by the water) and others at strategic points along the coast and in the hills and glens.

The Irish were not the only ones with their eyes on this corner of Scotland. Colintraive, like its neighbours, suffered raids by the Norse in their massive longships and endured colonisation. The Vikings came and outstayed their welcome. *Glenduisk*, Glen of black-water, became *Glen-da-ruail*, Glen of red blood, in the early twelfth century when Mekan, King of Norway and son of Magnus Barefoot, fought the Gaels and lost. When in 1263, King Hakon was defeated at the Battle of Largs, his ships retreated round into the Kyles of

Bute. The blaze of boats in Largs must have been seen in Bute and at Toward Point long before the fugitives sought sanctuary in the straits. The castle built in Rothesay by Magnus Barefoot around 1098 had gone back and forth between Norwegians and Scots for a couple of centuries but now the Scots were back in charge and the castle, like that at Dunoon, was seen as a strategic outpost from which the western fringe could be controlled. A stone castle was built at Dunoon in the thirteenth century and by the end of the fourteenth century it was a royal palace. Robert II is said to have enjoyed staying at Rothesay Castle and his son made the town a royal burgh in 1401. Later, James V added to it a part known as The Palace. In Dunoon, the strength of the Scottish kings was also being reinforced by a display of power architecture and in 1469 the castle there became the property of the heir to the throne.

The king could not spend all his time keeping a personal grip on the goings on in the west, however, and it was now that the major families, who had played their cards right, acted as advisers and supported the king with troops and cash received their reward – or perhaps their poisoned chalice. Colin Campbell of Argyll was made Keeper of Dunoon Castle by royal charter in 1472 and the Stuarts were given charge of Rothesay. The tiny village of Colintraive had the immense role of keeping the routes open for all the king's men. Law and order were kept from Dunoon's Tom-a-Mhoid – The Hill of the Court of Justice. There was Gallow Hill, too – but then, throughout Argyll, there were scores of places where gallows were erected to summarily dispatch those sentenced to death at heritors' courts: in Argyll, it was not only the state which dispatched justice. The royal presence, however, was felt much more in Dunoon and Rothesay, two towns more readily accessible than those of the more distant mid Argyll and Kintyre. The Campbells were to pay one red rose on demand in rent for the castle at Dunoon. Queen Mary came there in 1563 and was probably the most appreciative of this variation on a peppercorn rent.

Two decades earlier, the Stuarts in Rothesay found themselves on the receiving end of the Earl of Lennox's burn-and-pillage policy on behalf of Queen Elizabeth of England, and they were temporarily turned out of their hereditary stewardship. They were to suffer again a hundred years later during the violent century of civil war. Rothesay Castle was first held for Charles I and then Cromwell. The Roundheads left Rothesay Castle partially destroyed when they left it in 1659 and when the 9th Earl of Argyll unsuccessfully conspired with the Duke of Monmouth in 1685 to overthrow the recently crowned James VII & II, the Argyll Highlanders set Rothesay Castle on fire. That bloody century was a long nightmare for the leaders of Argyll. The Lamonts and Campbells used the civil war as a front to settle old scores which led to the Lamonts killing over thirty people in Strachur and Kilmun in 1644 and the Campbells retaliating with an attack on Toward Castle, a Lamont stronghold, in 1646. Campbell reneged on a deal to allow Lamont's men to go free, massacring some of them in Dunoon kirkyard. Some were hanged, some stabbed, some buried alive. A stone erected in 1906 by the Clan Lamont Society on Tom-a-Mhoid Hill belatedly honours their memory. In Loch Riddon, just north of Colintraive, the castle on Eilean Dearg (red island) was used by the Campbells as a stronghold against the Crown. In 1685 during that abortive attempt to bring William of Orange and his wife Mary (daughter of James VII & II) to power in Britain, the castle was stocked to the roof with ammunition and 180 prisoners were held there. When government vessels got too close, the Campbells blew the place up in an explosion so violent the foundations lifted. The safety of the prisoners, of course, never came into the equation.

Men around Dunoon and on Bute had made their living for centuries by raising black cattle – red, not black, in colour but so called to distinguish them from dairy cows – and on the meagre crops they could grow on the Cowal peninsula. The cattle were driven along the ancient drove roads to ferries which would take them to the mainland markets. Not all were such short crossings as the one at Colintraive. There was a passenger ferry at Dunoon for centuries. The Ballochyle Campbells of Kilbride Farm held the rights in 1618 and were obliged to take the Marquess of Argyll across the Clyde in a ten-oared ornamental boat whenever he desired. These rights continued until the early nineteenth century when they sold them to James Hunter of Hafton. Hunter's Quay, once known by the Gaelic name of Cammesreinach, or bay of ferns, became a byword for happy landings for myriad Glasgow day-trippers as that century progressed. There was not, however, a ferry for cattle at Dunoon although two unsuccessful attempts to build one had been made in the 1770s. So although there were cattle fairs – five a year in 1707 – at Dunoon, the cattle could not be shipped out from there and drovers had to take them up the coast to Ardentinny instead, which also linked with drovers coming from the west over the hill from Creggans on Loch Fyne.

Hunter's Quay (*Argyll and Bute Library Services*)

Industrialisation came to this eastern side of Cowal in the shape of a gunpowder factory at Clachaig. This was a custom-built village with a church and school erected by Curtis & Harvey in the early nineteenth century before they set up their venture at Kames and Millhouse. The Crimean War meant prosperity for the factory, which employed not only workers from the village but over 100 women who walked the ten kilometres every day from Dunoon to pack the japanned canisters of gunpowder. Sulphur, saltpetre and charcoal were brought by boat to Sandbank and then taken by cart to the factory.

In Colintraive, life remained unremittingly rural. The flurry of violent activity of earlier centuries gave way once more to peaceful occupations. There were tenanted farms, a smithy, a corn mill and by then the hunting lodge had become an inn. Much of the land belonged to the Marquess of Bute (and still does to this day) but a branch of the Campbell tree was rooted at South Hall, a property south of Colintraive towards Strone Point. Wealthy enough to build the local village church in 1840, the family then faced more difficult financial times by selling off feus in the manner of Arthur Scoular of Tighnabruaich. From secluded and poor, Colintraive was to be transformed into secluded and wealthy.

The sale of feus was changing not only Colintraive but the whole of the eastern coast of the Kerry peninsula. In 1822, some five years before Lord Teignmouth would dismiss the Kyles of Bute as a tourist attraction, James Ewing, the Lord Provost of Glasgow, feud land on Castle Hill in Dunoon. The first to be built was called Marine Villa (now known as Castle House). As in Colintraive, people were not so dismissive of the scenery as Lord Teignmouth and by 1833, when Dunoon first applied to become a burgh, there were over 200 new houses. Their owners had to come in small boats and land at one of the rickety ancient piers. With an eye on the main chance, James Hunter of Hafton, who by now had the rights to the ferry, set up a Private Joint Stock Company in 1835 and built a good solid pier capable of handling the new traffic. In 1845 this was improved by a new jetty which allowed the original structure to become a goods gangway. In 1896, the pier was bought by the town council for £27,000 and an even further improved pier was opened with great ceremony by one of Argyll's first families in the nineteenth century, Lord and Lady Malcolm of Poltalloch, who arrived at the pier in their own steam yacht during torrential rain.

That pier lasted until 1975 when it was taken over by Strathclyde Regional Council. The day-trippers had just about disappeared by then, lured away from the Costa Clyde by cheap holidays on the Spanish costas. Some £250,000 was spent on the pier in the 1980s and 1990s but Argyll and Bute Council inherited an ailing asset which today is threatened by shrinking local authority budgets. The pier had served a growing population: Dunoon comprised just 1,200 inhabitants in 1827, rising to 4,000 in 1871. In the early days of tourism, the new residents and summer visitors were served by 1,000 wells. The drainage was poor and there was no street lighting until 1868. As in Lochgilphead, a new gasworks provided light and employment. There had been schools since medieval times, but law and order became a problem and the nearest jail was at Inveraray.

Today, the emphasis on education continues with a high school serving the early twenty-first century population of 9,000 in Dunoon as well as young people from the rest of Cowal. It has produced many of the country's top figures, including the late John Smith, leader of the Labour Party, Lord George Robertson, former secretary-general of NATO, and New Labour minister Brian Wilson. Many of the local authority's offices are based in Dunoon; there is a sheriff court to deal with law and order; and this is a major consumer centre for Cowal. Forestry, agriculture, fishing. aquaculture, fish processing as well as tourism are the modern industries of this half of Cowal. But the magic of the nineteenth century bathing boxes has sadly gone. So has the Pavilion, opened in 1905 by the Duke and Duchess of Argyll – that Duchess who was Princess Louise, daughter of Queen Victoria. The bathing lido, opened in 1937 in the west bay, could take 850 outdoor bathers watched by 2,000 spectators from covered terraces. Today there is a modern swimming pool with a flume. The Cowal Games are a reminder of the popularity of Dunoon and its neighbours as a holiday resort, but the variety concerts which attracted top Scottish artistes are little more than a fond memory today.

The end of the holiday heyday, when going 'doon the watter' from Glasgow to the Clyde resorts was the year's biggest treat for thousands of workers, coincided with the beginning of a very different period of prosperity for Dunoon. During the Second World War, Holy Loch to the north of Dunoon became a submarine base. In 1961, the loch became an American naval base where Polaris nuclear submarines were berthed. Landladies, who were feeling the pinch as holidaymakers headed for Spain, now opened their doors to American sailors. Houses were built at Sandbank for officers from the USS *Proteus* and flats for ratings went up near the golf club. Taxi companies proliferated and burgers nudged fish and chips off the fast food outlet menus. There were protests against the nuclear presence but retailers and property owners reaped the benefits of this captive crew. For exactly thirty years, there was a sometimes uneasy relationship between the two communities but when the USS *Simon Lake* sailed back to the United States leaving the detritus of a naval base behind her, the economic climate plunged for Dunoon, Innellan, Sandbank and the rest. The presence of the local authority and health board has helped to ameliorate the situation, but it hardly matches the Gulf Stream comfort which US Navy pay packets ensured.

The colourful regattas which augmented the coffers of these Costa Clyde resorts before Polaris are history. The Royal Marine Hotel at Hunter's Quay was once home to the Royal Clyde Yacht Club, established in 1856 as the Clyde Model Yacht Club because its members then sailed craft under eight tons. In 1873, the club became 'Royal' and in 1876, Queen Victoria, who had a personal fondness for the West of Scotland following her 1840s yachting visit, presented a cup for the racing season. Sir Thomas Lipton, the tea magnate, often brought his yacht *Erin* to Hunters' Quay and the Prince of Wales who became Edward VII was a frequent visitor at the RCYC. In 1920, King George V came on the *Britannia*. These the local populace could take

Holy Loch (*Argyll and Bute Library Services*)

in its stride, catering to the needs of day-trippers and kings alike. They
were thrown, however, during an incident which caused the most
excitement since the civil war. A ship sailing from Spain to Glasgow
loaded not only with oranges but delayed action bombs planted by
a German agent exploded when the vessel was off Hunter's Quay. It
was not whisky but oranges galore, to the delight of local children
who had not seen an orange for the duration of the Second World
War. As they gathered these alien objects from the shore, they were
reported to have rationalised: 'If it bounces, it's a ba' – if it explodes,
it's a bomb.'

This shore had once been nothing more than a fringe of farms –
Crochan, Kilbride, Auchamore, Dunloskinbeg, Dunloskinmor,
Bogleha', Tom-na-ha, Ardenslate, Upper and Lower Dalling, Dalfauld
and Milton – interspersed with mills, quarries and castles. There was
a mill at Kirn (*quern*, millstone) and two quarries behind it which no
doubt provided stone for the castles at Dunoon, Innellan and Toward.
The castle ruins at Innellan date back to the fifteenth century and
nearby is a Campbell mansion built in 1650, right in the middle of
the civil war. Its ruins became the hideout for smugglers and distillers
of illicit whisky. In the hills behind Butt Woods, probably the site of
archery practice in medieval times, is the ruined village of Innellan,
last inhabited in the nineteenth century when sheep were taking the
place of black cattle as a source of wealth and replacing people in

Kirn (*Argyll and Bute Library Services*)

farming townships. The Victorian Innellan, where the sale of feus had started in 1851 after the pier opened there, was attraction enough to have Lord Byron write *A holiday in a quiet spot: watching the ships about Innellan*, in which he evokes 'pathless woods' and a 'lonely shore' where 'none intrudes'. Secluded though it may have been for a man used to the bustle of Venice, there were four coffee houses, four grocers, three joiners, two bakers, two masons, two dressmakers, a postman, a plumber, a tailor, a butcher, a milliner, a teacher, a carrier and an evangelist as well as the hotel, pier and post office. At its height of popularity as a seaside destination, it merited three churches to meet the needs of the fluctuating population.

Neolithic burial sites, early Christian churches, reminders of feuding Dalriadans, Vikings and Scots and the gentler history of the Clyde steamers are today the ingredients which attract visitors to Colintraive and its bigger neighbours. The strategic importance of this part of Cowal is highlighted by the presence of the grave of the executed Archibald, 1st (and only) Marquess of Argyll at Kilmun. Like Colintraive, this was an excellent hunting area enjoyed by kings and their followers – as well as an excellent place to play frontier power games. Kilmun was made a free burgh of barony in 1490 by James IV, giving the people the right to hold markets, fairs, and to conduct the business of bakers, butchers fishmongers and craftsmen.

Innellan (*Argyll and Bute Library Services*)

In 1650, the Campbells built yet another mansion to reinforce their status in the area. Eleven years later, the Covenanting Marquess was in his grave and his head was on a spike in Edinburgh *pour décourager les autres.*

These historical riches are the new industry of Cowal. Sea bathing is known now to be more pleasant in warmer climes, and the past is not just another country but a playground for the lovers of history and nature. The Rev. Mair Donald, minister of the parish of Kilmodan and Colintraive, says tourism is the key to keeping Cowal's head above the waves. Patricia Watt agrees. She says: 'People come for short breaks and love it.' They come for the walking, the fishing, the stalking, the wildlife – and the scenery of which Lord Teignmouth could make neither head nor tail.

8

NEWTON

'. . . under a necessity of thinning the population . . .' (*Earl of Selkirk*, Observations on the state of the Highlands of Scotland, *1805*)

Argyll had people planted in it for political reasons and people pruned from it for economic ones. For centuries, tenants were dealt with like expendable commodities, even by the best of lairds with the best of intentions. In the late eighteenth century when a degree of peace had broken out in the county and lairds were looking around for ways of maintaining their increasingly expensive habits, sheep were seen as much more profitable options than people and in 1805, the Earl of Selkirk wrote 'with pleasure' of an experiment being made at Ballure (Gaelic *baile ur*, new village or new farm), known today as Newton, on the old single-track road which clings to the eastern shore of Loch Fyne.

The project had begun in the early 1790s and was mentioned in the 1792 *New Statistical Account* as an interesting idea. It was conceived by Donald Maclachlan of Maclachlan, whose role as laird and clan chief was something of a part-time one as he was also an advocate in Edinburgh. In common with many landlords of the day, he had called in a surveyor to give him an accurate account of his property. George Langlands of Campbeltown also drew up plans for a new village on the shores of Loch Fyne which would allow Maclachlan to clear the hillside above the loch of small townships and put sheep in their place. According to the Earl of Selkirk, Maclachlan, finding himself 'under a necessity of thinning the population on several of his farms', chose ten or twelve cottars to live in his new village. They were some of his poorest cottars but men he believed were hard workers. He built three terraces of thatched cottages down on the shore, each with two rooms, and provided 'two substantial fishing boats of the best construction, with all their apparatus, on condition that their cost should be repaid to him from the produce of their industry'. Although the plan offered these families a better deal than that which faced many tenants on estates throughout Argyll – and, indeed, throughout Scotland – this was not an act of philanthropy

Built to take workers away from land more valuably used for sheep, Newton was the custom-designed fishing village (*Dr Alastair MacFadyen Collection*)

but a sweetener. The alternative was emigration to North America, possibly from the port of Crinan over the hills to the west of the ferry point on the opposite shore of Loch Fyne, or migration to the increasingly industrial Lowlands – Glasgow, Greenock, Paisley and the Vale of Leven, to the printing and bleaching fields and the cotton manufacturers. Those who crossed the Atlantic did so in appalling conditions and the weakest were unlikely to make it. Those who went off to the factories and sweatshops of Scotland's industrial heartland faced poverty and disease in overcrowded tenements. The fittest might make fortunes – for the rest, eviction from a highland cottage was tantamount to a death sentence.

Now here was a landlord prepared to set up a handful of tenants with a couple of boats at a time when herring was plentiful in Loch Fyne. According to the Earl of Selkirk, Maclachlan realised that fishing would not provide a year-round living and that cottars were rooted in the land. His pruning was judicious. The shoots he planted were hardy enough to be able to pay back the sum he had laid out for the two boats within a couple of seasons and to grub from the land such crops as the poor land given them would yield. There were crofting strips behind each of the twelve little houses and grazing rights on the hill at the back of them. This was part of a farm which Maclachlan turned over to them at a peppercorn rent, which he gradually increased to the full value so that the tenants would be obliged to fish in order to be able to pay the rent.

The tenants were, in fact, caught between a rock and a hard place. Although herring were abundant in 1790, the fishing was too precarious in subsequent years to guarantee maintaining a family – and the crofting could never be more than subsistence because of the quality of the land. But in those days there were no handy shops; no roads across the peninsula; no focal place called Dunoon, barring its few fishermen's cottages and the ruin of a medieval castle gifted by the king to the 1st Earl of Argyll in 1473. Buying food was not part of the culture and the villagers of Ballure had to produce enough crops to put food on their tables.

By the time Selkirk was writing in 1805, more tenants had been brought into the new village and the original land was subdivided. Selkirk optimistically saw a day when improved markets in Scotland would allow a situation in which Maclachlan could take all of their land and they would be able to sustain themselves without it. In the early years, they made enough to buy more boats and tackle and Selkirk claimed that some had 'accumulated considerable sums of money'.

They could not, of course, have survived on the proceeds of fishing had the market for their herring catches not been so near and so well organised. Selkirk admitted that in the remoter areas of Scotland, fishermen simply did not get the price for their catches, but he believed that if villages such as Newton were set up near the main fishing towns that fishing could become the saviour of the Highlands and Hebrides. It was something he suggested could only be developed slowly with loans such as Maclachlan had offered his twelve families as well as help in securing markets for catches. The Ballure catches were picked up from the boats by the herring busses and taken straight to the markets of Greenock and Glasgow. No gutting or curing ever took place at Ballure on a commercial scale and no ancillary trades ever developed there. What little fish was landed there was for the villagers' own tables.

An indication of the quality of the land Maclachlan of Maclachlan was trying to wean his tenants away from is seen in the valuation rolls of 1860, which put the Newton tenancies at £5 a year. In 1940, the valuation was still the same. This is gorse country where according to the Rev. Mr Charles Stewart, who wrote an account of Strachur and Stralachlan parish for the 1792 *Statistical Account*, the arable land was

Lives depended on the boats with their dark sails which went out from Newton to fish Loch Fyne (*Dr Alastair MacFadyen Collection*)

of little value. Mr Stewart explained that rent was given in proportion to the number of cattle each farm could sustain and at the time, the going rate was 13d an acre. The population at the time of the Newton project had dropped in the parish to fewer than 1,000 and already there were 12,280 sheep on the hills. Oats, bere and potatoes were the crops of the area which Mr Stewart said 'very nearly' supplied the inhabitants. Given the quality of the land at the back of the Ballure cottages, the crofting was not going to sustain those particular families by Mr Stewart's reckoning. Some of the potatoes were used in local distilleries which no doubt did supplement incomes but Mr Stewart would not have approved.

The landlords of the area who had trees were, of course, making a killing at the time and that included the Maclachlans. Directly opposite Newton on the other shore of Loch Fyne was the new furnace built by an English company for smelting iron ore. There was now a constant demand for wood, not just for traditional boatbuilding and house construction but for charcoal for Furnace, as the village unimaginatively came to be named. The woods, which covered 1,500 acres of the parish's 39,000 acres, were now worth £6,000. Just 700 acres were under tillage at the beginning of the 1790s.

Those who were not subsistence farmers worked for the local lairds. There were also a dozen weavers in the parish, who, according to Mr Stewart, 'wove coarse cloths and linens such as the country people wear', a mason, three carpenters, a blacksmith, five tailors, two ferrymen and two innkeepers. But many of the locals went off south for seasonal work even without the 'encouragement' of lairds to leave the land to the sheep.

Donald Maclachlan, a member of the Faculty of Advocates in Scotland, lived in what was described as a 'good modern house' fronting onto Loch Fyne near the medieval Castlelachlan, which was – and is – still standing. The estate stretched 11 miles along the lochside and between a mile and 1.5 miles inland. The farms of the estate bordered the loch but as Maclachlan had half of the woods in the parish he was not concentrating too much on developing his arable land. His neighbour, on the other hand, Lt. General Campbell, the Laird of Strachur, was farming in the 'English method', trying to produce green crops. He had developed Strachur Park as a stately mansion (his was reckoned to be the most ancient branch of the Campbell clan) and had built for his tradesmen, crofters and labourers stone houses with slate roofs – very different from the thatched cottages of Newton.

There was, as is always the case in parishes where there are two churches, rivalries between the villages. The Newton folk went to Stralachlan Church rather than the one in Strachur, a situation which remains to the twenty-first century. The work carried out by General Campbell in improving the area (and presumably to a lesser extent Maclachlan's building of the three little terraces at Newton) pushed wages for building labourers up from 1s to 1s 5d a day, but there was so little other work now that Maclachlan was clearing his land for sheep that parishioners were drifting off in their droves. Those lucky enough to be employed as farm servants living in got £7 a year and three pairs of shoes worth 12s, which was three times the wages of the 1750s. A young woman doing farm work was paid £3 a year and two pairs of shoes and Stewart reckoned that a farm labouring family in the parish could afford to educate their children. But the increase in sheep farming would change all that in the coming decades. While the Rev. Stewart looked on the Newton project as promising not just for the twelve favoured families but as a blueprint which the state should be encouraging in the rest of the Highlands, Maclachlan's tenants must have been wondering who was next to be 'thinned' from the land. Mr Stewart had seen sixteen families thrown out of their tenancies over the previous thirty years and four farms turned into sheep walks. By 1788 there were twenty-seven boats in the parish employing 108 men. The fishing at that time was providing the owner of each boat with a fifth of the clear profits and each man in the crew got between £12 and £15 sterling for working from July to Christmas. Now in 1790, Maclachlan was to manipulate a further twelve families into a situation where fishing had to be relied on for their main income. 'The sea', Mr Stewart said, 'opened its arms to the young and active.' But he also confessed: 'Many whole families emigrated to the manufacturing towns where a change of climate and diet shortened the days of the old and enervated the young . . . the district is now thinned of its inhabitants. The people have been forced to leave their native hills.'

Maclachlan's experiment led Mr Stewart to suggest in the *Statistical Account* that farms be joined together, that there should be more villages and they should be closer together – the distance between Argyll villages in the eighteenth century must have isolated people greatly and the ensuing lack of communication stunted progress – and that when families were moved from their homes, they should be offered resettlement close to their own neighbourhoods. Tenants should, he believed, be granted fuel accessibility, cultivable ground, decent housing and sponsorship of small industry by the lairds. Home employment for the women and children in wool and cotton industries would, in conjunction with these other factors, mean that 'emigration would never be thought of', he suggested. Maclachlan's Ballure greatly impressed Mr Stewart. 'It promises exceedingly well,' he said, and similar schemes would strengthen the state 'by sea and by land'.

But small individual projects, however admirable, can never change society without all the other pieces of the jigsaw in place – and in Strachur and Stralachlan parish there were a number of factors which disadvantaged tenants. Peat was available only on the hilltops and, as in so many other areas of Argyll, was so labour intensive as to keep whole families away from their farming chores at the very time of year when they were needed most. Waterborne coal, however, was too dear for the ordinary family in the 1790s when Ballure was built because there was duty to pay on it – although Lochgoilhead and Dunoon obtained their coal duty free because they came within the boundary of the Firth of Clyde. (In the 1920s, the *Jeanie* would bring coal to Newton and a horse and cart would offload it, duty free.) This added burden meant not only that that Newton houses were damp – peat may smell wonderful but it does not offer a blazing winter fire – but also that it was too expensive to burn coal in limekilns to make fertiliser thus delaying progress in agricultural methods.

To its advantage, however, the closeness of the parish to Greenock and Glasgow meant butchers came from the city and gave a good price for the black cattle. Whether the profits of these transactions were passed on to the stockmen or simply served to pile up coal in the grates of the 'good modern house' inhabited by Maclachlan is not recorded.

By the 1880s, when the *Second Statistical Account of Scotland* was pubished, it was Strachur which had become the main village, perhaps because it was nearer to Creggans pier where steamers from the Clyde landed. It had a post office with a savings bank and telegraph department, a good hotel and a cattle fair on the last Saturday of May and the first Tuesday of October. Despite Maclachlan's encouragement of the fishermen of Newton, the 200-year-old parish was commercially centred on Strachur and even its church, built in 1789 with 400 sittings reflected that status. Stralachlan Church, built in 1792 on the site of an ancient chapel, had just 150 sittings and by the late nineteenth century just forty-seven children regularly attended the Stralachlan school which had places for seventy-six. Sheep and black cattle were by now vying with 'visitors' as a source of income and Newton got its fair share of the latter, with villagers moving out into 'back houses' to allow holidaymakers from the industrial belt to rent their cottages for up to a month of the summer.

After the First World War, it was trees which dominated the Cowal peninsula. In 1929 Benmore House training school for foresters was set up with places for thirty students on two-year courses at the tree nurseries. From 1935, Argyll National Forest Park became the UK's first forest park and stretched over 60,000 acres. At the head of Holy Loch, which was to become world famous in the 1960s as the American Polaris nuclear submarine base, Bryant & May owned forest for the manufacture of their matches. In 1951, 5.5 per cent of the male labour force in Argyll was occupied in forestry work. The area, with its high rainfall and 250-day growing season producing three feet of growth a year, offered the best forestry conditions in Britain. Almost as many villages and townships were lost in the heyday of forestry as during introduction of sheep walks, but Newton survived, almost in aspic. According to the Rev. J. I. Crawford Finnie in the *Statistical Account* of the 1950s, forestry reversed the decline in population, which

At first there was scarcely a track to Newton, but by the early twentieth century a road allowed 'Montgomery's machine' to deliver goods and people to the village (*Alastair MacFadyen Collection*)

in 1951 had sunk in the Strachur and Stralachlan parish to 580. The high cost of living, poor soil and demise of the herring fishing had made it almost impossible for crofters to survive. New roads made it easier to leave the parish, but it also made it easier for outsiders to come in with their ready-made goods and food delivered to the door. The shoemaking and tailoring which had supplemented incomes were no longer viable when villagers could so easily avail themselves of 50 shilling suits in the city.

The Forestry Commission had by now bought six of the largest farms in the parish and had built thirty houses for their workers. The new roads meant the older children went daily to the grammar school at Dunoon – by now a town of note packed with summer visitors brought 'doon the watter' by the steamers from Glasgow. Back in the 1850s, people went there by coach and horses through Hell's Glen to Lochgoilhead and steamer to Glasgow. When a steamboat pier was built in the 1880s at Strachur, it brought direct transport to Glasgow and seventy years of profitable tourism to Newton. But just as the steamer had ousted the sailboat and changed the face of fishing, so motorised transport and improved roads ousted the steamboat – and cheap air travel changed society in Scotland. The Costa Brava became an easy option and the cheap modern hotels there seemed preferable to the cottages of Newton and the boarding houses of Dunoon. Even by the early 1960s, the pier at Strachur was derelict and the jolly blurred black and white photographs of Glasgow children frolicking in rowing boats off Newton became historical artefacts.

And yet as always in Argyll, there is a continuity. The Maclachlans of that Ilk, who have possessed these Stralachlan lands for some 700 years, are still in residence in the mansion house built on the shore next to the medieval castle. That castle was first mentioned in a charter of 1314 and has an internal double tenement structure found in only one other Scottish castle. Although the family lost their hereditary possessions when the 15th chieftain raised 250 men to support the 1745 Jacobite Rising, as was the way of things in those days, they were given back the lands of Cowal in 1749 when Robert Maclachlan succeeded. The population of the parish of Stralachlan declined from 433 in 1801 to 216 in 1951 as farms employed fewer workers. John, the 23rd chief, died in 1942 and his daughter Marjorie, Lady Marnie, inherited the clan chiefdom. Yet today, her descendants continue to take an interest in Newton and the surrounding villages.

Although little remains of the old crofts abandoned in the 1790s for the terraces at Newton (the stones were used to build walls around the fields), the houses at Newton are now probably in better condition than at any time in their history. They were electrified in the 1950s when hydroelectricity came to Argyll, but after the Maclachlan estates were partially broken up after the Second World War when death duties and taxes were the burden of every landowner, the tenants were, according to the Rev J. I. Crawford Finnie in the *Third Statistical Account*, 'virtually forced to buy their houses to ensure continued residence'. Most residents did, in fact, manage to buy their houses, often with a loan from a relative who had already left the area for the big city. They bought property which still did not have a public water supply, but that also was to come in the mid 1950s. Over the years, many of the houses have been improved but in the main without destroying the external features of the traditional cottages. Although few families now live there all year round, the majority stay in the hands of descendants of the original families, just like Castle Lachlan itself.

At the beginning of the century which saw the Maclachlans start to clear their land for sheep walks, Cowal had been a peninsula recovering from civil war and the currency was still black cattle rather than cash. They were not only raised on the inhospitable hills of Cowal but were driven through the peninsula on drove roads from the Isles and Kintyre. They crossed Loch Fyne at Otter Ferry (*oitir*, shingle bank), Strachur and St Catherines. Cattle from the Western Isles had a right to special stances and despite the lack of a good harbour at Dunoon, they were shipped in thousands from that stretch of coast and Ardentinny to markets in the south. In 1710 the main horse route was between Dunoon and Kilfinan and there would not even have been so much as a cart track to Ballure. Eighty years later in 1757, the Rest and Be Thankful pass through Glen Croe was built which eventually would take the emphasis away from the sea and focus travel through the hinterland – but Newton was built in an era when sledges of birch planks with hazel rungs were used on rough ground to transport goods and chattels. They called them cars, but would have made little progress over any distance and were as often pulled by men as by horses.

This was still a time of lawlessness, even though the days when Comhghall was gifted this peninsula by his grandfather, Fergus, son of Erc, subsequent Danish rule of Cowal, and the anarchy of clan ambush in Glendaruel were ancient history. It was in 1747, just four decades before Maclachlan's social experiment, that James Black, the innkeeper at Otter Ferry, was caught smuggling near Greenock in his yawl. Black cattle, Irish meal and, of course, illicit spirits were the main items of this trafficking – and James Black was not its only exponent.

When Donald Maclachlan, Advocate, suggested fishing to the dozen families he proposed to move to Ballure, it would not have seemed an outlandish scheme. Men did live by herring fishing and the bays of Castle Lachlan and Strachur had long provided good shelter for the tiny boats with their red sails. Newton bay itself provided a good natural harbour.

Dr Alastair MacFadyen, now retired from a career in teacher training in Glasgow, is one of the descendants of the Ballure experiment and one of Newton's permanent residents. Although the villagers bought the grazing rights when they were given the option of buying their cottages in the late 1940s, few have used those rights. Dr MacFadyen was brought up in Cumberland but always came to Newton on holiday as a child and remembers the cottages being 'like dolls' houses'. In the 1930s, the county provided grants to upgrade them and replace some of the roofs which by then were no longer thatched. At the end of the village was a stone building used to gut the fish for local use, which provided at least one Newton family with an income, but Dr MacFadyen explains that most families found seasonal work on the estate. The overseer's account records payments to Duncan MacFadyen for lifting potatoes, to Thomas MacFadyen for killing rabbits and Sandy MacFadyen for two days at the thatching.

The language of Dr MacFadyen's ancestors, like the rest of the Newton villagers, was Gaelic. In struggling to make himself understood in English, his great-grandfather Thomas MacFadyen, who was born in 1828 and died around 1912, told people: 'I'm a rabbit in winter and a yacht in summer.' His sons became in their turn Archie Rabbit and Sandy Rabbit. Thomas was employed as estate fisherman and given a rent free cottage, following in the footsteps of his father-in-law Duncan Crawford. A great-uncle was the estate factor. The timber on the estate was processed by contractors who sometimes employed local people and there was work for the women cutting reeds for the thatching and potato lifting.

Alastair MacFadyen is very aware of the Earl of Selkirk's phrase 'the poorest cottars and most industrious'. He says, 'Newton meant people could stay in the district,' but the work was not there for everyone who wanted to stay. His grandfather left for Cumbria and two great-uncles had to go elsewhere for jobs. Two great-aunts trained as nurses in the 1870s and 1880s and did well. Margaret and Annie opened a private nursing home in Colinton, Edinburgh – not long after Florence Nightingale had opened her own hospital. In time they bought a place at Dunoon as a summer residence for their patients, whose learning disabilities meant wealthy Edinburgh families preferred them to be looked after rather than being at home.

What Donald Maclachlan could not have foreseen, of course, was that fishing in Loch Fyne would virtually disappear by the twentieth century and that the estate itself would hit financial difficulties because of the rising cost of wages and the property and death taxes levied on the wealthy. Even as far back as 1893, the residents of Newton and Leachd, the neighbouring hamlet, petitioned the Maclachlans for a new road to their villages because of the summer visitors. They had put up with a rough track for a century and even the new road was an untarmacadamed affair which presumably was all the estate could afford.

That, says Dr MacFadyen, was the start of the 'back houses' – the stone outbuildings where families retreated in summer with a byre

The late nineteenth century brought tourists to Newton and young men like 'Tottie' Crawford augmented their income crewing for the 'toffs' in their yachts (*Dr Alastair MacFadyen Collection*)

underneath and living accommodation above. Visitors came by steamer, and those who did not sail all the way to Strachur might catch a boat to Minard or Inveraray and get a ferry across the loch. Tourists did not only mean the letting of houses, however. Men like Dougal Crawford found themselves working as crewmen on luxury yachts such as the *Iolaire* which anchored at Newton, one of the safest bays in the west. Times changed with the Second World War – many of the yachts were commissioned for service and were never seen again. In the changed social climate after that war, such yachts became less frequent visitors.

But not all was changed. There was still a Gaelic-speaking generation living at Newton, even if they no longer crofted or fished. Crofting finally disappeared in the 1920s. The Laird, John Maclachlan, told the Board of Agriculture in a letter dated 18 April 1928 that the crofts at Newton were Class Two, capable only of sustaining one cow and a follower and that only one now actually had a cow. He explained

Newton villagers moved out of their houses into sheds at the back to accommodate paying summer visitors (*Dr Alastair MacFadyen Collection*)

that the men were employed elsewhere as yachtsmen and that they let their houses out in summer. The estate had, he said, difficulty in letting vacant crofts because there was no employment in the area and the crofts themselves could not sustain a family.

Now the houses are not the estate's responsibility and no one makes a living either from the land or from the fishing. They do, however, still earn from the tourists and Alastair MacFayden says there is still the feel of a holiday place about today's Newton.

Although there is no doubt that Maclachlan was manipulating families when he moved them into his little fishing village, the alternative was much worse. Alastair MacFadyen says: 'This village enabled people to stay when in other parts of Scotland people had to leave, especially in the 1840s and 1850s. There have continued to be family links and I am a descendant of one of the first crofters here, John McVean. These are well-built houses made of two thicknesses of stone with rubble in between. They were thatched and glazed houses, there was a standpipe in the village and water closets at the back. Imagine what that was like compared with the hovels people like John left behind up on the hill.'

The children used to go to parties at Christmas at the big house and New Year meant a shinty match at the castle. In the 1940s, it was a day's journey to Glasgow and Dr MacFadyen can remember the crush and excitement of the boat from Gourock and the thrill of a trip on Montgomery's 'machine', a bus with wooden slatted seats which met the boat at Dunoon and drove over to Strachur (usually with pit stops for the driver who enjoyed his dram). Today, half of the castle is let out, children are bussed to school and Dunoon is a major small town with supermarkets, local government offices and the grammar school for the whole of Cowal.

Newton remains the 'hidden village' it has always been. Scarcely signposted, it nestles on the water's edge, a picturesque reminder of the 'thinning' of tenants a laird had to carry out to make way for more profitable sheep.

9
KILBERRY

Hic jacet Johannes Mauritii et eius filius . . .

Present-day Kilberry is a soothing backwater where unwinding is an art form. Perhaps it is not surprising, then, to learn that the first inhabitants of Kilberry Castle were poets by choice, warriors by command. The 'MacMhurrich' chieftains were bards to MacDonnel of Clan Ranald; harpists and poets who entertained and chronicled the famous – or infamous – Lords of the Isles. They must have gone to battle, of course, because one of the carved tombstones found around Kilberry Castle depicts a knight in armour with the inscription *hic jacet Johannes Mauritii et eius filius* (here lies John MacMurachie and his son) carved beside his helmeted head. The late Marion Campbell of Kilberry, whose life was so bound up in this castle overlooking the Sound of Jura, believed that Johannes was a descendant of the eleventh-century Murchaidh and that the MacMurachies probably built the first castle at Kilberry. They lived there from the fourteenth century by permission of the Lords of the Isles – those Macdonalds who were then in favour with Robert I and held the west coast of Argyll through a grant from him. But then, James III was not so impressed by the Macdonalds as Robert Bruce had been and in 1476 he confiscated the mainland possessions of the Lord of the Isles and chief of the Clan Donald. In the 1490s, the King instructed his Chancellor to set all of Knapdale in small portions on three-year leases to reliable tenants. The Chancellor, the Earl of Argyll, of course saw his Campbell kin as being 'reliable tenants'. He was fated not to see this particular task through, however. The re-assigning of Knapdale had to wait a while and the MacMurachies kept Kilberry almost to the end of the next century. Marion Campbell always felt that this period of forfeitures was much more the cause of the Campbell–Macdonald feud than the much later infamous event in Glencoe.

By 1600, Campbells were resident in Kilberry Castle and the harping days were over. These Campbells were descendants of Duncan, Lord Campbell, whose younger son Archibald founded the somewhat complex family of the Campbells of Auchenbreck with its offshoots at Knockbuy (Minard), Danna, Kilberry, Kilmory and Castle Sween. The Kilberry Campbells are descended through marriage from Colin Campbell, Auchenbreck's grandson, who at the end of the sixteenth century married Helen Wood.

However inaccessible Kilberry may seem now on its single-track coastal road between West Loch Tarbert and Ardrishaig, it was on the drove road north from Kintyre over the hills to Achahoish and its full-frontal position facing the island of Islay, lair of the Lords of Isles, putting it on the main seafaring route of every passing aggressor, missionary, craftsman and tradesman until the end of the eighteenth century. In his *Archaeological Sketches in Scotland: Knapdale and Gigha* (1875), Captain T.P. White clearly fell in love with Knapdale. Finding carved stones of a type he had not seen in Kintyre, undamaged except by time, he wrote: 'It is as though we had fallen upon a cellar of rare old wine, long forgotten and unprized, but mellow under the dust and accumulated rubbish of ages.'

Captain White's investigations in South Knapdale were sometimes informed more by local tradition than archaeological evidence. The cartographers placed an old parish church where White would have preferred to have seen evidence of the ancient monastery which local folklore claimed to have flourished there. There is no arguing, however, with his assessment that in Knapdale there were richer and older memorials of ancient times 'along with the glories of landscape, which add such charm to the researches of the wanderer in these solitudes'. But men who built monasteries and castles were unimpressed by the glories of landscape and solitude. What, then, set them to stay in what had by Captain White's day become this charming backwater?

In the earliest times there were the tribes who made their impressive mark with standing stones and burial cairns. Then came the early Christians (St Columba is reputed to have sailed for Iona from a consecrated cave near the chapel of Cove) whose teachings were consolidated in medieval times by those who built chapels and named them for Irish saints. The remains of a medieval church lie in the woods just 40 metres from Kilberry Castle and about 4 kilometres west-north-west of the present parish church at Largnahension. The name Kilberry could derive from St Berach of Cluain-coirpthe (Kilbarry in County Roscommon in Ireland) or from Berchan (Kilbarchan in Renfrewshire is named after St Berchan). Whoever it may have been named for, by 1392 the church at Kilberry had become a prebend of the cathedral of Argyll on the island of Lismore and the parson was presented by 'the king of Scots, the true patron'. In 1472, Angus, then Bishop of the Isles, petitioned to have a house at Kilberry – whether because he liked the spot or because it was in such a strategic place is difficult to know now. Certainly, the Kilberry church living was a pawn in a larger game and in 1492, John, Lord of the Isles, transferred his right of patronage to the Bishop of Argyll. Was it an act of defiance? It was certainly one of his last acts of authority before he had to forfeit all his lands and although a 1507 Charter of James IV confirmed John's transference, it was an empty gesture because the king had already given the patronage to the 2nd Earl of Argyll.

Control of church, strategic properties and those who lived in them determined the fate of the ordinary people trying to make a living. Who lived in Kilberry Castle was of enormous importance to the welfare of everyone living in the parish of Kilberry and Kilcalmonell, which by the Reformation included the southern shore of West Loch Tarbert where the minister normally lived. Kilberry Castle and the village which grew around it were on the main road south until what today is the A83 was built in 1776 on the east coast of Knapdale. As early as 1767, Colin Campbell of Kilberry and his tenants were required to build a line of new road north through Kilberry's land. In those days there were two ferries across West Loch Tarbert and sea traffic went past the door. The parish included other 'big houses' – Ormsary, Ardpatrick, and Dunmore – which with the castle provided the main employment for the area. According to the census returns of the day, men and women were farm labourers or domestic servants, provided services such as shoemaking and tailoring, or were smiths or carpenters. There were three licensed distilleries in 1792 and whisky was used medicinally – with sulphur three times a day, for instance, to flush away measles spots from children.

In times of peace, this narrow strip of land with its backbone of wooded hills was a place to grow crops and to raise cattle and, eventually, sheep. Place names perhaps give clues to the potential wealth of the area. Knapdale itself betrays the Viking influence and means hills and dales and this particular finger of Argyll is an undulating 21 miles long and 10 miles wide. The descriptive Gaelic names, such as *Allt Lairig an Uinnsinn* (Largnahension), tell of hills wooded with beech, ash and oak. Yet until the 1700s, woods were held to be of little value in Argyll and the constant skirmishing meant little time to cultivate with any long-term planning.

In the civil wars of the 1600s, Kilberry Castle was occupied by troops. In the next century, Colin Campbell of Kilberry would record that the church was burnt by the garrison of this castle during the 'Civill War, to prevent its covering any of the Royal army which then invested the place'. It is most likely that the damage was done by the troops of Alasdair Macdonald in the 1640s – though whether to wreak revenge on the Campbells for past injury or as part of military duties it would now be hard to unpick.

A meeting house was built to replace the burned-out church near to the castle. In the eighteenth century that was replaced by a house at Tiretigan until the church at Largnahension was built in 1821 'contiguous,' said the Presbytery of Kintyre, 'to the place called the preaching rock', which had been a traditional place of worship. The new church was designed by Leith architect Alexander Grant and contracted to builder George Johnston to complete 'according to a plan and specification showen to me by Mr Campbell of Dunmore'. It cost £573 and excluded the use of ornamental stonework – such stonework being seen in the early nineteenth century as surplus to requirements in a Presbyterian place of worship.

Today at Kilberry Castle, fine carved stones such as those commemorating John MacMurachie are displayed for visitors to see. For centuries, many of the oldest stones were treated with less respect: some depicting the Crucifixion were defaced at the Reformation; some were threatened with being ploughed up by Colin Campbell in the 1700s; some – as happened throughout Argyll – were used for the lintels of cottages or as part of dry-stane dykes erected when enclosure became the way forward in farming. The Campbell mausoleum itself has not entirely stood the test of time. It was erected by Captain Dugald Campbell of Kilberry, who held a privateer's licence in 1709 and later commanded HMS *Walpole* in the Mediterranean. Today his mausoleum shows the ravages of the west coast weather just as much as those stones tooled by the Kintyre and Loch Sween schools of carving in the fourteenth and fifteenth centuries.

There was a quarry near Kilberry Castle at Port a' Churaidh which provided stones for the castle's roof ridging around 1737–8 and the diaries of John Campbell, the laird in the late nineteenth century, record the finding of a large carved slab in the sea off the castle which he believed had been destined to be a church lintel lost overboard

The hub of industry in Kilberry for centuries, the castle was still the main provider of work in 1902 (*John Campbell of Kilberry Collection*)

before it could be transported by boat to its destination on Eilean Mor. The Kilberry stone was, according to Thomas Menelaws, who renovated the castle after a fire in 1772, extremely hard and expensive to cut – harder, said his employer Colin Campbell, than that used by the Duke of Argyll to build the castle at Inveraray but 'very durable and pritty' and so presumably not suitable for carving. It was, perhaps, suitable for grinding corn. An incomplete millstone was used in 1789 as a headstone to mark the burial place of William Dawson at Largnahension.

Had William lived, he may have been on the 1797 Militia List for the Parish of Kilcalmonell and Kilberry along with weaver John McAlchallum from Clachan and Duncan McCallum, an apprentice wright from the same township. By then, military service was no longer to serve clan chiefs but for the service of king and country – but if a man wanted to work in peacetime South Knapdale he was still reliant on the goodwill of his laird. That state of affairs was to continue into the twentieth century, but there were very different

A constant stream of guests dined at Kilberry Castle in 1902 on lobster caught by fishermen employed by the estate (*John Campbell of Kilberry Collection*)

lairds over the centuries. Colin Campbell was the man who quarrelled with the parish about his digging up of headstones and objected strongly to paying the window tax he found himself liable to after improving the castle following the 1772 fire. Then from 1788 to 1839, Kilberry's landlord, 'Jamaica John', was absent and only came from his home in Minard to collect the rents for the farms and for shooting. Born in Jamaica, he was brought up at Minard, inherited Kilberry from a cousin and did not seem to have much affection for the place. The next incumbent was John Campbell of Knockbuy, who employed Edinburgh architect Thomas Brown to extend the modern baronial mansion when he sold the Minard property and moved to Kilberry at the time of the birth of his son in 1844. According to legend, the old castle had been plundered and burned by an English pirate called Captain Proby in 1513, and was rebuilt after the fire in Colin Campbell's day. It was John Campbell who, with other local heritors, took a courageous anti-establishment stance in support of the people of Tarbert during the herring trawling crisis and won the affection of local fishermen.

During his lairdship, dairy farming and wool spinning and carding were principal activities at Kilberry. It cost this John Campbell £26 5s 4d for the work of fifteen men, including Colin Bell, Donald Bain, Hector Clark and Duncan Weir, on Kilberry Farm in 1843. Two stones of wool spun (or *spined* as the vernacular then had it) for Kilberry cost £1 12s. John McPhail's wife was paid 1s 3d a day for ten days at the shearing and 8d a day for fifteen days at the potatoes, while Mrs Campbell was paid 7s 6d for carding wool. Buchan the gamekeeper lived at Achaglachach and Neil Malloy the parish constable lived at Carse. Many of the working families reared orphans, whom they described as servants on the census forms. This John Campbell let out Kilberry Home Farm hill to George Hamilton for grazing, then Allan Pollock rented the farm from Whitsuntide, 1855 for ten years. According to Marion Campbell, his great-granddaughter, there were large numbers of small tenants of houses and smallholdings who were not shown on the rent books of the time.

This was the time of the potato blight, a contributory cause of the tragic famine in Ireland. Because there were no potatoes available by late 1846, cash was given in lieu as part of the wage packet of the farm servants. John Martin, for instance, who usually was paid coal, peat and potatoes as part of his wage, was given £2 from the Kilberry estate that year. In 1856, Neil Galbraith, another Kilberry farm servant, whose annual pay was £23, received with his half-yearly wages oatmeal and £5 for the keep of a cow. John was an improving laird – the first wire fence went up on the Kilberry land in 1849.

When the next John Campbell succeeded in 1861, he was serving in India and did not come home to Kilberry until 1870. Then he, too, set about making improvements. In 1873, architects Peddie & Kinnear further modernised the castle. John Campbell had inherited an estate of some 20,000 acres with an annual value in rents of £2,173. The arable land in the south-west of Knapdale was rich and very productive according to the *Statistical Account* of the late nineteenth century. Just one-eighth of the land was under tillage, however, and around 2,000 acres were covered with woods and plantations. In 1699, the 9th Earl of Argyll had commissioned Dougall Campbell of Kilberry as Forester of Sliabh Ghaoil, the wooded spine of hills running down from Ardrishaig to Tarbert. Dougall was to 'debarr strangers from pastuering their goods thereupon' as well as manage and oversee the forestry and deer. The late 1700s had seen some intensive afforestation by the Duke of Argyll, Lord Stonefield, Sir James Campbell and Captain Campbell of Kintarbert. Captain Campbell had 20,000 trees of valuable timber in his natural woodlands in 1794. At the time, oak bark was fetching 12 guineas a ton and an acre of good twenty-year-old oak wood could produce just over a ton of bark. The Crinan Canal company was also buying timber at 7 shillings a foot – almost three times the usual price – and in coming years, deciduous trees were bought up by the ironworks at Furnace and Bonawe.

The John Campbell of the second half of the nineteenth century added considerably to the Kilberry estate woodland. On 25 December 1871 he took delivery of 12,000 forest tree plants from Downie, Laird & Lang of Edinburgh. The servants may have had a 'blow out of food and dancing' that Christmas Day, but on the 27th, John had 'all hands at planting trees'. On the 29th, while his wife Maggie gave the local schoolchildren 'a blow out of food and tea' for Christmas, the farm labourers were still planting, but by the following day the job was finished – just in time, it seems, because John recorded in his diary that a 'very stormy night' followed and on the last day of the year, snow was seen across the Sound on the Islay and Jura hills and the wind 'blew very hard indeed at night'.

The more modern Kilberry had always been an outpost of the Knockbuy empire until John's father sold the Minard property and resolved to live at Kilberry because 'it was the family place'. He had described it not as a place of beauty as seen by the artist and archaeologist Captain White but as 'a bare, flat, featureless, half-reclaimed moor'. While he did not rate the place quite as highly as the more poetic Captain White, he had enlarged the home farm. Now his son John would increase the home farm still further in 1881.

The Rev. Dr John Smith had deplored absentee landlords in his *Statistical Account* of 1794. Although this latest laird was actively involved when he was at home, he still headed off to Edinburgh and London for part of the year and spent time in Italy and other European resorts. Yet he was always to come home to an exuberant welcome from farm hands and domestic staff alike. His diaries record being met by tenants and servants waving flags on 30 April 1870 (his homecoming after his India service), having made his way the previous day from Glasgow to Greenock by train, by the steamer *Mountaineer* to Tarbert and from Tarbert to Ardpatrick by 'Ardpatrick's trap'.

Arriving at Kilberry, his tenant McCalman headed the welcome party and a piper led the procession on foot to the castle where 'we had some speechifying and whiskey' [*sic*].

Just as wages were paid part in cash, part in kind, the records for Kilberry Castle from the eighteenth century show rents paid similarly. The castle accounts show that produce was sold in bulk – butter by the stone cost £4 Scots in 1733 and had risen to £5 Scots in 1745. Cheese in 1733 was £1 13s and 6d a stone and soap 4 shillings a pound. Servants were clothed rather than paid well: a pair of shoes for the kitchen boy in 1738 cost 2s 6d. The price of plough horses fluctuated wildly in the 1740s from £21 to £40 and back to £33 – perhaps the horses themselves reflected the prices paid for them. Sheep and milk cows were also recorded in the accounts of the day. The estate was the industrial heart of Kilberry.

As the present-day century John Campbell of Kilberry says, 'Everything centred on the estate and it kept the area going and the people employed.'

There was a smithy to shoe the plough horses needed for five farms and those used for traps, carriages and riding. There was a carpenter and a plumber, a beekeeper and a laundry maid, game-keepers, gardeners, farm workers and domestic staff. By the time of John Campbell, the laird who kept such meticulous diaries in the late 1800s, employees were needed to run the gas plant which, from the 1870s, piped methane gas to the castle.

Although jobs were handed down through families and the estate looked after its own, there were still people who fell through the net. Even in the heyday of the estate in the 1870s and 1880s, there were those who ended up in Lochgilphead's Combination Poorhouse. Janet Cunie, 49, a former domestic servant from Kilberry, was recorded in the 1881 census as staying in the poorhouse. Fellow inmates included former farm servant Margaret Hamilton, 67; Mary McDougall, 60, who had worked as a domestic servant; and Dugald Walker, 50, another former agricultural servant. One of the youngest inmates, Margaret Connor, 11, was yet another Kilberry-born individual. The sad histories of these folk born in an area of prosperity but reduced to seeking charity are now lost. In 1890, Dr Duncan MacMillan, medical officer of Kilcalmonell and Kilberry Parish, reported that in Clachan, 'two or three of the houses are hardly fit for human occupation, the cattle and the fowls living under the same roof with the household'.

When John Campbell was in residence, his duties within the

The castle's laundry was done here throughout Victorian and Edwardian days (*John Campbell of Kilberry Collection*)

community included the parish council, the 'lunacy board' of the new hospital in Lochgilphead and the law courts and licensing courts. On a stormy and wet day in May 1870, he went to a 'parochial meeting' at Whitehouse with Ardpatrick (the laird of Ardpatrick House, another Campbell). He records: 'The principal business was connected with the sanatory [sic] condition of Tarbert which has to be greatly improved according to a new law.' He added: 'The only men who ought to have the power of legislation for the sanatory condition of the village are those who have interests at stake there. However Stonefield [another Campbell, another laird] at present does not seem to see this in the proper light. He will not feu any land there and merely gives building leases of from 30-35 years so that men will not build sufficient houses for the demand.'

Married in Rome to Margaret Lloyd of Leghorn in February 1871, John Campbell and his new bride were home from honeymoon in June and that August travelled via Tarbert to Inveraray to meet the also recently married Marquess of Lorne and Princess Louise, daughter of Queen Victoria. A gift worth £1,500 from the worldwide

Clan Campbell was presented to the princess – a necklace of pearls and diamonds with a locket and a pendant book of all the names of the subscribers – and she made a thank you speech which John Campbell found lacking. The princess, he said, was 'rather embarrassed and did not speak very well'. Out on the loch were 100 yachts and there was a great deal of celebrating among the landed gentry in the Inveraray Hotel.

This was a time of general prosperity and the Kilberry Campbells shared in it. While John Campbell took his duties as laird very seriously, diary entries about road meetings at Tarbert and his wife's examination of the schoolchildren with the local minister are interspersed with shooting trips in which anything which moved was bagged in true Victorian style. Although the shooting had been let along with Kilberry House while John was still away in the Army, once he was home it became sport for his many house guests. The income for the estate came from the five farms – the rents from those which were tenanted and the profit from those which were managed. On a fine warm day in February 1873, he recorded: 'We killed in the morning a small Highland Heifer which I have been feeding on turnips and corn for a month or six weeks. She weighed 400½ pounds.' On 1 October of the following year, he wrote: 'Managed to get all my corn (6 small stacks) stacked before dark. The corn was not in very good order owing to the great quantity of rain which has fallen since it was cut.' On the 9th, 'My horses and men still helping McCalman to get in his crop.' And on the 21st: 'Six lobster creels which I had lying at Port a Hoorie on the rocks disappeared.' There had been a gale which also caused damage to corn and hay at Tarbert which was still in the fields. And on 5 November that year, John bought a 'good fat black cow for £10 10s.'

Early in 1875 he was in the process of re-letting Keppoch Farm. On 10 February, his diary records that a lot of men came to look at Keppoch and on the 18th he inspected Barr farm, 'whose tenant is leaving it'. On 3 March, John and Alexander Snodgrass from Clochkee Farm near Campbeltown came to 'close the bargain for a lease of Keppoch which is now vacant.' Campbell says: 'I have had a good many offers but not more than two or three from men who I would care to have so close to me.' The Snodgrass men were 'in every way desirable' – not least, perhaps because they offered £400 a year for the first five years' rent and £430 for the rest of the eighteen-year lease. The previous rent had been £360.

By 1890, the story was very different. Farm rents had hit their peak and were on the way down. The depression caused by a fall in grain prices was affecting everyone and when John Campbell chaired the 2 October meeting of the Lunacy Board in Lochgilphead it was decided not to take a new lease of the farms held by the board from Auchindarroch. Campbell said that the lease taken eighteen years previously had been £380. Now it was just £178. He said: 'A great comedown but not more than I have had to submit to in the cases of Coulaghailtro and Keppoch. In 1878 I let Coulaghailtro to McCalman for £640 a year and now I have just relet it to him for £300 and I have to spend £150 on repairs etc. Keppoch is now let for £150 and within the last 20 years it has been let several times at rents from £400 to £360.' Just a few days later, Archibald Turner decided to take a new lease of Tiretigan for five years from Whit Sunday 1891. He had given up Keppoch and Tiretigan but now wanted to retake the latter at a rent of £155.

Timber was a main source of income and felling provided plenty of work – around Torinturk the estate harvested 2,868 tons of oak, 2,263 tons of birch, 825 tons of ash and 800 tons of alder. Sheep, too, became a mainstay for the estate. In 1881, Campbell handed over 1,017 sheep to the incoming tenants of Keppoch Farm, John and Duncan Morrison, stock which was valued at £1,648.

The family went off to the dentist in Glasgow, to the theatre in Edinburgh, to parties and balls in London. The workers went to Tarbert Fair on 27 July and enjoyed the estate's New Year balls which were held around the 'old' New Year's Day, 12 January. Families were invited from all over the parish, heritors and workers alike. Relatives of farm workers and domestic servants who came to the party walked from Tarbert and changed into their dresses at the castle. There were also January ploughing matches, shinty games and summer Highland games with prizes. Sometimes John Campbell could record that there was a good 'blow out' but no drunkenness – on other occasions there were tears before bedtime. On 13 January 1875, he dismissed his cook for drunkenness and the following day had her removed from the premises by a doctor and the police. On 11 April 1889, the butler, on being found drunk in his bed, was sacked and told to leave. He asked for his wages, was 'very impertinent' and stole beer on his way out.

But mainly this was an efficient working unit which saw the heifers being sent off to summer at Achaglachgach and the Tarbert butcher McSporran coming round to inspect Campbell's crossbred

The estate ran a home farm and its other farms were tenanted. Hay making
was still a communal activity in 1915 (*John Campbell of Kilberry Collection*)

lambs, which in June 1889 he bought for 26 shillings each. There
were harvests to be got in, ewes to be clipped, wedders to be bought
and fruit to be picked. That July it was a wonderful summer and
the gardens at Kilberry Castle abounded with apples, strawberries,
cherries, raspberries, gooseberries and plums for the many guests.
Typical of Argyll summers, which can either offer incessant rain or
fierce heat, that one brought burnt grass on thin soil but 'grand crops
of all sorts on deep land'. The sun must have gone to some people's
heads: the vet came to see a colt at Kilberry Castle and was apparently
drunk when he arrived. John Campbell remarked drily: 'Tarbert Fair
has not agreed with him.'

This was the heyday for such estates, but a few good summers like
the one of 1889 were not enough to guarantee that such an essential
hub of the community could survive on the profits accrued from farm

Coal came by boat to Argyll estates and villages alike. This load landed at Kilberry Castle in 1926 and was brought ashore by horse and craft (*John Campbell of Kilberry Collection*)

rents, timber cropping and sheep and cattle sales. Kilberry Castle could maintain only ten domestic servants and twenty agricultural staff and support the local ancillary trades with the help of investment. After all, the smithy existed because of Kilberry Castle. Legge the vet could afford to get drunk because of Kilberry Castle and other 'big houses' around Tarbert. The owners of the SS *Lochnell* which delivered Peruvian guano from the Farmers' Supply Association of Scotland in Leith to the beach at Kilberry Castle were able to do so because the custom made it worth it. Even the coal merchants who a couple of times a year delivered coal to the castle – first the sloop *Margaret Wotherspoon*, registered in Gigha; later the steam lighter *Pointer* – were dependent on the patronage of such estates. On 24 February 1890, Pointer arrived in the evening with 97 tons of coal from Ayr. The freight charge was 6 shillings a ton and the coal was 11s 6d a bag. It was a splendid sight to see the boat offshore and the horses waiting patiently in the water while the carts were loaded to take the coal to the castle store for distribution to tenants over the coming months.

Such estates needed regular injections of cash to maintain them in the manner to which not only the lairds but the workers had become accustomed. In the eighteenth century, that injection was provided for Kilberry from new properties in Jamaica established by the family to produce sugar and rum. The Kilberry Campbells were not among the first to claim land in the West Indies and so did not make a killing, but there was income enough to keep Kilberry going. When John Campbell inherited in the 1860s, it was his wife Margaret, an heiress, whose money allowed the castle and estate to be modernised. John and Margaret's heir had a much more difficult time of it and when he died, his widow and daughter, Marion, became dependent on the Campbell family network to see them through. The castle and estate eventually came back to Marion Campbell but at the end of the Second World War she was forced to sell off much of the estate in a very different world to the one in which her grandfather had lived.

Today's John Campbell, who inherited from Marion, admits such estates are poisoned chalices in the present social and economic climate. The castle and 15 acres of woodland remain in family hands and John makes his income elsewhere, coming home like so many of today's Kilberry residents at weekends – some stay for just part of the year. Many of the original families have left the area and there has been a latter-day 'plantation' of incomers. The Kilberry Inn, once a traditional Black House, has become famous for its food and employs some local people, but the cottages let as self-catering holiday homes do not offer large-scale employment and today's mechanised agriculture provides far fewer jobs than in the nineteenth century. The Forestry Commission planted trees as the nineteenth century John Campbell did – but until that timber is ready for extraction, no workforce is needed. Only the fish farm up the coast at Ormsary employs people in any numbers. The loss of a hundred jobs in a rural area like Kilberry has the same devastating effect as the loss of thousands in an industrial zone.

The present John Campbell produces splendid honey in his remaining woodland – a legacy from his namesake's days in the 1870s and 1880s – and lets out the former laundry to holidaymakers. Many neighbours are retired people who have come to enjoy the beauty and tranquillity so admired by Captain White when he made his archaeological sketches in the 1870s. There were always people who left Kilberry, such as Archibald Arbuthnot who was born in the parish on 1 January 1816, and died in Hutcheson Town in Glasgow at the age of forty in 1857, having spent his working life as a soap-maker's labourer and soap-boiler journeyman in the city. There were always people who fell through the security nets which the big houses like

Kilberry provided. In 1876, the logbook of Ormsary Public School records that some pupils were absent for 'want of boots' and in March 1881, a girl was absent for the same sad reason. At a time when many lairds were turning their tenants off the land to establish more profitable sheep, the more benevolent were providing practical help. Margaret Campbell was involved with the school and the church and provided all those summer and winter 'blow out teas' while at Ormsary Mrs Tarrant's New Year gift to the local schoolchildren on 20 January 1874 was 48 yards of material for shirts.

John Campbell says now: 'Unless there is a big turnaround in agriculture, the only answer for Kilberry is leisure and tourism,' and, of course, these modern industries, along with the recording studio near Kilberry, generate work in the wider area, just as the estates once did. But few property owners can afford to transform derelict byres and former farm workers' cottages into the kind of holiday homes which the discerning tourist demands. John Campbell believes that financial support is necessary if areas like Kilberry are to be sustained. He says: 'People who come here are full of praise for the area and they come back time and again. We have something special here but these days it does not produce much work. A lot has changed even in the last forty or fifty years and leisure will play a large part in Kilberry's future.'

10
CRINAN AND BELLANOCH

The Royal Route

One day in 1819, 525 Scots sailed from Crinan to North America. They went in ships which were subject to an Act of Parliament aimed at protecting the lives of emigrants, but even so they faced a miserable journey in overcrowded conditions with little to eat. As they herded into the little harbour on the west coast, they saw this journey as a better alternative to life at home – a means to an end preferable to the conditions of poverty and oppression under which they subsisted at home. The Highland Society had been created by some benign heritors to try to maintain the population of the Highlands and Islands, but too many other landowners had replaced men with sheep, and the fishing industry could never guarantee an alternative living, even in sometimes herring-rich Argyll. Jobless and homeless, the 525 souls who crammed into Crinan to await their departure had every cause to feel as powerless as the black cattle which had been herded through the harbour for centuries on their way from the islands to major mainland markets.

This was just two years after the Crinan Canal had been finally completed after many setbacks. The costly project had been designed to avoid the long voyage around the Mull of Kintyre. It had provided labouring work for decades, often undertaken by Irish immigrants and itinerant workers from Glasgow and the Lowlands. It had given heritors with extensive woodlands excellent prices for timber and work for those extracting the felled oaks. It would now allow the herring fleets easy access from the Firth of Clyde to the West Coast and it had the potential to create profitable trade routes for merchant shipping.

None of this was enough to keep those 525 Scots at home – and, curiously, none of it was enough to turn Crinan from a tiny strategic harbour into a bustling port.

Why did Oban become Oban while Crinan remained Crinan? It may be a question that has been asked for three millennia, because that is how long Crinan – or Portree (*Port righ*, Gaelic for 'the king's port') as the southern settlement on Loch Crinan was called until the coming of the canal – has been a focus of industry without ever growing into something more than a village.

Today its foremost industry is as a tourist and conference centre. When psychiatrists come from around the globe to discuss the latest findings in their field with the distinguished professionals from Argyll and Bute Hospital – built in Lochgilphead in 1863 as the first of its kind to have been established following the Mental Health Act of 1857 – they look from the windows of the Crinan Hotel across the masts of yachts on the canal, beyond the Crinan Moss (*Moine Mhor*), over the hilltop which was once Dunadd Fort, seat of the kings of Dalriada, to the far-distant snow-capped splendour of Ben Cruachan. The hydroelecricity marvel housed within the bowels of that stately mountain on the shores of Loch Awe is the first hint of heavy industry within that beautiful landscape. Except for Crinan's chemical factory which extracted naptha from birch wood (there was a twin plant in Carsaig) in the 1850s, it has always been so.

Yet from the earliest times, Crinan was a maritime crossroads, a trading centre, a landing place, an international melting pot. Our ancestors came into these waters, perhaps sailing coracles into Loch Crinan and up the snaking River Add. There is evidence that people were raising cattle here in the Bronze Age. At Bellanoch, according to an archaeologiocal study carried out by Marion Campbell, there was a stock enclosure near the road which today goes up from the canal bank. Graveyards, enclosures and early forts followed the route away from Crinan Harbour. Near Cairnbaan, now on the banks of the canal but believed to have once been the head of Loch Crinan, fifty flint and stone axes were found in the peat moss. The area abounds with standing stones, burial cairns and cup-and-ring marked stones – those enigmatic designs which give away nothing about the artists who carved them on smooth rock faces so many generations ago.

Crinan was where people came from the islands and Ireland in the west and from the Clyde in the east. These sea routes crossed two major land routes: one which went by Loch Awe to the Tay Gap and the other which found its way by land and water through the Great Glen to the north. The people who settled around Crinan – who themselves probably had ancestors from central Europe if not Asia – traded from earliest times with the Lake District, Cornwall and southern Ireland. Mesolithic Man brought meal to Scotland. He fastened his clothes with buttons and made artefacts from tin sourced in Ireland or the Cornish mines later colonised by the Romans.

Crinan loch was the start of a highway across Scotland from Neolithic times
(*Author's Collection*)

Nor was it a one-way traffic. Copper and lead were found around Crinan and that meant local people had goods to export. Crinan was a centre of trade and also of culture, because as long ago as the late Bronze and Iron Ages, Celtic art was developing. Metalwork provided weapons but people wanted jewellery and decorative objects too. It was an age when wealth was measured in cattle and the cattle bought attractive trappings. A jet necklace was found dating from the era on the Poltalloch estate to the north of Crinan across the Add. Decorative bone and bronze pins and amber jewellery were fashionable. Brightly coloured enamels brought colour to lives far more sophisticated than we care to admit could exist so long before our modern age. The evidence on show in Kilmartin Museum cannot be denied, however, and nor can the astronomically precise standing stones and henges be dismissed as proof of ancient knowledge long lost.

St Columba knew Crinan. In the year 574 when he came to annoint Aidan as the first Christian King of Scotland (and indeed the first Christian monarch in the British Isles), he carried out the ceremony at Dunadd, a heron's wingspan from Crinan harbour. A harbour at the doorstep of kings is an important place indeed.

In later centuries, the area which today is the line of the Crinan

A stone's throw from Crinan was Dunadd Fort, seat of the kings of Dalriada, scene of the anointing of the first Christian king in Britain by Columba (*Author's collection*)

Canal was the northernmost border of the lands held by Suibhne or Swene. His territory stretched on the west from Rudhnahaoran in Kintyre north to Crinan and on the east from Cour up to Loch Gilp. His stronghold, Castle Sween, built in the late twelfth century, was seen as the key to Knapdale and its position on Loch Sween gave protection in that complex corner of peninsulas and lochs. Over the coming centuries, power would move back and forth between Argyll's major players. MacMillans and MacNeills, McTavishes and Campbells would hold some or all of North Knapdale but the MacSweens, once the peers of the sons of Somerled, lost power when they took the 'wrong' side in the Wars of Independence. After the horrors of the civil wars and the depredations of the Campbells, North Knapdale became a Presbyterian parish in 1734, formed out of the larger old parish of Knapdale. It included the port of Crinan, the village of Bellanoch and included the islands of Danna and Ulva. It was an area of wood and water, encompassing twenty-one fresh water lochs, springs impregnated with lime, burns powerful enough to turn mills and with a waterfall near Inverlussa Church. Woods and plantations covered more than 2,000 acres and only an eighth of the parish was under tillage. The Malcolms of Poltalloch had by then become the main landowners.

In the late eighteenth century, with no roads to speak of and a canal still at the discussion stage, the people of North Knapdale were resigned to walk any distance to a central point for their essential needs. The parish church was then at Kilmichael-Inverlussa and the school at Bellanoch. The school was built for eighty-six pupils but fifty-four was a realistic attendance figure as most children were needed on the land. Schools in Argyll were often a moveable feast and the 'teachers' were often 12–15-year-olds who went from house to house teaching younger children all winter for £1 and their keep. Bellanoch in 1798 had just two houses – a decrepit one with a barn rented by Alexander McTavish and a good dwelling house with a barn where Malcolm McAlpine lived. When the *Statistical Account of Scotland* was published in the 1790s, the fishing was good some years, bad others – a fluctuation echoed down the centuries. In the herring season, many of the young men left behind their weaving and shoemaking and went north to the fishing grounds. Farm labourers were paid £6 a year and shepherds got £7–£8.

The Rev. Dugald Campbell of Glassary wrote in the account of his parish, which was about to be skirted by the proposed Crinan Canal, that 'whatever may be the advantages of this arduous undertaking to the public, it is probable that during the execution of the work, this and the neighbouring parishes may reap some benefit'.

In the parish of Kilmartin, one of those neighbouring parishes set to benefit from the canal, the Rev. Mr Hugh Campbell was even more enthusiastic, but then Mr Campbell was a man of enthusiasm. His praise of Loch Crinan was fulsome. It was not only the best harbour in this parish, he said, 'but is considered as the best upon the great tract of the western coast'. The whole of the buss herring fleet was anchoring in Crinan harbour in the 1790s along with 'a vast number' of vessels from Great Britain and Ireland. The Bay of Crinan itself

Crinan harbour and the chimney of the pyroligneous acid factory (*Mike Murray from a collection by Jim Souness of Edinburgh*)

abounded with cod, ling, turbot and sole but Mr Campbell criticised the local people for not being 'skilful in catching them'. Herring, he said, were frequently taken in Loch Craignish and Loch Crinan, 'but not to any extent'. Oysters were 'the finest that are anywhere to be found, and in great plenty', and there was plenty of seaweed to be used for 'manuere' on potatoes. The runrig system which had seen farms tenanted by four families was coming to an end and land was being amalgamated into single-tenancy farms raising black cattle. But although the farms were bigger, the houses were poor and damp. Rheumatism was one of the area's most common ailments.

Herring at Crinan were bringing around a shilling a hundred. In the early years of the 1790s, between twenty and thirty boats had earned £500 in four to five weeks. But bad weather could often keep the boats in Crinan harbour for weeks at a time waiting for a fair wind, as the Rev. Campbell said, to take them round the Mull of Kintyre for the herring in the Firth of Clyde. And of course, this was the main reason for considering a canal between Crinan and Ardrishaig. The Rev. Campbell said that a recent survey had found it 'practicable' to make a navigable canal for large sea-built vessels to make the crossing to Loch Gilp. 'Mr Rennie, an eminent engineer', had surveyed for the canal and believed it could be done at moderate expense with plenty of water for boats, barges and larger vessels.

The enthusiastic Mr Campbell was beside himself: 'It is hardly possible to express the astonishing advantages with which the opening of this communication will be attended to the people of this part of the kingdom.' Not only would fishermen avoid the rigours of the Mull of Kintyre but there was a ready market out there just waiting for people 'to pursue a variety of kinds of industry, to which they have hitherto been strangers'.

Salt and coals were two commodities which would become more readily available to ordinary people, but Mr Campbell wanted more than a canal to improve the lot of his flock: 'If the duty were taken off the salt and rock salt allowed to be imported, the people in this country would be as happy as they are now miserable and they would be under no temptation to leave their native soil to try their fortunes in America.'

That salt tax, of course, made it unprofitable for small-time fishermen to compete because they could not afford to cure their catches. The people of Crinan and Bellanoch needed many strings to their bows to survive. They could earn a little at the fishing, a little at the farming – although by now there were 6,000 sheep in the parish of Kilmartin and crops of oats and potatoes were mainly for home consumption. People from 15 to 20 miles around Kilmartin went to the thrice-yearly markets there, bringing webs of linen, woollen clothes and parcels of lint to sell.

When the canal did go ahead, it was not quite the answer to everyone's prayers that the Rev. Campbell of Kilmartin had envisaged. It was built in that twilight zone before the steam engine had transformed maritime vessels and never allowed for the length and beam of the modern commercial vessel. There were those who asked why it had been built at all – why Crinan and not Tarbert, which was the far busier fishing village? But built it was and it did allow vessels of 200 tons to move from the Firth of Clyde to the Firth of Lorn avoiding the 70-mile trip round the sometimes perilous Mull of Kintyre.

James Watt and James Rennie both surveyed the route of the canal. When Rennie costed the project in 1793, he estimated a price of £63,678. The same year, James Campbell, 5th Duke of Argyll, was elected to run the Canal Company and he appointed Rennie chief engineer. By the time it first opened in 1801, the actual cost had been £141,810 and still more loans had to be negotiated. The Canal Company was in debt to the tune of £67,810 by 1814. The canal was cut through chlorite schist and rose to a height of 59 ft between Loch Gilp and Loch Crinan. The stretch between Loch Gilp and the summit had eight locks and there were fifteen altogether: thirteen were 96 ft long and 24 ft wide and the other two 108 ft long and 27 ft wide. The average depth of the water was 10 ft and was fed from reservoirs in the steep hills which form what is reckoned to be one of the most dramatic backdrops to any canal in the UK.

Those hills had provided hiding places, lookouts and fortification since people first trod the soil of Argyll. They were where the MacTavish family lived and the Pont map of 1634 shows a castellated building called the Tawes of Dun-ArdRigh. The castle came down so the canal could be built.

This estate ran from the line of the present-day canal towards Kilmartin and it was one of those properties which went back and forth between heritors. It had been granted to the Earl of Argyll when he was in favour with the Scottish kings, but by 1686 after the 9th Earl had been executed for conspiring to overthrow James VII & II, Campbell lands were confiscated, Dun-ArdRigh along with them. The depredations against the Campbells of Argyll were perpetrated around Crinan and Bellanoch just as elsewhere. In 1686 when the Macdonalds took the opportunity to take their revenge against the Campbells under the guise of avenging the government, there were plunderings throughout the whole of July in the area and Widow MacTavish of Dunardry had her boats stolen – all the worse, she reported, because that summer there was a remarkable take of herring and she and her neighbours could not fish for their share. They were not the only victims. Neill Campbell of Duntroon and his tenants 'within the paroch of Kilmartine' were plundered by Macleans of Mull. Angus McCallum and his two brothers in Poltalloch were raided by Jon Maclean, brother to the laird of Torloisk, on the last day of June and first day of July 1685. McCallum lost cheese, butter, meal, linen yarn, wool, coats, shirts, plaids and weapons as well as houehold goods, farm tools and crops, all valued at over £180.

In the wake of such depredations, the people of North Knapdale were impoverished. Records say that the trade in black cattle was crippled and that the eighteenth century opened in scarcity and poverty with a succession of bad harvests and a long period of unseasonable weather.

In 1704, Dunardry land was given back to Duncan MacTavish, but by 1718, the family left for Inverness-shire. This was not the only family to leave in the early eighteenth century. Colonel John Campbell, grandson of the Rev. Dugald Campbell who lived in North Knapdale from 1599 to 1673, went off to Jamaica, acquired the Black River Estate and a fortune of £10,000. Campbell then invited others to go over from Knapdale and many settled there and prospered. More sailed from North Knapdale in July 1739, under the leadership of Duncan Campbell of Kilduskland and Dugald MacTavish of Dunardry. Back home in November 1741, word came that this group of émigrés had settled at Cape Fear in North Carolina and they were expecting poorer folk to follow.

It is not difficult to imagine why people would want to leave Crinan, Bellanoch, Kilduskland or Dunardry in those troubled times. Dunardry itself had rarely been settled and its history was bloody. It had been gifted to John Carswell, Bishop of Argyll, when he first was at Carnasserie Castle, north of Kilmartin. More than a century later, it was part of the bloody goings on which dogged Argyll during the Covenanting struggles. Carnasserie was defended by Sir Duncan Campbell against the Duke of Atholl. Although it was surrendered peaceably, Atholl's men despatched its defenders in cold blood, hanging Dugall MacTavish of Dun-ArdRigh over the gateway of the castle. In 1615, the Campbells of the area were ordered by the king to stand against Sir James Macdonald, whose status as Lord of the Isles had been stripped from him. The Earl of Argyll landed from England at Crinan to muster troops at Duntroon. From there, the Earl marched down to Tarbert with 400 government troops and hundreds of local men obliged to fight for him under the terms of their tenancies. On the way he sent 800 men and a fleet of galleys to the island of Cara to surprise Macdonalds there. The infamous Coll Ciotach (Colkitto) fought for Sir James Macdonald, but even so, Sir James ended up fleeing Kintyre and seeking refuge in Spain. Coll Ciotach returned to Islay and later became an Argyll partisan.

But the Union of the Parliaments put an end to this warfare in the hills and although many decided to leave to seek their fortunes elsewhere, life slowly began to improve. A new road was built from Dunardry to Bellanoch under an Act of Parliament aimed at bringing civilising elements to the west of Scotland. In May 1760, a local law was passed preventing droves of cattle passing the new line of road in the parish of North Knapdale, although they were allowed to go through the lands of Barnakill 'as usual'. In May 1763, the inhabitants of North Knapdale sought help from the Commissioners of Supplies for public funding to help build the new line of road from Dunardry to Bellanoch, 'much used by travellers'. This stretch of road was to continue to cause local problems for years. In May 1764, according to the Commissioners of Supply Minute Book of 1744–94, droves of cattle were to be hindered from passing this new line of road – presumably changing the drove routes of centuries. Two years later, plans were drawn up to build a new quay at the ferry house 'from Creenan to North Knapdale'. This was where cattle were brought ashore from Jura to be driven along trackways to Kilmichael Tryst at the Add bridge. In 1774, the new stretch of road was still causing problems – Neil Campbell of Duntroon petitioned the Commissioners because of his fears that crops along the road from Bellanoch to Dunardry would be damaged by cattle passing along that way.

By the end of the eighteenth century, arguments over roads must have seemed petty in the face of excitement over the creation of the canal. The whole idea of it seemed to set minds whirring. In 1789 there was a proposal to create a British Fisheries Society village just north of Crinan Ferry as a planned village – one of many such communities which societies and enlightened landlords were establishing to improve living standards and create wealth. This idea went nowhere, and a similar fate awaited a brainwave of Alexander Campbell, who had been the somewhat eccentric minister at Kilcalmonell and Kilberry for the previous twelve years. In 1793, the Rev. Campbell issued a prospectus 'on the propriety of joining Loch Awe to the Crinan Canal', just one of many ideas enlightened minds were having to link all the canals of Scotland. There were many schemes in the 1790s to extend from Crinan Canal to Loch Awe and on to Loch Tay – an interesting connection. Saint Columba, sometimes known as 'the apostle to the Highlands', had travelled to the mouth of the Tay and is recorded as the teacher of the 'tribes of Toi, a river in Alban' (*Alba*, Scotland). Three hundred years later, Crinan de Mormaer, son of the Lord of the Isles, became lay abbot of Dunkeld. He was also grandfather of King Malcolm III, whose marriage to Margaret (St Margaret of Scotland) moved the church in Scotland from its Celtic roots to the influence of Rome. Was this the link that gave Crinan its name? Or was Crinan de Mormaer named for the port of the king known to Columba?

Alexander Campbell did not only want to extend the canal. In

1794 he was making improvements to Small's plough to make it suitable for the hilly land of North Knapdale and he received the Highland Society's gold medal for his work. Sadly, many of his ideas for improving agriculture in the area were never put into practice.

A paradoxical situation was emerging in North Knapdale. Poor farmers using ancient agricultural methods remained poor, living in huts and plagued by rheumatism, while the marvels of modern engineering were being executed on their very doorsteps.

There were few jobs for the local unskilled labourers of Knapdale when the canal was built – work mainly went to the teams of itinerant diggers and engineers who travelled from one new marvel of irrigational engineering to the next. The canal did, however, improve and change local lives despite its many setbacks, such as the dramatic collapse of its banks in 1805. The rent books of 1809 show a merchant listed in Bellanoch, and Duncan Miackellar was the innkeeper. By 1837, Bellanoch had a sub post office because the Bellanoch basin was now an important point along the canal's nine-mile length. At Crinan itself, there were two inns run by Margaret Kerr and Margaret McLachlan.

During the building of the canal, the Crinan Canal Company bought oak from local landlords for as much as seven shillings a foot at a time when the usual price was 2s 6d. According to the Rev. John Smith in his assessment of the agriculture of Argyll at the time, deciduous woods in the county also became more valuable because of the two English companies which set up iron forges at Furnace and Bonawe. Charcoal was also a source of income for those with woodlands and oak bark was sold to tanners. In 1795, oak bark was worth as much as 12 guineas a ton.

There were those who immediately saw the benefits of the Crinan Canal and Henry Bell, the entrepreneur who initially built the *Comet* steamship to transport guests from Glasgow to his hotel in Helensburgh, was soon running a regular service with the speedy little ship from Glasgow to Fort William until her sad demise on the Craignish rocks. The links with the newly opened Caledonian Canal regenerated trade routes as far as Inverness. Thomas Telford, the bridge, road and church builder, redesigned part of the canal in 1816 after problems with the water levels and collapsing locks. Although defects in the canal were becoming even more apparent in 1845 when yet another plan to open a canal from West to East Loch Tarbert was floated, Queen Victoria's trip along the canal in 1847 cemented its success as a tourist route. She had travelled with Prince Albert and their children from Dartmouth on 12 August in thick fog, sailed up the west coast to the Isle of Man by 16 August and on to the Mull of Galloway. They went on to Arran the following day, reached Greenock at 12.30 p.m. and as they set off for Loch Long in the steamer *Fairy*, they were followed by thirty-nine steamers buzzing the royal entourage. It was 18 August when *Fairy* set out once more, this time up the Kyles of Bute and on to Inveraray to the Castle, traditional home of the Dukes of Argyll (in 1871, the queen's fourth daughter, Princess Louise, would marry the 9th Duke). After what the Queen called a reception 'in the true Highland fashion', the Royal party rejoined *Fairy*, sailed down Loch Fyne to Loch Gilphead, which she described in her *Highland Journal* as a small village, and were driven in a carriage lent by Sir John Orde to the canal. The Queen enjoyed the decorated barge pulled by three horses but found the process of going through the locks 'tedious' and was not best pleased that the journey took so long that by the time they reached Loch Crinan and the Royal Yacht *Victoria and Albert*, which had sailed round what she called 'the Mull of Cantire', it was too late to sail to Oban that night. They stayed the night at Crinan instead, enjoying the panorama of hills 'from the Cruachan range to the Paps of Jura'. Perhaps it was Victoria's description of Crinan as 'a very fine spot', or perhaps simply that people were keen to follow in royal footsteps, but the future of the Crinan Canal as a centre of the tourist industry was sealed on that fine August night with its half moon and clear skies.

Two years later, the statistics were showing a decrease in the population of North Knapdale because of famine. The price of meal had risen to three shillings a stone, at a time when a man's wage was £6 a year and a loaf of bread cost a shilling. There were also a number of cholera outbreaks and there was migration and emigration. The industrial expansion of Glasgow and Greenock meant jobs on the Clyde, and deputations from Canada to persuade people to leave for a better life across the Atlantic met with success.

As a fishing port, Crinan's heyday was already over, and the pyroligneous acid factory, known locally as the 'vinegar factory', like its twin at Carsaig, which used birch wood to provide acid for the textile and dye works at Renton in the Vale of Leven, did not provide enough jobs to keep people from emigrating. The works were leased by heritor Neill Malcolm of Poltalloch to Timothy Philips, who retained the lease until around 1879 when Messrs Turnbull & Co. took

Crinan harbour foreshore, where emigrants huddled before setting off in their hundred for a better life in America (*Mike Murray from a collection by Jim Souness of Edinburgh*)

over. They kept the lease until the last mention of the works in the Valuation Roll for 1888–9 and rather than creating employment in the area, workers from mid Argyll drained away to the Turnbull works in the Vale of Leven where thousands were employed in the bleaching, dyeing and printing industries which used the pyroligneous acid manufactured in this remote corner of Argyll as a main ingredient in their processes.

From 1875, as farm rents peaked and the combining of farms reduced the number of people on the land, summer visitors became more and more important. Plans in 1857 and again in 1907 to improve the canal to take large vessels were never funded, although in February 1859 work had to be carried out to clear a mile of debris in the canal when the hillside burst and washed away part of the banks. The government paid for the £12,000 repair job, which must have come as a relief to the Commissioners of the Caledonian Canal who managed Crinan Canal from 1818. Revenues from the canal seem rarely to have been sufficient to cover maintenance and repairs. Although 33,000 passengers, 27,000 sheep and 2,000 cattle were transported along the canal in 1854, takings for 1864 were £3,602 and expenditure was £4,545. By the late 1870s the financial tide fluctuated favourably and in 1879 takings were £5,730 against expenditure of £4,929. That was hardly coining it in, however, even if 2,668 passengers on their way from Glasgow to Inverness did travel along the canal that year

The tiny *Linnet* steamer which plied the Crinan Canal at the height of its popularity with day-trippers from the industrial belt (*Mike Murray from a collection by Jim Souness of Edinburgh*)

on what was advertised as the 'elegant, roomy and well-appointed steamboat conveying passengers between large steamers at Ardrishaig and Port Crinan'.

As the twentieth century progressed, the canal was increasingly left to private yachts. In 1929, *Linnet* made her last trip after fifty years conveying passengers on the canal. The lock at Crinan Harbour was excavated in the 1930s and there is now a sea lock leading boats into Crinan Loch and from there to the Sound of Jura. A £3 million renovation programme was completed in 2003. Once the fastest way to travel from Glasgow to Inverness was via the Crinan and Caledonian canals. Today the motorways make that journey a short morning's work but there are still some 2,000–3,000 vessels using the Crinan Canal, which is now the responsibility of British Waterways.

The industry of North Knapdale in the second half of the twentieth century became forestry, not fishing or farming. In 1950, there were 1,213 cattle registed in the area – no longer was wealth measured in black cattle – and 7,187 sheep. Sir Ian Malcolm of Poltalloch had sold his Achnamara estate in May 1930 to the Forestry Commission and in total the Commission acquired enough land in North Knapdale to plant 19,000 acres from Craigmaddy to Scotnish. The remnants of traditional forest – now once more being encouraged to flourish and fast becoming yet another tourist attraction – were swamped between Sitka and Norway spruce, European and Japanese larch, Scots pine and Douglas firs. Forestry, however, brought jobs. There was a forestry holding scheme under which four crofters were given a guaranteed minimum of five months' work in the forest as well as whatever they could make from the land. The Forestry Commission employed fifty-eight people in North Knapdale and replacing the now derelict old townships were twenty-four new wooden Swedish-style houses at Achnamara with a rent of £20 a year rising to £22 a year when electricity was installed. Of course, forestry work is spasmodic – the planting and the harvesting are generations apart and in between the maintenance does not require big work forces – but the Commission did set up a training school and workshop at Cairnbaan.

The changes in fishing have not only been affected by new-style nets, factory ships and European rulings. At the beginning of the twentieth century, 16-ft boats with jib and mainsail used to take nets out to Corrievreckan, Eilean Mhor and Carraig Island off Keills to catch saith which were salted for winter. The saith oil was used for household lamps. By 1960 when the *Third Statistical Account of Scotland* was written, only a handful of rowing boats were going out and no fish were cured for the winter. There were many more changes. The ice-house at Crinan Ferry was no longer in use. It had been built along the lines of the east coast houses in 1833 by William Frazer for the Malcolms of Poltalloch's flourishing salmon fishing industry and salmon from Loch Crinan were packed in ice there for transport to market. The 'vinegar factory' had closed by the First World War, although its distinctive red chimney remains a landmark long afterwards. It had been generations since black cattle negotiated the paved shallows at Bellanoch Basin on their way to Kilmichael Glassary market or lime had been produced at High Barnakill opposite Dunardry locks. Those had been the days when Gallanach on the northern shore of Loch Crinan was known as the Bay of Tears because of the emigration from the area and dozens of small crofts in the hills stood deserted.

Loch Sween, once a seat of clan power, became the site of research into marine cultivation in the 1940s. Today the castle itself is swamped by a static caravan park. The parish's tailor, shoemaker, joiner, cartwright, wheelwright, builder, miller and blacksmiths disappeared, to be replaced by those who service the tourist industry or who cleverly use the latest technology to allow their home industries to flourish in some of Scotland's most beautiful scenery.

Modern times have not been without their excitement. Clan warfaring is happily a thing of the distant past, but the Second World War impinged on the peace of the area. Children from Glasgow and Dumbarton were evacuated to North Knapdale and prisoners of war were held in a camp at Cairnbaan – causing a stir when Italians escaped in 1944 and were recaptured in Tayvallich after having spent nights in the hills.

Today, Bellanoch Bay is a long-term marina but many pleasure craft head instead to the marina up the coast at the twentieth-century village of Craobh Haven. There is a scallop farm in Crinan Bay but fishing boats are a rarity now. Mike Murray, whose catamaran *Gemini* takes thousands of visitors out from Crinan harbour each year to explore the surrounding coast and neighbouring islands, says that one or two shellfish boats come in and when fishing boats from Banff and the Isle of Man are in the area they stop by.

Mike Murray has lived at Kilmahumaig since 1975. A chapel there was dedicated to the seventh-century abbot of Iona, St Commine. The township itself, where slate was quarried for local floors and roofs for centuries, appeared on maps long before the name Crinan did and was in the record books as far back as the 1340s when a fugitive from the Lord of the Isles was apprehended there. Its current owner says: 'For centuries, everything was subsistence living. Kilmahumaig was owned by the MacNeills and then the Mackays and the property was tenanted by poor farmers.' But when the canal was to be built, Stevensons, the quarriers and distillers, got wind of it and speculatively bought up all the land south of the River Add from Kilmahumaig to Tayvallich. Stevenson, who was manager of Ballachulish quarry, brought his own men with him to work on the canal and some of them signed legal documents when Stevenson cleverly sold off this tract of land for £1,500 to Malcolm of Poltalloch, making him, as Mike Murray says, 'a tidy profit'. The Malcolm family continued to rent out the farms on this land, along with the rights to graze a cow and grow potatoes, until it was sold to the Forestry Commission in the 1930s. Tenants of the Forestry Commission had the right to buy in later decades and many incomers now own the houses in and around Crinan and Bellanoch. Because they own their properties, there is perhaps a degree of 'protectionism' in the area and it is questionable whether the canal would be built today if it were muted as a new idea – let alone be greeted with the enthusiasm expressed by the likes of the Rev. Campbell in the 1790s. Tobermory Race Week and West Highland Week, two major yachting events, no longer start from Crinan but from Craobh Haven and although 'tourism totters on', Crinan village cannot cope with significant numbers, according to Mike Murray. 'There's been no village hall or shop and no petrol pump for years and there is a limited boatyard and chandlery facility, although the boatyard is thriving because it has engineering facilities,' Mike says. 'We are geographically limited and Crinan has become a commuter village with the majority of people working in Lochgilphead or elsewhere. A few work in the hotel, one or two of us run boat trips, a few work on the canal and there are a few holiday houses. But we are not going to fall off the map. This is a pretty location and it will always attract a number of people. It fluctuates with the decades as enthusiastic young people take over various aspects and inject new life.'

11
Tayvallich

The house of the pass, the vinegar factory and the charcoal burners

It was one of those nights. At this distance, we do not know if it was one dram too many, an old feud or just a touch of summer madness, but Donald Leitch laid into Robert Cameron, who that July was staying with a fellow tailor at Barbreck. Days later in August 1852, Leitch was charged with the assault, which had been witnessed by Sarah McAlpine or McLean, the publican in Tayvallich and by Angus Smith, the manager of the local factory. The attack happened outside the factory – the charge sheet referred to it as 'the vinegar works of Tayvallich on the lands of Ardnafadmore' where Turnbull & Co. were manufacturers of vinegar. History tells us that this factory on the short road between Tayvallich and Carsaig did not actually manufacture vinegar, but pyroligneous acid. This was extracted from birch bark and used, as was the product from the twin works at Crinan run by the same company, in the manufacture of dyes for linen.

Tayvallich played a very small role in the Turnbull empire, but the presence of the factory at Carsaig was one of the few times in history when the Tayvallich peninsula ever got close to being a hub of industry.

Turnbull & Ramsay, linen printers and colour makers, had set up a pyroligneous acid works in Camlachie Street, Glasgow, around 1813. In their early years, they also opened subsidiary factories but these were far more short lived than the parent company which was in operation until 1965. Around 1825 the company was a manufacturing chemist. By 1831, the firm's name had changed from Turnbull & Ramsay to Turnbull & Co., Manufacturing Chemists and Vinegar Makers, and their main works were at Camlachie. Branches were set up in Balmaha on Loch Lomond, Crinan, Carsaig, Kilkerran, Perth, Renton and Stirling. Pyroligneous acid is made through the dry distillation of wood – a development of the traditional process of charcoal burning. Birch, alder, oak and beech can be used, and the Tayvallich peninsula with its remnants of ancient forest was a source of all four. The wood had to be cut into uniform lengths, placed in ovens and fired. The

Scene of the rammy between Donald Leitch and Robert Cameron in July 1852, site of the short-lived 'vinegar works of Tayvallich on the lands of Ardnafadmore', which played a part in the dye industry of Alexandria (*Angus McInnes Collection*)

vapour from the process was then distilled and condensed into barrels where the acid rose to the top over a few days and tar, the by-product of the process, settled at the bottom. The company used some of this acid in the manufacture of paint dye while the tar was exported to paint the base of rubber trees in outposts of the empire.

Armstrongs did not choose the sites of their branch works at random. Charcoal production had a long tradition in mid Argyll and around Tayvallich there are semicircular stone platforms once used to burn charcoal. Some of it went to Furnace on Fyneside to make gunpowder in the nineteenth century, but these platforms pre-date gunpowder (and the vinegar factory where Leitch attacked Cameron) by some three thousand years. Our mysterious ancestors with their standing stones and chambered burial cists settled in these ancient forests on the Tayvallich peninsula and built forts – Dun Mhuirich between the ancient chapel of Keills and Linnhe Mhuirich; Dun a'Chogaidh; Dun Taynish and yet another on Barr Mor – looking out to Jura and Islay or down Loch Sween to protect themselves from invaders. This remote spot on the modern road map was open to the prying eyes of waterborne Romans, Irish and Vikings. But until the incomers of the twentieth century, the landscape changed little. In

The house of the pass – Tayvallich village grew up because drovers took their cattle through the pass on their way to Kilmichael Tryst (*Angus McInnes Collection*)

her memoir of Tayvallich and Taynish, Veronica Gainford notes that over a dozen farms and houses named on the Blaeu map of 1654 are still to be found.

Tayvallich means the house of the pass (*tigh*, house). The indents of Carsaig Bay on the sound of Jura (Carsaig Bay) and *loch a' bhealaich* (loch of the pass) off Loch Sween create a narrow waist for the peninsula. Tayvallich village is particularly protected from the elements by its geographical position – the ideal spot, in fact, to stop after a dreich walk from Keills following a rough crossing from Islay and Jura with cattle destined for markets at nearby Kilmichael Glassary and then perhaps as far away as Falkirk. The land on Tayvallich peninsula is not rich and fertile. Even its trees were no permanent source of great wealth in the past, though they did in their time provide charcoal for the gunpowder manufacturers and acids for the linen dye makers to pollute the waters of Leven with their 'turkey red'. But the peninsula is an ideal staging post: land at Keills, walk the length of Linne Mhuirich and come down into Tayvallich to a welcoming peat fire, a dram of locally distilled whisky and a night out of the wind while the cattle rest before setting off over the hills to Loch Crinan, Bellanoch and Kilmichael Glassary.

This was a drovers' village: the old drovers' inn is still marked to this day. North of that 'waist' of land is Gleann Sabhail, the Pass of Moine and the now deserted village of Arichonan – once another lively landmark on the way to Bellanoch and Kilmichael Glassary until police and Poltalloch estate workers evicted cottagers in the nineteenth century to make way for sheep. The modern road brings the traveller down to Kintallan Point along the shores of Caol Scotnish, just one more loch in this corner of Argyll where land seems scarcely to have emerged from the primeval waters. Taynish peninsula, which drags through the water south of Loch a' Bhealaich, has become a source of interest to modern visitors because of the remains of ancient forest, charcoal platforms, the wildlife and the ruins of Taynish mill. It was the MacNeills who built the mill and Taynish House around 1650 when a cadet branch of the Campbells were living at Ardnackaig. The mill would then have been a focal point for all the tenants of the MacNeills, obliged by the terms of their leases to bring their bere there for grinding. It was an act of faith to build a mansion house in that grim century, because Knapdale was by no means isolated from the effects of the civil war nor from the retribution meted out by Montrose's commander Alexander Macdonald when he set about devastating Argyll in revenge against the Earl of Argyll's role in the war. John MacIlvernoch of Oib, north of Tayvallich, and John Campbell of Ulva, the area south of Taynish, were part of the Earl's rebellion against the insidious Test Act of 1681 but as that century passed some form of peace was imposed on a peninsula which had always been a backdrop to the violence of clan skirmishes, the brawls of drovers, and a backwater of a bigger war.

It was in 1695 that legislation was passed requiring all parishes to provide schools and MacNeill of Taynish petitioned the Synod of Argyll in 1696 for a school in Tayvallich. But what were the lads being educated for? That question must have been asked (and continued to be asked up to the end of the nineteenth century) by many a parent who wanted his children at home to help on the land or in the house. Farming was the industry which put meals in most bellies in Knapdale, even if it was all too often at subsistence level. The 1792 *Statistical Account of North Knapdale*, written by the Rev. Archibald Campbell, claimed that the pastures of the area produced the best cattle which appeared in the English markets from the Highlands. Eilean Mor was said to produce top-class mutton and beef – but such small areas of land were never going to feed the nation, and quantity rather than quality was the only way of making a profit. Drovers who landed black cattle from Islay and Jura at the stone jetty at Keills had a hard life, walking cattle hundreds of miles. They probably had more cash in their pockets, however, than the farmers who raised the beasts on the Tayvallich peninsula for their lairds. Right up until the Second World War, Taynish cattle walked to Lochgilphead market – but by then the men were able to jump on a bus to come home after the market.

In the old days, the crofters grew black oats and bere. Flax was an important crop in the Tayvallich area but was for domestic use rather than as a cash crop – the women spun it and wove it into coarse household linen. The soil was good but overstocked with cattle and in the days of runrig farming too many tenants were trying to make a living from one farm. When potatoes were introduced, they became a source of income and in the 1840s, when Ireland's crop had failed, Barrahormaid Farm, halfway between Tayvallich and Keills, was exporting 70 tons of potatoes a year to Irish merchants. Today, even in Kintyre where potatoes used to be grown for export for many years, the farm gate price is too low for them to be a viable crop.

Tayvallich peninsula has been the scene of a number of economic ventures. Kelp was the crop of the moment in the late eighteenth and early nineteenth centuries and heritors made a killing during the Napoleonic Wars, producing kelp for the glass, soap and linen-bleaching industries. It was, of course, the tenants who hauled the seaweed up above the tide line, built pits lined with stones to burn it, kept the fires burning for anything between four and eight hours and returned to pound it into saleable ash.

It was the seaweeds Ascophullum spp. and Laminaria spp. which were used from the late 1600s to provide soda and potash. The Tayvallich peninsula was not the only place to benefit from the discovery – the whole of the Western Isles and Orkney experienced something of a bonanza at the time. The discovery of this new source of the chemicals was significant because previously they had been available only from Spain. Now Britain no longer had to depend on this continental source. A century later, this was invaluable when the Napoleonic Wars isolated Britain, and the shores of the Tayvallich peninsula were let out to contractors who arranged the collecting and burning of the seaweeds. The price of kelp rose in 1790–1 from £6 to £10 a ton. Because 20 tons of wet seaweed were needed to produce a ton of ash, the process was not only labour-intensive but back-breaking. In Orkney, there was a rise in the number of cases of arthritis during this boom. No one logged a similar rise in Tayvallich, where the wet climate must have seeped into workers' bones even without such exacerbation. In the short period it was produced, kelp was a significant source of income, but although the heritors made money (this was an industry worth the modern equivalent of £7.5 million a year to the Hebrides alone) the tenants did not directly share in the bonanza. Some were even encouraged to leave their agricultural work from June to August by landlords anxious to cash in on the kelp boom and this obviously had an adverse effect on the tenants' meagre incomes.

It all came to an end, however, when mineral deposits of potash were discovered in Stassfurt in Germany in the early years of the nineteenth century and the kelp industry collapsed. The short revival when a process was discovered for extracting iodine from kelp ash did not impinge on the Tayvallich peninsula. Lady Gainford wrote that her family was approached in the winter of 1935–6 by a company who hoped to extract iodine from the kelp, but then decided that it was not the right area or the right kelp. In any case, by then mineral deposits of iodine had been found in Chile.

So many skills have been forgotten in this area: what, for instance, happened to the artisans who were such skilful exponents of the Loch Sween school of stone carving in medieval times? The five different medieval schools of carving were based at Iona, Saddell, Kilmartin, Loch Sween and Oronsay. The famous Campbeltown Cross was carved by the Iona school from an enormous single slab of bluish-green calc-chlorite-albite schist quarried at Doide between Castle Sween and Kilmory Knap – a quarry close enough to the shore to make transporting the stone easier. The Loch Sween school was seen as the most accomplished of the mainland carving schools and examples of work are found around Argyll mainland and on

Fishing and subsistence farming were the industries which sustained Tayvallich

neighbouring islands. At Keills itself – once known as Kilmarcharmic and a relic of the Celtic Christian mission to Argyll from Ireland – evidence of the craft of the stone mason is still preserved.

Like the kelp trade, of course, stone carving was done at the instigation of those who held power. Most inhabitants of Tayvallich peninsula have met the needs of their landlords and only the whims or economic ventures of those landlords have changed the direction of everyday life.

Arable farming was done to produce food for local use. Fishing in Tayvallich was not an industry but a provision occupation. The blacksmiths, weavers and tailors served the community headed by landlords like Duncan Campbell of Taynish who in 1803 contracted his tenants Peter and Archibald Brown to bring their grindable corn and bere, seed and horse corn to the mill at Duntaynish 'to be grinded thereat, and all their ironwork to the smithies upon the estate to be worked therein' – protectionism at its most unassailable. Other mills at Oib, Danna, Keills and Taynish Loch were operated by their own heritors in a similarly dictatorial manner.

Timber was felled by the tenants for the profit of the landlords. There was a boom in the eighteenth century with the opening of the Argyle Furnace Company at what became the village of Furnace. But some heritors sold off their assets rather than their produce. The woods of North and South Scotnish and Coishanfad were sold to the Fyneside company in 1786 for £220, excluding woods around tenants' homes. Other Tayvallich peninsula landlords did, however, sell the timber and kept the land. The new roads would have made this trade easier and more profitable. The Commissioners of Supply had broadened and drained roads in Knapdale and by 1750 there was a road taking today's route along the shore of Loch Scotnish to Tayvallich but with no branch to Carsaig. From there, it followed the high ground traditionally taken by the drovers down to where the ferry crossed to Castle Sween. Although by the end of the eighteenth century many of these roads were 20 ft wide and well maintained by previous standards, travel was still difficult and the need for two inns – one at the bottom of Glean a'Ghaolbhan, the other in Tayvallich itself – was never questioned. Yet in the 1890s, the licence of the Tayvallich inn was not renewed and the village remained 'dry' until the 1970s. There was, of course, an abundance of illicit stills in the Tayvallich peninsula as elsewhere in Argyll and the spirit produced by them may well have been responsible for the many brawls and skirmishes which legend records in the area.

One road which was not improved was that running north from Carsaig to Ardnackaig and Dounie, both houses of importance. Dounie is where the poet Thomas Campbell from Kirnan House in Kilmichael Glen was tutor to the sons of Colonel Napier who was away in the Indian Army. The house belonged to Napier's father-in-law Robert Campbell who opened its doors to his daughter and grandchildren while Napier was abroad. Thomas Campbell enjoyed the peace but evidently not the isolation – the family had to travel by boat to Crinan or Tayvallich and Campbell spent much time wandering the hills behind the house. The location did not seem to adversely affect his pupil, who grew up to be Sir William Napier of Milliken. In the twentieth century, Dounie was revived and a garden created, but by then most of the area was in the hands of the Forestry Commission and planted over. At Achnamara on the eastward peninsula skirting Loch Sween, the Commission built a model village for its workers, which in time was given over to Glasgow Corporation for children's holidays. The twenty-first century sees the Tayvallich peninsula as a playground for walkers, cyclists and yachtsmen and for those interested in the flora and fauna which have survived while other areas have been subsumed by foreign fir trees.

The various grand estates, farms and townships have in the main disappeared. The latter were the first to go when cottagers were evicted to make way for sheep or migrated to seek a living in Glasgow, Greenock or North America because it was too harsh a life at home. The industrial revolution took many away – preceding the pyroligneous acid down the road to the Vale of Leven where the factories, bleach houses and mills offered plenty of jobs. At home there were up to four tenants on each farm. Rents on the Tayvallich peninsula might have been £168 a year and some of that was demanded in produce. Twelve dozen eggs and a dozen chickens had to be sent up to the big house at Taynish by one tenant. Peats had to be dug for the laird and he could ask for 12 days' service of man and horse when required. The laird would often stipulate that the kelp, the oysters and fish were for his use only. When the Malcolms bought out the Poltalloch Estate, much of the Tayvallich peninsula came with it – and with the land went rights for oysters in Linnhe Mhuriche. Houses were built for workers similar to those on the Poltalloch Estate. But in the 1930s, this land was sold to the Forestry Commission and an area which had once been almost bare of trees except on the Taynish peninsula was clothed in fir trees. Now those firs are mature, but forestry has changed considerably and mechanisation and a policy of contracting out means that the harvesting of these trees does not mean jobs for local people.

Tayvallich may have had a school, a post office, a church and all the trappings of a village, but life remained that of a remote Highland village well into the twentieth century. Electricity eventually came in 1955 – and that was only as far as Tayvallich; Keills kept its candles until Jura was powered up at the end of that decade. The school had no sanitation in the early years of the century and in 1920 the teacher's house still had no water supply. But the school has stayed open, despite temporary closures because of falling rolls, and today there is also a flourishing shop, a café, a restaurant and pub of repute. New houses have been built and a caravan site brings tourists to the area. And of course, the yachts flock to Tayvallich just as in the days when Captain Neill, the man who skippered tea magnate Sir Thomas Lipton's yacht *Shamrock*, built Keills House at the turn of the twentieth century.

Its remoteness meant that Tayvallich remained untouched by modernity to the middle of the twentieth century (*Angus McInnes Collection*)

Farming became less focused when lairds used their big houses for pleasure rather than to sustain their families. In the days when it was a working farm, Taynish House had a separate road for farm vehicles so that they did not pass the main gates of the house. By the nineteenth century it had become a shooting estate rather than a farm. Its dairy became a gunroom and a summer house was built with facilities for health-giving saltwater baths. Lillie Langtry, the music hall star and special friend of the Prince of Wales, was a frequent visitor at Poltalloch when her daughter married Sir Iain Malcolm. She came to Taynish to take these hot saltwater baths according to Veronica Gainford. The gardens were developed with the help of fine topsoil brought over in boats from Ireland as ballast when they came to buy slate from the quarry at Tayvuillin. The slate was not top quality but was used to roof the older houses at Cairnbaan. The quarry itself had closed in 1909 but reopened for a brief spell in 1936.

The privacy maintained by the successive owners of Taynish House and those like it may have created an unequal society in their day, but in the twenty-first century we benefit from the unspoilt nature of areas like the Taynish peninsula, acquired by the Nature Conservancy in the mid twentieth century.

Boats, however, are what we most associate with Tayvallich in the twenty-first century, and they have, in their many forms, played an enormous role in the history of the peninsula. Coracles brought from Ireland St Cormaig and his followers to Eilean Mor in the seventh century. Then came the cattle boats from Ireland and the islands, carrying cattle to Keills and Carsaig for the Falkirk tryst. Puffers brought coal to Carraig pier, which in 1928 had a wooden extension added.

There was no real fishing fleet but, according to Rhona Erskine and Margaret Docwra writing in Lady Gainford's Tayvallich and Taynish memoir, rowing boats were built by Peter Gillies of Tightuath and Archie Graham on Danna. Then came the yachts and in the 1920s an annual regatta began. Tourists came up Loch Sween in steamers and convoys of merchant ships started out from Loch Sween for their perilous journeys across the Atlantic during the Second World War. And Loch Sween became one of the first centres in the country for wind surfing and water skiing as well as hosting small craft sailing races.

With the Faery Isles at the head of Loch Sween designated a Scottish Wildlife Trust reserve and many areas of the Tayvallich peninsula recognised as sites of special scientific interest (SSSI), there is no question but that the area has become a place for leisure rather than industry.

Angus MacInnes was born and raised in Tayvallich, as was his son Colin. Wife Mae and daughter-in-law Lynda have brought up their families in a village a dozen miles from the nearest supermarket. They have seen many changes in their own lifetimes and Angus, born in 1931, can recall the glory days of estates like Keills House when there was employment for a chauffeur, handyman, gardener and maids. He can remember when farming was still part of the local scene. Now, he says, there are just three farms left in the area and the Forestry Commission owns the rest of the land: 'The Forestry used to be a big employer – about eight or ten men in the 1950s – but now there's only one man working for them from the village.' The early plantations have been harvested and replanting is done by contractors from outside.

Most people now work in Lochgilphead. Lynda is an exception, having a couple of jobs in the village. Colin and Angus have worked on lorries and buses all their days. In the last two decades of the twentieth century, many 'incomers' came to Tayvallich. They have been welcomed and have brought new life to the village. Mae says: 'They have kept the village alive and the young families have kept the school going. New technology also means people can work from home, although most commute elsewhere to work. Their presence keeps people as a community and brings money and some employment to the village.'

The yachts and holidaymakers are the biggest source of income and the MacInneses see the village prospering – although this is a pocket where property prices have gone 'sky high', pushed up by what locals refer to as the 'yellow wellies' – people from the south whose property transactions allow them to pay inflated prices for houses and cottages near their beloved sailing grounds, leaving young local couples gasping at what has for them become an unattainable market.

Mae remembers electricity connecting Tayvallich because she and Angus married in 1955. 'We had gas cooking before that although we'd got mains water in 1947.' Water – but no pub. The licence was not given back to the pub until the mid 1970s. Travel was difficult. The steamer went Monday to Saturday (no Sunday sailings, of course) from Ardrishaig to Glasgow but there was no bus to connect with the steamer. The Christmas shopping outing to Clydebank which so many people from Argyll undertake without a thought today was never a viable option for Tayvallich folk in the era before cars were commonplace.

The MacInneses say Tayvallich has doubled in size. There are new houses where the vinegar factory was and there are resident artists such as John Lowrie Morrison (who signs himself Jolomo) who attract yet another type of visitor to the area. There is little memory of the pyroligneous factory according to Angus, but there is, he says, a good community feel about the place. So no more fisticuffs ending in charges for assault outside the vinegar factory.

12

SLOCKAVULLIN

'. . . only a dream after all'

The quote from Mary Malcolm, sometime television celebrity and daughter of the Poltalloch Estate, refers to Poltalloch House rather than to Slockavullin. This grand mansion, built in the early 1850s, was the Malcolm family's Scottish home until harsh taxes prompted them a century later to take off its roof and retreat to Duntrune Castle which guards the north flank of Crinan Loch. During Mary Malcolm's childhood it was a magical place filled with guests of great status from all around the world. When the family travelled north from London for its sojourns in Argyll, she could never quite believe that Poltalloch would really be there at the end of the long and complicated journey. For a century it epitomised grand living and an 'Upstairs, Downstairs' social order. According to Robin Malcolm, who represents today's very different generation of Malcolms, the industrial heart of the Poltalloch Estate, which enabled the house to run like clockwork and present its face of perfection to the world, was the village of Slockavullin.

The village had existed long before the Malcolms came to be such powerful landlords, owning not only Kilmartin Glen, Kilmichael Glen, swathes of Knapdale and parts of Cowal, but also grand houses in London and Lincolnshire and estates in Jamaica. The first laird of Poltalloch, named Donald McGillespie O'Challum in the charter which granted him the property from Campbell of Duntrune in 1562, lived on a small estate now know as Old Poltalloch on the shores of Loch Craignish. Some forty years before that grant, there was a smiddy at Slockavullin (*Slochd a' Mhuilin*, mill in the hollow) to which young Duncan Campbell of Lairig na huinnseann (later known by the English translation of Ashfield in North Knapdale) took his sword for sharpening. According to the *Genealogist*, when the sword was ready, Duncan swung it round to test its balance – and cut off the smith's head. He was, of course, drenched in blood and became known as Donachie na fola, or Bloody Duncan. The name of the village suggests a grain mill and the fact that there was a smith there

Slockavullin became the heart of the Poltalloch estate's industry and the quality of cottages built for the workers reflects the value of the late nineteenth-century Malcolm family placed in keeping the wheels oiled (*Sheena Carmichael Collection*)

in 1520 with a reputation that brought young men with swords a dozen miles across country indicates a well-established settlement. Perhaps not surprising – Kilmartin Glen had been inhabited for millennia, although even in the 1790s the minister would say in his report in the *First Statistical Account* of Argyll that there were 'no antiquities of note' in his parish. The cairns, cists, standing stones and henges dating back 3,000 years before the Christian era and the carved stone grave slabs of the medieval age either failed to impress the minister or were out of human view – they had frequently been cannibalised to build houses and much later stone walls.

The parish of Kilmartin, named for St Martin of Tours, contained much evidence of early settlement, mostly on land which would become the Poltalloch estate. Dunadd itself, where the Dalriadic kingdom was cradled, stands above Crinan Moss (*Moine Mhor*) which the Malcolms attempted to drain to improve their agricultural land some 1,500 years after Columba crowned Aidan there. At Ardifuar, just north of Duntrune Castle, there are Iron Age forts. Slockavullin is skirted by and no doubt sits upon some of the most important pre-Christian remains in the British Isles. An early Christian stone slab used as a fireplace lintel was incorporated into the renovation of Trevenek, a cottage in Upper Slockavullin. The parish perhaps gained in importance when lands were granted to John Carswell, variously described as the Bishop and the Protestant Superintendent of Argyll and the Isles, titles which say much about the progression of Scotland's religious reformation. Mary, Queen of Scots gifted the keepership of Carnasserie Castle to him and it was there that he translated the Book of Common Order, known as John Knox's Liturgy, which when it was published on 1 April 1567 became the first printed Gaelic book. Translations of the Bible into Gaelic were undertaken by several ministers, including Archibald Malcolm of Poltalloch, in Kilmartin, Kilmichael Glassary and North Knapdale over the next century, some of which were lost in the ensuing civil wars.

If a favoured bishop – or Protestant Superintendent – gave importance to the remote area of Argyll, so too did the presence of the county's most prominent family, the Campbells. Their involvement in the area, of course, was as complex as most involving Clan Campbell. In 1665, Archibald MacConnochie Campbell succeeded to Inverawe. He had married Mary MacNeill in 1657. Mary was the widow of Campbell of Duntroon and daughter of MacNeill of Taynish and the marriage created a legal tussle over the inheritance of Duntroon which lasted for several years. She had been promised £1,000 in 1656 and a further 500 merks in 1657 but did not get her money until 1663. Then in the early 1670s, Archibald Campbell bought Kilmartin from the then incumbent of Duntroon, Neil Campbell – a negotiation which brought Neil a gown for his wife. This then was the local cast list which experienced the depredations carried out on the Clan Campbell throughout Argyll in 1685–6 in retribution for their role against the Royalist cause in the civil war.

Neil Campbell of Duntroon 'and his Tennents within the paroch of Kilmartine and division of Argyle' were plundered by Donald McCharles McLeane and his two brothers in July 1685, '18 days after rebellion and disorders in the Countrie were crushed and silenced'. The value of the property looted from Campbell and his tenants amounted to £3656 13s 4d.

It was all downhill for the Campbells of Duntroon (or Duntrune as it was beginning to be spelt) after the tribulations of the seventeenth century. The parish was in a very poor state after the civil war and

Commissioners of Supply were appointed to sort things out. In the Commissioners' Minute Book of 1766, Neil Campbell of Duntroon referred to the quay being built at the ferry house from 'Creenan to North Knapdale'. A petition was made in June 1767 about the condition of the bridge over the water of Kilmartin which was 'so ruinous that passengers cannot cross thereon in safety' and was so narrow that cattle were injured or fell from it. The Commissioners allocated £10 for repairs.

In 1775, Neil Campbell of Duntroon was still one of the road trustees as a member of the Justices of the Peace and Commissioners of Supply Trustees. The family may have played its role as part of the ruling classes in Argyll, but it was badly embarrassed financially and in 1792 the Duntrune estate was sold to Neill Malcolm of Poltalloch. The Malcolms of what will now be referred to as Old Poltalloch had been lesser gentry than the Campbells. Their route from Old Poltalloch township to Kilmartin may geographically have been by tracks made by the feet of cattle but in social terms it was a journey undertaken with a certain shrewdness and perhaps a little luck. Alexander Malcolm, who became the 9th Laird in 1756, had farmed in mid Argyll since 1719 and was an elder in Kilmartin Kirk. He married the schoolmaster's sister and through her inherited property in Jamaica in 1746 which his son Dugald administered. Some West Indian enterprises brought Argyll families nothing but heartache and ruin. The Malcolm venture took some time to get into order. Fever, runaway slaves and badly kept books hampered Dugald and then his cousin George. Dugald died before his father, Alexander, and it was Neill Malcolm who purchased Duntrune in 1792. In the new century, the profits from Jamaican sugar were reinvested shrewdly and were to transform not only Malcolm lives but the whole of mid Argyll. Although their contemporaries may have read in *Candide* that the true price of sugar was the beaten and mutilated slave, this form of labour was accepted as the norm and the Malcolms were by no means unique in founding their fortune on slave labour.

The Malcolms by this time had properties in London and spent much time there, but always retained strong links with mid Argyll. Old Poltalloch was abandoned and Duntrune Castle was to be a summer residence with Neill's son in charge of restoration of this ancient pile on its rocky promontory. Dugald McIsaac from Slockavullin was employed to carry out the work and seems to have been slow to complete the task. In 1797, James Gow – a man brought in to oversee agricultural improvements rather than house makeovers – had to report that Mr McPhail the plasterer 'tells me that he will require about ten hundredweight more of stucco to finish off the castle'. By 1800, a gardener had been appointed and the work done.

But the castle and its grounds were small beer compared with the much more farsighted plans which Neill Malcolm had for the area. He had invested in the Crinan Canal right from its conception in 1785 and now he wanted to drain Crinan Moss. He by now owned 3,000 acres of Moine Mhor and wanted to turn it into arable farmland. He employed James Gow, seen as something of a drainage expert because of his role in improving Trafford Moss near Manchester, to oversee the project and from 1795, acre after acre came into cultivation.

Experiment Farm, now rebuilt as Barsloisnoch, was up and running in 1801 as the headquarters of the newly drained areas. Advice was sought from the engineer John Rennie, who was still involved with the Crinan Canal, and water-powered threshing mills were installed. From peat bog to waving fields of corn was quite some feat, and although the cost was considerable, the value of the estates crops rose from £200 to £1,000 in the last four years of the eighteenth century.

The second Neil Malcolm developed the whole estate, enclosing land, building dykes and ditches and offering opinions on fertilising the land. He sent trees from his estate in Kent to Duntrune and in his time planted oaks, larch, firs, thorns and mountain ash, changing the complete landscape of the nine mid Argyll estates he owned, including Kilmartin Estate which he bought from the Campbells of Kilmartin. Gow ran the agricultural enterprises as one of the new breed of estate manager while the Malcolms continued to move between their London, Kent and Lincolnshire properties. The third Neil Malcolm was MP for Boston in Lincolnshire in 1826 while a succession of his relatives managed the growing Jamaica plantations. When they came home to Argyll, they stayed in Kilmartin House, but as transport improved (trains meant it no longer took weeks on horseback to get from London to Poltalloch) it made sense to have a home of comfort and style to which they could invite their increasingly powerful circle of friends and acquaintances. Queen Victoria was making holidays in Scotland the thing to do and her visit to the Crinan Canal would in time put Duntroon on the map. A house and park were planned and Slockavullin came into its own as the powerhouse of the enterprise.

Instead of a corn mill, there was now to be a sawmill in the village.

The smithy was still much in use. In time there would be a gasworks serving the new house. A tileworks went up nearby and two terraces of cottages were built to house estate and domestic workers. This was a time of great production – and of great destruction. Gow had started his career as a young farm manager in Perthshire. Now he introduced modern agricultural methods to mid Argyll and dozens of labourers lost their jobs with the amalgamation of tenancies and the automation of farming. Houses with gardens went up at Kilmartin and Slockavullin but cottages were abandoned and left to decay on the hills as farms were brought together with fewer tenants. People, turned out of their cottages on the hills, were asked instead to rent the red brick houses built by the estate and to seek work within the estate. At the turn of the century, the Malcolm properties had been surveyed and many were scarcely fit for human habitation, with their turf walls and badly thatched roofs. There had been little investment in these houses and Neil Malcolm wanted to clear newly bought estates like Oib in Knapdale but was prevented by his factor John Campbell, a lawyer in Inveraray. Even so, in the first decades of the nineteenth century many estate families were deprived of their homes and traditional livings and told to live elsewhere and work in other capacities.

Those who ended up in a new brick house with a slate roof like those the Malcolms built throughout their Argyll properties, and who received cash for contract work, may have felt they had moved into a new world. Those like Donald McCallum of Tighachan who were evicted sometimes begged for any corner on a hillside to live rather than leave the district. Around eighty tenants were put off the two Ardifuir farms and in 1848, the sad affair of the eviction of a community of some 100 people at Arichonan above Loch Sween which led to five tenants being sentenced to eight months in Inveraray jail cannot have made for comfortable laird/tenant relationships. A modern sheep fank had been designed for Arichonan and people were in the way. From the 1830s to the 1870s, the population of Kilmartin Parish dropped from 1,475 to 869 and by the beginning of the twentieth century was just 663, mostly due to emigration and to amalgamation of farms.

It has to be said that the Malcolms did assist people to emigrate to Canada in the 1840s during the potato blight and many families from Argyll ended up in Australia working on the vast Malcolm acres there. And while some were made homeless in Argyll, others were employed

The house the Malcolms built on the strength of their colonial and UK fortunes: Poltalloch House in its glory days (*Sheena Carmichael Collection*)

to build the magnificent pile that was to be Poltalloch House with its nearby chapel. Kilmartin Church itself had been rebuilt in 1835 on the site of the 1601 building but that was, of course, a Presbyterian church. The Malcolms were Episcopalians and an Episcopal clergyman was employed for many years at the new St Columba Chapel, where in 1850 the Malcolms took the Kilmichael Glassary cross 'for safe keeping'. This stone-carved crucifix with a Celtic design on the reverse originated in the fifteenth century at Kilneuair on the shores of Loch Awe and had presided over the Kilmichael Glassary tryst for centuries.

The new Poltalloch was built in the neo-Jacobean style designed by William Burn for Neil Malcolm in 1849 at a cost of £100,000 – although some say this figure included the terraced gardens and the chapel. William Burn was one of Scotland's leading architects in the mid nineteenth century and was much sought after to create country houses throughout Britain. One of his design skills was to create spaces in which owners, guests and servants did not encroach on each other's privacy. The third Neil Malcolm and his wife Louisa felt they needed such spaces for entertaining and the house, built of imported sandstone, was huge even by baronial hall standards. The chapel was intended as an integral part of the building but was eventually built

Poltalloch estate brickworks produced the raw material for the laundry
(*Author's Collection*)

at a distance from the house to drawings by Thomas Cundy between
1852 and 1854.

The house had a billiard room, conservatory and public rooms
looking across the park across to Crinan. In 1849, a brickworks was
built on the estate to provide bricks for interior walls and the walled
gardens. A house at Ballymeanoch and the cottages at Kilmartin were
constructed from this brick. Other buildings on the estate were planned
with English Jacobean features, including the tall chimneys of the
laundry at the top of the Long Walk. At Dunadd Farm, Slockavullin
and Kilmartin, this meant an odd mix of architecture. When the local
authorities of the twenty-first century demand that new houses are
built to a 'traditional' Argyll style, it would be interesting to know if
the 'tradition' includes the Malcolms' neo-Jacobean influences.

The house employed an enormous staff managed by a butler and
a housekeeper. Most lived in and there were also quarters for the

The Poltalloch guests, including royalty and captains of industry, sometimes arrived by train and Loch Awe steamer and were taken by brake to Poltalloch House (*Sheena Carmichael Collection*)

servants of visitors. The gardens produced blooms for their London house and there were flowerbeds, terraces and lawns laid out by landscape gardener W.A. Nesfield. Neil Malcolm built a network of roads around the estate, opened a girls' school, built the Victoria Halls for the community and the Royal Hotel (now the Grey Gull) at Ardrishaig for his guests coming off the steamer. Some guests would travel by steamer down Loch Awe. Neil Malcolm, creator of Poltalloch House, enjoyed it for little more than a decade before his death in Brighton in 1857. He was succeeded by his brother John, who was laird until 1893 and entertained the great, the good and the not so good. Some guests bemoaned the fact that a perfectly good snipe bog had been drained to create 'indifferent farms' and that sentiment might be echoed for other reasons by today's environmentalists. However, today there is a part of the moss which invites visitors to enjoy the rare wildlife – unlike the late nineteenth-century visitors who wanted to shoot it or pin it under glass.

The gasworks built at Slockavullin became semi-redundant in 1910 when a generator was installed in the stables at Poltalloch House and the house electrified. Bathrooms were then installed – six for the twenty-five guest rooms. Sir Ian Malcolm and his successors lived in the main block of the house when they were in residence although the main hall of the house, known as the corridor, was always used as a meeting space for family and guests. There was a tenants' ball in the house at Christmas. Sir Ian came north almost every month and there were house parties all winter which involved shoots. Local beaters were paid by the day and 400 brace of birds might be shot in a day. The beaters were required to wear uniforms, even though they were casual labourers, and the indoor staff had quite elaborate outfits. In the 1920s and 1930s, there were five footmen, a butler, odd job man and a pantry boy. Before the First World War, twenty-one women worked in the house but after the war this number was reduced. Four men were employed to look after the cars, there was a head gamekeeper and six other gamekeepers, and there were kennel staff to care for the Poltalloch terriers, a breed developed on the estate.

As late as the turn of the twentieth century, there was a factor living in a substantial house, Ri Cruin, an estate clerk of works and forty-five estate tradesmen, including joiners, slaters, stonemasons and forestry workers. But all this was to end. There were no new injections of cash into the family to keep up such standards, and although Sir Ian was active at Westminster (he was Parliamentary Private Secretary to A.J. Balfour) and consorted with kings (Feisal of Iraq was a guest at Poltalloch) he was not the same kind of entrepreneur that his ancestors had been. Society was changing much more rapidly than ever before and the financial stability of Edwardian Britain evaporated between the First and Second World Wars. After 1945 there was a Labour government seeking to create an egalitarian society. Rented houses were to be made fit for human habitation. The Malcolms were not alone in putting many of their substandard properties up for sale to sitting tenants. They had already sold off properties on Loch Awe and Keills at around the turn of the century and the North Knapdale properties in the 1930s to the Forestry Commission. Now the Argyll empire which had been theirs was contracting ever more rapidly. The family moved back into Duntrune Castle for the first time in a hundred years and converted the mighty Poltalloch House into flats. The final retrenchment was to remove the roof on the house in 1957 to avoid paying crippling rates.

Sheena Carmichael has witnessed the many changes which the twentieth century brought to the Malcolms and to her birthplace,

Not all the houses on the estate were of smart new brick and slate – the traditional thatched cottages like Auchachrome at Slockavullin survived into the twentieth century (*Sheena Carmichael Collection*)

Slockavullin. Her father was Mr Wilson the butler at Poltalloch House and his family lived in this ancient village in one of the brick terraces with their slated roofs. Her grandmother and grandfather MacNair had lived in the top terrace. Granny MacNair came to Poltalloch from Ross-shire to work as a laundry maid at the big house and she met Sheena's grandfather who was a stonemason on the estate. Sheena's family lived in the bottom terrace with her two sisters. Born in 1920, she was only eight years old when her father died of pneumonia. She says: 'Although the Malcolms let us live on in the house, we had no income.' By then, Granny MacNair had come to live with them and the two women's state pensions as widows amounted to £1 a week.

'My mother asked for a bathroom,' Sheena recalls. Until then, they had a shed at the back. Now the estate added a bathroom to the house (the cost to be paid back, of course) and Sheena's mother was able to take in a boarder to make ends meet.

Sheena remembers the village as a busy one, although already not everyone worked on the estate. One neighbour was a tailor in Ross's shop in Kilmartin. Another ran a motor hire business. But most worked at Poltalloch House and Sheena says: 'There was a huge staff inside and outside and the sawmill and the gasworks were still working – it served the big house, the church and maybe the Episcopal minister's house. The big house was getting electricity as well but we all had paraffin lamps. My grandfather has been a mason working on the estate. The cottages were comfortable and we used to run down the wee wood to school at Kilmartin and came home at lunchtime.'

Kilmartin was always the bigger village and had the school, church, hotel and shops (today, of course, it also has its award-winning museum), but Slockavullin was where the industrial work of the estate was done. Today, both are on the tourist trail and excite visitors interested in history and archaeology, as well as the wildlife of the Moss and the surrounding woodland walks. Many people work in Lochgilphead or further afield or offer bed and breakfast to the tourists. Yet within Sheena's memory, every cottage belonged to the Malcolms and most people worked for them. She recalls Sir Ian Malcolm as a vague figure but Lady Malcolm used to visit tenants. Then after the Second World War, the family could no longer get staff. Sheena says: 'They turned the place to flats and there was a man who worked in the bank lived there. It became a sad ruin of a place and then they took the roof off. By that time there wouldn't be many working on the estate.'

In the glory days she remembers the guests at Poltalloch House coming by steamer to Ardrishaig and staying at the Royal Hotel on the way back. 'They had their own chauffeur and their own little bus with canvas sides. Sir Ian moved in theatrical circles and Lady Malcolm was the daughter of Lillie Langtry. Their daughter Mary Malcolm, the BBC announcer, loved Poltalloch.'

Lillie Langtry, famous actress of her day and companion of Queen Victoria's son the Prince of Wales, had been a visitor to Poltalloch in the late nineteenth century. The ghosts of such guests may hover around the ruins of Poltalloch House, but there have been changes too in Kilmartin and Slockavullin – changes which Sheena found hard to come to terms with at first. The cottages at Slockavullin were added to and altered; Kilmartin became a busy place on the main road to Oban. Now, however, the residents of Slockavullin have formed a preservation society and as a community are working together to keep the integrity of a village which has survived the ravages of history and the fluctuating fortunes of a family.

13

KILMICHAEL GLASSARY

Colkitto, courts, kirk and cattle

It was the church and the cattle which gave Kilmichael Glassary ideas which now seem so much above its station. Once it was the bustling crossroads of Argyll, a place of noise and wealth and synod meetings. It was on the main road from north to south and had such a splendid area of grazing that it was considered to be *the* place to stop on the road east from the islands to the major markets of central Scotland. But its place on the drove road, its role as an ecclesiastical centre of some note and the presence of a law court and jail are by no means the first evidence of Kilmichael Glassary's prominent place in the sun. On the hillside above the vibrant primary school is the smooth slab of rock carved with some of the finest cup-and-ring marks in Argyll – and, because of their keyhole shape rather than the more usual whorls and circles, some of the most intriguing. These enigmatic carvings, still undeciphered by the archaeologists, indicate a place special to the inhabitants who walked this land in the millennia preceding the Christian era. Running parallel to Kilmartin Glen – considered today to be one of the UK's most important archaeological sites, despite the local minister's laconic verdict in the 1790s that Kilmartin was a place of 'no special antiquities' – Kilmichael Glen has perhaps kept secret most of its ancient treasures. Those forts, standing stones, cairns, cists and intricate rock carvings which do remain visible suggest a valley where Neolithic man sheltered and prospered.

At the fork of the two glens lies Dunadd, site of the coronation of kings. The River Add's sinuous exit to the sea through Loch Crinan may seep into the Moine Mhor at the foot of Kilmartin Glen, but it flows from two head streams 600 feet above Kilmichael Glen and its length tumbles and twists its way through this more easterly valley. These hills once lay under the ocean and there is evidence of its mighty strength in the shapes of the rocks which look out across to Jura high above the explosive plug which became the seat of kings. There are forts up there which guarded the sacred places of both glens millennia before the Christian era. When Columba crowned Aidan

Torbhlaren Farm in Kilmichael Glen, witness to the ravages of the civil war, the struggles of the Covenanters and the depredations of the Campbells (*Author's collection*)

the first Christian monarch of these islands in the sixth century, both glens must have shared the reflected glow of the royal court and their inhabitants drunk the wine traded from French vessels to the Dalriadic court.

By medieval times, the lands of Glassary were owned by a powerful family called Scrymgeour, whose western properties were mainly centred on Lochawe. The dean of Glassary in 1240 was named Malvin and it was the church of Kilneuair (reputed to be a chapel of St Columba's) near their castle at Fionncharn (Finchairn) which was then the major focus of Christianity in mid Argyll. When it fell into disrepair in 1563, the church at Kilmichael Glassary took on the imposing role of ecclesiastical centre of the old Lordship of Glassary. The names Kilmichael and Kilbride indicate that early monks had prayed and evangelised in the area, perhaps from the days when Columba walked the banks of the Add and climbed Dunadd rock to anoint the king of Dalriada. These two cells or chapels are on either side of the ridge which separates Kilmartin and Kilmichael glens. Today, Kilbride is a ruin surrounded by mystery and legend like the church at Finchairn (at the former, blood-curdling screams are said to be heard; on the latter's door frame legend places the scratch marks of the Devil's hand as he scrabbled to catch a tailor who sought sanctuary within the sacred place). The present Kilmichael Church was built in the first half of the nineteenth century to replace the by then decrepit medieval church. In the graveyard around the church, centuries-old slabs depicting armoured men testify to the generations who have worshipped there since the Irish saint brought Celtic Christianity to Argyll.

The Scrymgeour lairds held the patronage of Kilmichael Church from the early fifteenth century and treated it as part of the family 'business'. At least six Scrymgeours were rectors of Kilmichael, although not all of them enriched the souls of their parishioners. James was sacked in 1423 because he could not speak or understand the Gaelic spoken by his flock. Whatever the damage done to them by effectively being without a spiritual guide for the eighteen months he held the post, he was moved onwards and upwards to become a canon of Glasgow and dean of Aberdeen. Later in the century, Hercules (or Arculyus) Scrymgeour became canon of Argyll and held land from the Constable of Glassary. He was one of the clerics assaulted in 1452 when the less than popular Bishop of Argyll, George Lauder, was attacked on Lismore (the seat of the bishops of Argyll in those days) by an angry populace. In the 1500s, yet another clerical Scrimgeour – note the variant spelling of the name – found fame when he tried through diplomatic means in France to spring Archbishop James Beaton from jail. The English referred to him as 'one naming himself parson of Glaister' – just one of the variations on 'Glassary' (*glas*, grey; *glassra*, a greyish strath) down the ages. The last vicar of Glassary before the Reformation was Henry Scrimgeour, a scholar who had worked with Calvin in Geneva.

When the Rev. J. G. Mathieson wrote his account of Glassary for the 1961 *Statistical Account of Argyll*, he said that the 94 square mile parish could 'claim to be the cradle of the Scottish kingdom,' because Dunadd stands in the parish. So, not only the cradle of Christianity but of Scotland itself. No wonder Kilmichael Glassary had aspirations above its modern status. In 1814, a Celtic iron bell in a bronze case bearing a depiction of the Crucifixion was found at Torbhlaren farm to the north of Kilmichael Church (although the Rev. Donald Campbell, minister in Kilmichael from 1852 to 1906, whose uncle and grandfather were ministers in the parish back to 1779, believed the bell was found at the back of the manse on the site of the old church). Cast in the twelfth century, it is now in the care of the National Museums of Scotland, tangible proof of the days of prominence and influence.

Wherever it was found, it is possible that the bell was rescued from the old church during the tragic times of the seventeenth century when blood flowed in Glassary as elsewhere in the name of king, country and religion.

In 1638, it was the 8th Earl of Argyll who helped to launch a 5,000 word manifesto, later to be called the National Covenant, which pledged loyalty only so long as the King upheld ancient liberties. In other words, it was a statement in favour of the Presbyterian form of worship against the Episcopal system then being imposed. Charles I had rejected similar documents, but this one had 300,000 signatures from all around Scotland – a powerful enough force to ignite the bloody conflict which would last fifty years. In 1645, Charles was imprisoned in England but the Marquess of Montrose and Sir Alexander Macdonald (a descendant of the Lords of the Isles) campaigned on his behalf. Known as Alasdair macCholla and called *fear tholladh nan taighean* (the house burner), Sir Alexander was said not to have left 'a fruit tree nor a fishing net' along Loch Fyne as troops made their way through Campbell country. On May Day 1647, Alasdair macCholla (son of Colkitto – *Coll Ciotach*, left-handed) marched through the hills from Kilmichael Glassary to Loch Awe. At the top of the pass at Loch Leathan, the defenders of a small outpost killed a man at macCholla's right side. He marched on without attempting to revenge the act and when he reached the foot of the pass he accepted a challenge to single combat with Zachary Mor MacCallum, leader of the local guerrilla force. He lost the contest and when he asked the name of the place where he had met his match and was told Mill of Gocumgo, he said his childhood nurse had told him his luck would run out at a place with that name, turned on his heel and led his army back to Knapdale and down the drove road to Kintyre over Sliabh Ghaoil. He retreated to Ireland and was killed there that November.

Among those who suffered in those years of turmoil was Patrick Campbell and his wife Jean. Patrick was to have been minister at Inveraray but the religious unrest meant he was out of a job and a home. He went to stay with his father in Knapdale and the couple had their family there. The youngest boy, John, was baptised in Kilmichael Glassary in 1673 because by then his grandfather had installed Patrick and Jean in Torbhlaren Farm across the River Add from the Kirktoun and in the shadow of the rock on which once stood Torbhlaren's ancient fort. At first, the family was able to raise enough to feed the children, although in those days there were no staples like potatoes or field turnips.

They lived through a period when the population tried everything from peaceful protest through civil disobedience to armed resistance. They were up against legislation and martial law imposing a rule and religion they refused to acknowledge. There were demonstrations in Kilmichael, prayer meetings in the hills and battles in the glen. In some areas of Scotland, ministers were shot on their own doorsteps. In Glassary the cup-and-ring marked stones were used as communion tables by the Covenanters. Patrick held services in Gaelic even though by 1679 preaching at a field conventicle carried the death sentence and attendance at such a meeting meant a devastating fine for worshippers.

This was a time of open war in Scotland and the Earl of Argyll was in the forefront of the battle. The Duke of York devised the tricky Test Oath in 1681 which had to be sworn by all and there was a ban on discussion of politics and religion. That was the year Elizabeth Campbell, oldest of the Torbhlaren children, was married to the newly appointed sheriff clerk. Her brothers took jobs and they felt secure with the support of relatives in the glen. But Patrick was to fall foul of the system. When the Earl made his abortive attempt in 1684 to bring William of Orange over from Holland, suspected supporters like Patrick were taken off to Inveraray jail. He received a life sentence which could be commuted only on payment of a fine far too big for Jean to pay. The economy of the whole country was now running on an empty tank and ordinary families like this minor branch of the Campbells could raise money only by selling their cattle and their household goods, the only capital they had. One of the daughters, Jean, got a job as a domestic at Carnasserie Castle at the age of just thirteen. It was one less mouth to feed. When Charles II died in 1685, Patrick was about to be deported, but somehow got ashore. Although the family was pleased he was alive and free, the extended family finances had already been wiped out to pay the bond for his release.

Young Jean followed in the family footsteps as a heroine of the cause by eating vital papers which would have incriminated Sir Duncan Campbell of Auchenbreck, her master, as soldiers searched his carriage.

The whole of Kilmichael Glen's agricultural wealth was trampled underfoot during this lengthy period of bloodshed. Soldiers were no respecters of property. When revenge was to be wrecked on Campbells, the devastation of crops was deliberate. Carnasserie Castle was sacked, hostages were hanged from the trees, Auchenbreck's elderly lawyer was lynched as the avenging armies marched from Lochgilp laden with plunder, and the distress of cattle, women and children was audible across mid Argyll.

Elizabeth Campbell, a relative of Patrick, was a widow in Kilmichael Glassary who ran a small shop. According the records of the Depredations on Clan Campbell, she lost 'goods, furniture, wares and money, in all worth £500'. Jean herself made no claims, not even when still more marauders passed through the Glen – including the Lochsweenside MacNeills, MacAllisters from Tarbert and others from Glenary. Government forces were allowed meal and meat from local sources, although men and women over sixty were supposed to be exempt from such requisitions. The Marquess of Atholl may well have issued orders to protect some householders, but his troops could not read. The exiled Patrick Campbell's family were in the path of these marauders at Torbhlaren farm and Jean's biggest fears were for her fifteen-year-old daughter Bessie. As a family, they survived. but the trials and executions went on and still more avenging troops came later that year and cleared any remaining cattle. There was no harvest in Kilmichael Glen that year. A Kilmichael brewster and merchant was plundered in July 1685 and ten Kilmichael men and three from Torbhlaren township – Charles McIlmun, William Stevison and Thomas Dick – were tried and fined for their part in the uprisings against the government. Where on earth did they get the money to pay?

The parish lost 805 cattle, 155 horses, 195 sheep and 92 goats as well as tools, bedding and personal clothing.

And yet by 1687, with a swing in government (James was attempting appeasement), Patrick had got his parish back and the family moved from Torbhlaren back to Inveraray and spent thirteen relatively peaceful years there under subsequent monarchs. Jean the letter-eater grew up to marry MacIver Campbell in 1692 when he came from Caithness to be minister of Glassary. They bought the farm next to Torbhlaren and raised six children there. In fact, the whole family's fortunes changed. Patrick's son Dugald inherited Kilmory Estate from a childless cousin. John, the youngest, joined William and Mary's army and was a military escort for the ill-fated Darien scheme and then set up in Black River in Jamaica, became an administrator and encouraged poor Glassary lads to follow him to make their fortunes.

With hindsight – and possibly at the time – it is obvious that the venom and savagery which that century of political and religious turmoil wrought in Argyll had a clan subtext. There had always been bickering between the clans over cattle and property. The Campbells had ousted the Scrymgeour lairds from much of their lands in the parish of Glassary two centuries before these civil wars began, although in 1601 Sir James Scrymgeour of Dudhope complained to the Privy Council that Colin Campbell of Otter, Duncan Campbell of Danna and Dougal Campbell of Kilmorie had come to his lands of Glassary and threatened his tenants. The King summoned Campbells and Scrymgeours to Dunfermline and told them to settle the matter amicably, but Duncan Campbell of Auchenbreck raised 1,500 men with 'hagbuts and pistolets' and went on the rampage in mid Argyll with other cadets of the Campbell clan. In time, they became the main family in mid Argyll, with cadet branches scattered in every corner. It was confirmation of the power they had sought since medieval times – there is record of Sir Cailein Mor (Campbell) of Loch Awe being killed by the Clan Dougall in 1296 and it was in the thirteenth century that 'Cambel' was first used as the clan surname. Sir Duncan Cambel of Lochawe may have been made the first chief when he was created Lord Campbell in 1445.

Their power was also a thorn in the flesh of the former Lords of the Isles – the Macdonalds and their followers – and the visitation of macCholla had far more to do with clan vengeance than the bigger political picture. Yet despite such seventeenth century savagery, the Campbells were to hold onto Glassary until James Campbell of Duntrune became bankrupt and sold out to the Malcolms of Poltalloch, who would be the main landowners in Glassary until after the Second World War. It was then that the government legislated for housing improvements. Landowners were required to make homes fit for modern habitation with running water and electricity. In common with lairds throughout Argyll (2,178 houses were seen as unfit for habitation in Argyll in 1955), the Malcolms sold their tenanted properties rather than face the crippling cost of such modernisation, although they still, of course, have Duntrune Castle and the much contracted Poltalloch Estate as their seat.

But in the glory days of Kilmichael Glassary, the land belonged to Campbells, and Campbells frequently held the rectorship of what was considered to be a plum ecclesiastical living, having as it did a large glebe stretching down to one of the curves of the Add.

Black cattle did not only pass through Kilmichael. They were raised there and sold there and the community's wealth was built on their hooves. An indication of that wealth comes in the accounts of the depredations of the Campbells. Patrick and Jean were not alone in losing everything and nor was Patrick's shopkeeping sister, whose lost fripperies indicate a clientele with money to spend. Duncan Grahame, 'a merchant in Glassarie', was paid an avenging visit in July 1685. His 'household plenishings, clothes, bracelets and furniture' worth £200 were looted along with an aquavitae pot worth £100 and a brewing cauldron worth £72. Angus Campbell in Kilmichell of Glassarie had been cleaned out the previous month while the Earl of Argyll was losing his head at the market cross in Edinburgh, where it was affixed to the Tolbooth. Angus may have been looked on as almost lucky in the circumstances, having lost not his life but '25 great coues worth £400', other 'coues', sheep and two horses, and 'from his tenants 40 great coues' worth £640. Shops were overturned and houses looted. Women, children and old folk shared the fears of Jean at Torbhlaren and fled to the hills in Kilmichael Glen to escape the pillaging.

Their lives may have been blighted by the warfare – the peace seemed little better. From being villagers who could afford to buy fine lace in the local shop and to keep cows valued at hundreds of pounds, they found themselves foraging in the woods 'without a morsel to preserve a miserable existence'. The Synod of Argyll recorded a famine in 1650 caused by a late harvest, hard weather and the many foot soldiers who pillaged what food there was. After the war, grants were given to the heritors to bail them out, but their tenants did not benefit and it was hard to recover from many so years like that one. Scotland as a country had no money, no trade and the taxes were doubled. Many of those who stayed in Kilmichael were dragged off to jail or deported to the plantations – lacking their ears. Local jails (there was one at Kilmichael Glassary itself) were full to overflowing and many from Argyll found themselves in Dunnottar Castle in Kincardineshire on the other side of the country, confined to filthy dungeons.

The lairds of mid Argyll, as elsewhere, had maintained their own gibbets to carry out the most extreme sentences of their own courts. The Campbells of Achnabreck had held theirs at Kilmichael Glassary. In 1748 after the second Jacobite uprising in which the local laird, Sir James Campbell of Achnabreck was imputed, the abolition of heritable jurisdictions meant local kangaroo courts could no longer take place and tenants were no longer at the mercy of their landlords. Schools were founded and roads were planned in the later years of the eighteenth century as the warring subsided and 'civilising' legislation was directed at the unruly west of Scotland. The previous century of war, famine and plague had taken its toll and landlords were bankrupted, leaving tenants vulnerable. It was a time for drastic change.

David Campbell of Dunloskin had set up a business manufacturing coarse linens in Dunoon which employed around twenty to thirty women. He then opened a college there to teach women and weavers in Cowal the trade and in June 1749 he was writing to the Commissioners of Supply to suggest setting up more manufacturing companies in Cowal, Inveraray, Oban or Easdale, Tarbert or Kilmichael Glassary with a college at Campbeltown. This did not seem to come to anything, but it was indicative of the excitement being engendered by the mood of the Enlightenment. A request for a parochial school was made in Glassary in 1753.

The Rev. Dugald Campbell was minister in Kilmichael Glassary in the 1790s when he was asked to contribute to the *First Statistical Account of Argyll*. He approved of the change from the runrig system of farming, where tenants had managed their allotted strips of land and ploughed and sowed as a commune, to the joining of several tenancies into single farms – although this obviously made many tenants homeless. Because of the wet climate, the land in Glassary parish was, he said, only fit for green crops and in the previous quarter of a century the most adventurous had combined several small farms and were raising and finishing black cattle. There were large tracts of land at that time being turned into cattle farms and two heritors were beginning to introduce sheep to the land – the scourge which would see still more subsistence farmers turned off the land they worked to make room for a more profitable 'resident'.

The population fluctuated. The parish as a whole had in 1755 held 2,751 souls. By 1792, the population was 2,568. There were then six main landlords in the parish and a number of smaller ones. Rents ranged from as little as £6 to £2,000 a year. The total rent value of Glassary Parish property in 1793 was £5,700. There were five blacksmiths in the parish (every farm had its plough horses, of course, and every man of note travelled on horseback), thirty-two weavers, six shoemakers and what were described as 'inferior shoemakers' who also did odd jobs like fencing and ditching and perhaps went off to the herring fishing in the summer. Around forty young men called themselves fishermen and worked on the thirty boats harboured on Lochfyneside. This was before either Ardrishaig or Lochgilphead were villages of any standing. The area supported two masons, six millers, six tailors, three boat carpenters, three joiners, two wheelwrights, two tide waiters, and two surgeons. The rest of the population was sustained by fishing or farming.

Property was beginning to be enclosed by the heritors to increase value and improve farming. Much timber had been planted in the parish and oats, barley and potatoes were the main crops grown. Already the sheep were outnumbering the cattle – there were 3,200 black cattle in the parish compared with 12,000 sheep. There were still a few of the small white-faced native sheep around but although their wool was superior to that of the Galloway sheep, their weight could not match that of the incomers. White wool at the time was fetching 7s 6d a stone.

As the heritors began to balance the presence of man versus sheep, there were some tragic scenes as tenants were thrown out of their houses and off their land. From 1831 to 1851, Argyll saw a time of emigration, of vacant crofts and farm amalgamations. In 1848 when such evictions were at their height, Archibald McCallum, a 23-year-old farm servant working for Neil Malcolm of Poltalloch and living at Kirnan Mill in Kilmichael Glen, gave a statement against Catherine McLachlan or Campbell of Arichonan in North Knapdale. Neil was one of a deputation of twenty-five workers from the Poltalloch Estate and nine local policemen who went to Arichonan to carry out Neil Malcolm's eviction notice on Catherine and her neighbours. The people of Arichonan did not take kindly to the men knocking on their doors, reading the eviction notice and forcing their way in to throw out the tenants' personal property. They were accused of rioting and mobbing on that summer's day and according to the National Archives of Scotland what came to be known as 'the matter of Arichonan' reached the Inveraray autumn court circuit. Archibald swore that he saw a red-haired girl strike Mr Martin, the Poltalloch factor. James Ormiston, the 44-year-old farm overseer at Mr Malcolm's 'Experimental Farm', went along with the police and

John Gillies the Sheriff Officer who were executing the Decree of Removing. He claimed to have seen Mrs Campbell seize Mr Martin the Poltalloch factor by the neckcloth and pull it 'as if she wanted to choke him'. She probably did, poor woman, as she fought to stay in her cottage. The children threw stones, the women pounded these burly men with their fists – but the eviction still went ahead.

This was a bold and brave rebellion. Tenants relied on their landlords for their very lives. In the late 1700s, labourers who were not fed by their employers were paid around one shilling a day. A male servant given his meals by his employer would get between £5 15s and £6 6s a year. Female servants who got their board were paid around £3 a year. The tailor and shoemaker would make up to 10d a day with meals while a joiner or mason working on a temporary job would get between 2s and 2s 6d a day. The married worker employed throughout the year by a farmer got a house, kailyard, peats, grass for two cows, land to grow potatoes and a stone of meal a week, which with his pay was worth the princely sum of £12 a year.

Even the minister's style of living was dictated by the local heritors. The Kilmichael Glassary manse had been built in 1763 and it was damp. There were few manses built at the time in Argyll and this one turned out to have been a shoddy job despite the boast of sixteen windows. In the 1790s it already needed repairs. The minister's living was worth £120 a year, including meal, oats, the manse and the glebe (six acres of arable as well as the use of grass from the neighbouring farm). Mr Campbell of Knockbuy (Minard) was the patron of the church. Now that the modern roads to Minard go via Lochgilphead and the coast, Minard seems distant from Kilmichael Glassary, but the parish stretched from Lochawe to the boundary with Knapdale (the line of the Crinan Canal) and from Kilmichael Glassary over the hills to Fyneside at Lochgair and Minard. And that was the way people, and cattle, travelled to Fyneside, over the hill at Glashan Loch, an area which today is heavily afforested.

The 1563 church had survived clan skirmishes, civil war and the bitter Covenanting period. When it was at its most important in the seventeenth century, with Synod meetings held there regularly, Archibald Malcolm of Poltalloch in the Parish of Kilmichael was one of the translators of the Bible into Gaelic – the first translation to be made into Gaelic was begun under the direction of Bishop John Carswell at Carnasserie Castle in the 1500s. Now Kilmichael Church was in disrepair. It had been patched up twice between 1760 and 1790

Kilmichael church, manse and steading. The old manse and steading are still visible, with the wide passageway for cattle to be driven down to the Tryst on the banks of the Add (*Author's collection*)

but the Rev. Campbell felt it was time for a thorough overhaul. He would have to rely on the heritors to provide the finances, however, as the Sunday collections were evidently poor. Little wonder – the 'ordinary' people in his congregation were living in what he described as 'huts' damp enough to make rheumatism ubiquitous. A parochial school had been set up in the middle of the century but Dugald tells us that 'since private education became fashionable' that school was in decline. There was also an establishment set up by the Society for Promoting Christian Knowledge with a salary to pay a sewing and knitting mistress, so it can be assumed girls were getting some form of education, even if the emphasis was on the domestic rather than the academic. Rector Scrimgeour would still have found it difficult to preach in the area because the language was still Gaelic, although most by the late eighteenth century could understand and speak some English.

The Tryst Fair was held on land west from the church to Leacach Luaine or Dancing Stones, a pair of fallen stones on the rise south of two standing stones near the two-arched Bridge of Add, built in 1737 as part of the efforts by the Commissioners of Supply to improve river crossings, and about 500 yards from Dunamuck township. At that time, the fifteenth-century Cross of Argyll from Kilneuair was in the centre of that field. The cattle from the islands and the north came along the ancient drove roads to be sold on to markets in central Scotland. Staff were hired at the fairs and there was bustle and trade for the blacksmith, the drove inn, the cartwrights and horse-traders. But life was changing quite drastically. The superiority of the church and the importance of the cattle market and hiring fair were beginning to diminish and that would be because of changes welcomed by the Rev. Dugald Campbell. First came a new road following an Act of Parliament in the 1770s which demanded one shilling in the pound road 'stent' – in effect a demand for the local heritors to make modern roads. According to the Rev. Campbell, some heritors in Glassary borrowed money on their own security to finish road lines in the parish. A magnificent 12 miles of road 24 feet wide (far wider than many of today's single-track roads) helped to join up the dots between Inveraray and Campbeltown (what is today the A83) and another six miles were created from Lochgilphead going west and north-west towards Lorn – in other words, the line of the modern road from Lochgilphead to Oban. The clergyman's report that there were insufficient funds to maintain the roads after they were built could almost have been a prophecy of what Argyll's road network would become in future centuries.

These roads were intended to 'civilise' the wild west and to make it more accessible to governing forces. The effect was to give Lochgilphead and Ardrishaig a starring role on the map, turning them into prominent staging posts between the places already considered to be important. It had been Kilmichael Cross which was universally known as the crossroads of Argyll. Now Lochgilphead feus were sold by the main heritor, John McNeill of Gigha, with the intentions of creating a model town. Inns were built, dwelling houses went up in that distinctive late eighteenth-century style McNeill dictated – and

Kilmichael Cross. The fifteenth-century Celtic carved stone cross which survived a journey from Loch Aweside to Kilmichael Glassary, where it presided over the Tryst for centuries until taken to Poltalloch by the Malcolms for safe-keeping. (*Author's collection*)

suddenly there was a place of note on the map. When Ardrishaig became the eastern terminus of the Crinan Canal, a waterway which the Rev. Campbell saw as a bright star on the economic horizon of Glassary parish, it, too, took on an importance which slowly began to eat away at the status of Kilmichael Glassary.

Market forces had already attacked that status in the 1760s. On 30 April 1762, the Commissioners of Supply appointed a committee to investigate a scam allegedly being perpetrated by dealers from the 'Low Country' (Dumbarton). They were deliberately not buying black cattle at Kilmichael Glassary so that the centre of the trade could be shifted. Farmers and grazers in the West of Scotland had actually advertised in the *Glasgow Journal* that instead of going to Kilmichael Glassary they would hold a tryst on Dumbarton Moor from 2 to 5 June 1762, and that this would become an annual event. A Minute recorded by the Commissioners of Supply in Argyll that year recommended that farmers should not be intimidated by this advertisement and that any black cattle not bought at the end of the Kilmichael tryst would be bought up by the Commission. It was just the first salvo in a long battle.

The committee's next move was to put notices in the press advertising stages with grazing on the way to the Low Country. By May 1763 the problem was still a major concern and the go-ahead was again given to buy black cattle at the Kilmichael Glassary Whitsunday market if sales were slack. Naively, perhaps, the commissioners believed the 'combiners' would 'soon be wearied of the scheme' and the local trustees were empowered to use the same interventionist tactics at the next Whitsunday market and given permission to borrow up to £500 if necessary to keep sales up. In 1773, yet another committee was appointed to support Kilmichael Glassary's market and to safeguard the one held at Whitsuntide. The following year, that committee was still following the tactics of buying up cattle to keep the market in the black – this time with the authority to buy up to 1,500 head. The market may have lost some of its caché at this time, but it continued to be a valuable local market for many years to come.

Piggott's Directory records that in 1837, 7,000 to 8,000 head of cattle were presented at the 'much frequented' Kilmichael fairs. In 1843, the Campbells of Kilberry bought 25 head of black cattle for £105 9s at 'Kilmichell' – the spelling in the home farm manager's account book reflecting the pronunciation still used today. In October of the following year, the Kilberry farm manager sold 'six stotts at Kilmichell market' and charged his boss John Campbell five shillings for going. When he went with some of his men on 26 May 1844, he put in for 12 shillings expenses. No doubt they had a good day out at the Horseshoe Inn while they were at it and fortified themselves for the 25-mile walk home. Temporary courts were held at the time of the markets at Kilmichael Glassary to keep order.

So, the descent from the dizzy heights of hosting the baron-bailie courts of the Campbells of Achnabreck was a gradual one. The old medieval church was replaced in 1827 by a splendid new building with 1,300 sittings. Three years later, lightning struck and although it was repaired and improved, it was taken down less than four decades later and a second new church was built by the heritors 'on a scale better suited to the population'. This time there were only 300 seats, an altogether more modest affair. Twelve years later in 1885, the *Ordnance Gazetteer of Scotland* described Kilmichael Glassary as having 'dwindled to a mere church hamlet'. But there was life in the old place yet. The school could take 100 pupils (although 80 was a more realistic turnout) and despite all the Dumbarton shenanigans there were still two cattle fairs at the end of the nineteenth century. They were held on the last Wednesday of May and the Tuesday before the last Wednesday of October. They were hiring fairs where labourers and servants sought new contracts as well as a place for selling on black cattle, horses and sheep, and a market for household wares. Cloth was bought there and measured out on a fallen stone which may once have fulfilled a role in pre-Christian rituals. It became the accepted measure for cloth throughout Argyll – an indication of the importance of the market rather than the convenient size of the stone.

It is hard now to imagine the presence of thousands of head of cattle seething in a black mass down the drove road through the glen to the church, being herded left by Gaelic-speaking, plaid-dressed drovers at what is now the village hall (then the court house and lockup for use at the market) and through wide droveways cut into the stone walls heading across the valley. These droveways were to help the drovers muster the cattle when they were setting out again to Crieff or Falkirk.

It is equally difficult to imagine the clusters of houses – townships – around Kilmichael and up the glen. There were cottages at Achnashellach (a centre of industry even in Neolithic times when flint axes were made there). At Dunamuck, overlooking the tryst, around sixty people lived in a cluster of cottages as late as the nineteenth century. It was home to the Glassary Stewarts who had lived in the area since the late 1600s, probably having migrated from Greenock during the seventeenth-century influx of lowlanders to Argyll. According to the privately published *Records of the Glassary Stewarts* by Alexander Donald Stewart, oral tradition has it that the family descended from Shaw-Stewarts of Greenock and Blackhall. Archibald Stewart, who married Margaret McTavish in 1781, was tacksman in Balliemor in 1816. They had moved into the area when runrig was still the farming system. As they became established, heritors like the Malcolms of

Poltalloch were combining the runrigs together to make bigger farms with fewer tenants. The evictions may not all have been as dramatic as that attended by the Poltalloch henchmen from Kirnan and the Experimental Farm but many in Glassary parish were put out of their cottages – Auchoish, Ardnaheir and Achnaba were all turned over to sheep with only one tenant as shepherd. Alexander Stewart bought a share in a house in Lochgilphead in 1862 and became a full-time herring fisherman when his township at Achnaba was cleared. A number of elderly men and women from Glassary parish ended up in the poorhouse, according to the 1881 census – among them Elizabeth Kerr, 81, a former domestic servant; and Donald Black, 80, a former agricultural labourer. Some were younger: Janet Turner, a widow of 55; Christina Muir, 33, a former domestic servant; and young John McPhail, 26, another former agricultural labourer, were all inmates of Lochgilphead Combination Poorhouse at the time of the census.

From the mid 1800s, Stewart descendants were tenants at Dunamuck, farming 70 acres at first but by 1871 had taken on 800 acres, of which 170 were arable. In the cottages around the farmhouse, twelve of a family were living in two rooms. The 1871 census recorded that of the fifty-two people living in the township, just one was employed by Archibald Stewart, the tenant farmer. In 1841 there had been 134 people living in twenty-three houses – probably little better than the 'huts' described in the 1790s in the *Statistical Account*. They were certainly thatched with heather, had earth floors and cow dung plaster on the walls. As tenant farmer, Mr Stewart would have been more comfortable and certainly much better off. The inventory taken at the death of Archibald Stewart in 1875 put the capital value of stock, crops and implements at £960 with a cash value of £430. The annual rent was £295 for Dunamuck which was offset by £42 rent due from the cottars round his door. The arable land of Dunamuck had been reclaimed from the moss – the Moine Mhor expanse of peat stretching from the Add towards Kilmartin. By the 1790s, malaria had been on the decline as this land was drained.

The Poltalloch Experimental Farm, established as a model farm complex with an expert brought in from the north-east of Scotland to improve fields, drains, crops and husbandry, was created from the Moine Mhor. But such improvements seem to have passed by Kilmichael Glen. Duncan Blair, born in 1915 in Kilmichael Glassary, recalls thatched cottages throughout Kilmichael Glen with no electricity or running water. He lived in the building which is now the village hall. There was a shop there and it once housed the post office, although the Horseshoe Inn at Bridgend also had the post office in the early twentieth century. The building, Campbell's Land, extended further east in those days. There had been houses up above the school where Duncan's father was born. His grandfather had been a contractor, mainly making drains on the Poltalloch Estate.

Duncan's grandfather had ten children. The blacksmith at Bridgend had fourteen – one son and the rest girls. The shop at Campbell's Land sold sweeties, but how many of those children could afford them? Duncan's grandmother fed her family on poached fish (in the criminal rather than culinary sense), rabbits, eggs from her own hens and she made a little cash by keeping bees. It was a hard life and Duncan's father's generation did not all stick at the drainage contracting. Two brothers went off to South Africa, but Duncan's father stayed for a while before becoming a gillie on the Malcolm Estate. Duncan says: 'The estate was becoming poorer but my father was employed at Kirnan Lodge for shooting and fishing. There was quite a lot of poverty when I was a child and my mother used to write letters for those in the glen who could not read or write.'

Duncan remembers the old townships and the days when the Horseshoe Inn had its own farm. Carrots grew in the sandy soil near the river and turnips and potatoes were cash crops. The blacksmith and joiners were the hub of activity at Bridgend in the 1920s because all the farmers still had horses and carts. The first tractor did not come to the area until 1922 and was then much denigrated. At Torbhlaren Farm, where Patrick and Jean Campbell had attempted to raise their children in the turbulent 1600s, Robert Miller was breeding fine Clydesdale horses and exporting them abroad. In time he went to South Africa to visit a brother and died there, and the brother gave money to build the Lachlan Miller Memorial Hall – the conversion of the building where Duncan Blair was born. A tailor at Bridgend opposite the Horseshoe Inn made MacBrayne uniforms and his sister was a seamstress until the Glasgow 50 shilling Tailor made it impossible to compete. Duncan is saddened by the disappearance of cottages throughout the glen – some have simply disintegrated, some disappeared into the forest planted by the Forestry Commission when he was a young man. His childhood coincided with the final decline of Kilmichael Glassary as a place of note. The market went to Lochgilphead, that fine place with its gasworks and ropeworks and its wide streets designed to allow the run of cattle through them on market days. The licensee at the Horseshoe gave up the licence because trade was so bad and the blacksmith and joiner's shop closed. Duncan says: 'The joiner's shop was a cartwright and he made carts when I was a boy. They had apprentices then.' But the combustion engine had arrived and the blacksmith saw no future – his apprentice went off to New Zealand.

The landlords were experiencing huge changes too. As a child, Duncan Blair, who grew up to be a nursing officer at Lochgilphead Hospital, went to children's parties on the estate and was awed by the richness and splendour of it all. Malcolm family birthdays were celebrated by grand firework displays. But in the 1930s, most of the Poltalloch estate, stretching from Loch Awe to Achnamara, was sold off – mainly to the Forestry Commission. Coates the thread people from Paisley had been tenants of the Malcolms at Achnamara. Now it was put into the hands of Glasgow Corporation as a holiday place for the city's children. The grand occasions of 'rent day' – the six monthly day out when tenants paid up to Poltalloch and made an outing of the trip to the factor's office – were coming to an end. After the Second World War, all the Poltalloch tenants were able to buy their homes and business at sitting tenant prices when legislation called for unaffordable improvements to property.

When the Forestry Commission first took over the land, many local people were employed because the draining, fencing and planting were all done by hand and the work was labour intensive. There was a sawmill in the glen and the houses at Balliemor above the church and school were built to house forestry workers, joining houses built there by the council. The place was described as being of a 'pleasing and picturesque design' by J.E. Mathieson in his contribution to the 1961 *Statistical Account* of the county. New life was injected into Kilmichael Glassary and there was even electricity after 1955.

Even then, tourism was beginning to be an important industry for the glen. Foundry boys used to come from the Clyde towns for their holidays and stay in farm outbuildings, The Paisley mill girls stayed in the barns at Dunamuck where the Stewarts had worked so hard to farm the land. They came on the steamers to Ardrishaig in the days before cheap flights could whisk them to sunnier climes.

Today's tourism in the glen is very different. Walking, cycling and stalking are just some of the activities people enjoy. Stalking holidays are offered at Kirnan House, once the home of Thomas Campbell the poet, a descendent of the Rev. Dugald Campbell of

The alpine garden of R.E. Macauley, the botanist who transformed Kirnan House. Plate from the Journal of the Royal Horticultural Society, vol. lix, 1934 (*Royal Botanic Garden, Edinburgh*)

Knapdale, one of the most influential figures of the early seventeenth century. Thomas was to become one of the Scottish Enlightenment's luminaries but he did not forget the glen of his childhood. A later tenant was R.E. Macauley, who transformed the bleak hillside into a rich alpine garden in the early years of the twentieth century. He bred gentians there (Gentiana Macaulyi became a common rockery plant and as predicted in his obituary in the *Gardener's Chronicle* of 25 December, 1937, has kept his name alive) and was known as a generous gardener willing to show visitors around and to swap plants with other keen gardeners.

A scholar, athlete and East India merchant, he died at his home in London, but was never happier than when in his Argyll garden or meeting like-minded spirits at the Royal Horticultural Shows. He was given an Award of Merit in 1931 by the Royal Botanical Gardens for his new gentian and today, the gardens at Kirnan House still boast specimen trees introduced by the adventurous Mr Macauley. Duncan Blair remembers half a dozen gardeners being employed at Kirnan and experts coming to see the beautiful gardens. Today, mechanisation and the economy have reduced employment in agriculture and

Kilmichael manse and Balliemor. The manse was built in the 1830s when Kilmichael Glassary's medieval church was replaced by a new one. Behind are the forestry houses built in the 1950s – the village's industry of the mid-twentieth century (*Argyll and Bute Archives*)

forestry to a minimum. Kilmichael Glassary has become a haven for tourists and a dormitory for those who work in Lochgilphead – which has stolen Kilmichael's status as the seat of government not only for Glassary but the whole of Argyll and Bute.

ACKNOWLEDGEMENTS

This book is informed by the following:

First, Second and Third Statistical Accounts of Scotland.
The Agricultural Survey of Argyllshire by Rev. Dr John Smith,
    Mundell and Sons, Edinburgh, 1798.
General View of the Agriculture of the County of Argyll, Rev. Dr John
    Smith, Richard Phillips, 1805.
Still Books of 1811–17.
Origines Parochiales Scotiae.
Tarbert Past and Present by Dugald Mitchell, 1886, Bennett &
    Thomson,
    Dumbarton, 1886; reprint by House of Lochar, 1996.
The Campbeltown and Machrihanish Railway by D.A. Farr, Oakwood
    Press, 1969.
Kintyre in the 17th Century by Andrew McKerral, Oliver & Boyd,
    1948.
Kintyre Country Life by Angus Martin, John Donald, Edinburgh,
    1987.
Records of the Glassary Stewarts, written and privately published by
    Alexander Donald Stewart
Queen Victoria's Highland Journals ed. by David Duff, Webb &
    Bower, 1980.
A Memoir of Tayvallich and Taynish by Veronica Gainford.
Archaeological Sketches in Scotland: Knapdale and Gigha by Captain
    T.P. White, Wm Blackwood, 1875.
Depredations on the Clan Campbell, published in Edinburgh 1816
Archive material of Argyll, including John Campbell of Kilberry's
    diaries, made available with patience, enthusiasm and great
    knowledge by Murdo Macdonald.
Kilfinan Parish: History and Memories, booklet ed. by Alan Millar.
Tarbert, Loch Fyne: The Story of the Fishermen by Ronnie Johnson,
    www.tarbertlochfyne.com

The late Marion Campbell of Kilberry's conversations and notes, which included her great-grandfather's account books.

Campbeltown 1700–1950: a souvenir booklet, edited Angus MacVicar, Campbeltown Week Publications, 1950

Memories of Dunoon and Cowal, Renee Forsyth

Dunoon Pier, Ian McCorie

Dunoon of Old, Angus McLean

History of Cowal, A. Brown

Place Names of Cowal, MacLean

Innellan: The Popular Resort of the Clyde Coast, Rev. John C. Hill M.A.

Clyde Piers: A Pictorial Record, Ian McCrorie and Joy Monteith.

PHOTOGRAPHS come from collections of: Maureen Bell, Drumlemble; Neil and Marie Kennedy, Campbeltown; Archie Smith, Tighnabruaich, Sheena Carmichael, Ford; James & William Wallace, West Drumlemble Farm; Mike Murray, Crinan (from collections of Jim Souness, Edinburgh); John Campbell of Kilberry, Kilberry; Dr Alastair MacFadyen, Newton; Angus MacInnes of Tayvallich; Argyll and Bute archives, courtesy Murdo MacDonald; Marian Pallister; Debbie White, Royal Botanic Gardens of Scotland, Edinburgh.

THANKS to the following for information, conversation and sometimes cups of tea and biscuits: Kilmartin Museum staff; Murdo MacDonald, Argyll and Bute archivist; Maureen Bell, Drumlemble; James Wallace, Drumlemble; Audrey Houston, Argyll Arms Hotel, Southend; Graham Hardy, librarian, Royal Botanic Gardens, Edinburgh; Rev. David Kellas, Tighnabruaich; Alan Miller, Tighnabruaich; Archie Smith, Tighnabruaich; Catriona Maxwell, Kames and Millhouse; Andrew Gemmill, Ifferdale farm, Saddell; Robert Millar, chairman of the NFU in Argyll, High Catterdale Farm, Southend; William Leitch, Tarbert; Dr Alastair MacFadyen, Newton; John Campbell of Kilberry; Mike Murray, Crinan; Peter McLardy, Slockavullin; Sheena Carmichael, Ford; Angus, Mae, Colin and Lynda MacInnes, Tayvallich; Duncan Blair, Kilmichael Glassary; Rev. Dr Roddy Macleod, Furnace (for his Gaelic expertise).

Particular thanks go to Bridget Paterson for her additional research in eastern Cowal.